WEEKEND IN MUNICH

WEEKEND IN MUNICH

ART, PROPAGANDA AND TERROR IN THE THIRD REICH

ROBERT S. WISTRICH

CONSULTANT: LUKE HOLLAND

PAVILION

To my youngest daughter, Sonia

This edition published in Great Britain in 1996 by
Pavilion Books Limited
26 Upper Ground, London SE1 9PD

Text copyright © Robert Wistrich 1995
Foreword copyright © Luke Holland 1995
Colour photographs copyright © YILDIZFilm/ZEF Productions 1995

All the colour illustrations are based on the original colour archive footage that featured in the Channel Four (UK)
documentary *Good Morning, Mr Hitler!*, first broadcast in May 1993, produced and directed by Luke Holland (ZEF Productions), Paul Yule
(Berwick Universal Pictures) and associate producer Alexander van Dülmen (YILDIZFilm). Enquiries regarding the availability of video-
tape copies of the 52' programme or further use of the illustrative material should be directed to ZEF Productions Ltd, PO Box 2023,
London W1A 1FJ

The illustration Leda and the Swan on p.77 is reproduced courtesy of Bavarian National Library

Translations of transcripts from the documentary by Luke Holland and Sabine Pusch
Translation of the poem on p.60 by Gerty Holland
'So it was' by Gerty Spies reproduced from *Im Staube gefunden: Gedichte*, published by Chr. Kaiser/ Gütersloher Verlagshaus, Gütersloh

Designed and typeset by Grahame Dudley Associates.

Set in Janson 10 on 15 point

The moral right of the author has been asserted.

A CIP catalogue record for this book is available from the British Library.

ISBN 1 85793 7988

Printed and bound in Great Britain by
Butler & Tanner Ltd, Frome and London

2 4 6 8 10 9 7 5 3 1

This book may be ordered by post direct from the publisher.
Please contact the Marketing Department.
But try your bookshop first.

CONTENTS

PREFACE

THIS BOOK arose out of a Channel Four documentary *Good Morning, Mr Hitler!*, which I had the privilege of being associated with as commentator and historical adviser. I wish to warmly thank its co-producer and co-director, Luke Holland, for suggesting that I write a book based on the pictures that appear in these pages. He was kind enough to put at my disposal a considerable amount of material relating to the Day of German Art festival organized by the Nazis in Munich in July 1939. This was the original starting point from which a wider project grew, still based on the images which had appeared in the Channel Four film. The story of that documentary and its importance is integrated here into a wider-ranging study of the interaction between different facets of art, propaganda and politics in Nazi Germany.

This book is to some extent an experiment, though it does not lay claim to absolute novelty. In my work as a historian for many years I have written about the Third Reich and even prepared an encyclopaedia on the subject. But this is the first time that I have focused so intensely on the aesthetic dimensions of Nazism and their implications. It is also the first time that I have been confronted with the problem of writing with and *against* a large body of images derived from the Third Reich. The dilemmas that this poses are discussed in the book itself, which I hope not only contextualizes the pictures but also neutralizes some of their potential seductiveness. My commentary has been written to stand in its own right as an interpretation of the period rather than to match the pictures in a direct manner. Nor have the

pictures, except in a few special cases, been selected as a visual accompaniment for the words. Nevertheless, there is a more subtle connection, perhaps even a dialectic of word and image, which implicitly underlies the presentation. The aim is simultaneously to convey some of the visual appeal of Nazism while deconstructing its meanings and deflating its pretensions. There is a delicate line to be trodden here between the need to understand a phenomenon in its own terms and the strong emotions of repugnance that it can arouse. Without some kind of imaginative effort to get inside the heads of even such repulsive historical actors as the Nazis, it is difficult to arrive at any fresh or illuminating insights. At the same time this is a topic that demands a sense of moral reponsibility from the historian and a special sensitivity to its many nuances. As one who was born when the Nazi era was already over, I feel a certain freedom to view this dark history in a new and more detached way. As a humanist with a deep abhorrence of fascism and as the son of Polish Jews who narrowly escaped the Holocaust, all my sympathies are unequivocally with the victims.

It is perhaps symbolic that these words are being composed in Israel on the eve of the Feast of Tabernacles. For it was from this land that the Hebrew prophets first thundered against idolatry and graven images. Their message still retains its freshness and meaning for our civilization if it is to overcome those sources within itself from which the Nazi creed was born.

Robert Wistrich
JERUSALEM, SEPTEMBER 1994

FOREWORD

IN VIEWING the colour images in this book, it is important to remind oneself that they were not recorded for the printed page but were intended for projection as a sequence of moving images. They were drawn from approximately thirty minutes of 16mm film footage shot by a group of enthusiastic and extremely competent amateurs – all members of Munich's Amateur Film Society. The film stock was Kodachrome, which had become available only a year or two before this film was shot in 1939. The Munich amateurs were effectively experimenting with an exciting new medium.

By reproducing these pictures here, for the most part as single, static frames, one runs a number of risks, not the least of which is that one is rendering accessible a series of potent, and potentially dangerous, images. One also runs the risk of humanizing Hitler and his Nazi henchmen – applying seductive flesh tones and colour co-ordination to their fascist finery. For those of us who experienced the Nazi era only in the grainy newsreel of another time, Hitler and his strutting henchmen had receded into the archival past. They had been consigned to history. The disconcertingly rich colour of the Munich home movie brings them striding into sharp contemporary relief. Suddenly the newsreel has taken on the immediacy of the news and Hitler has re-surfaced with the sometimes shuffling, blotchy immediacy of a prime-time politician.

Hitler was unique and his genocidal regime was uniquely awful. Comparisons are not always instructive. Nevertheless, the colour footage, espe-cially the 'seductive' images of the fascists at play in pre-war Munich, may provide us with another template through which to view both the past and the political landscape of our ever-present future. The abiding hope is that this book, with its some-times alarming images and Robert Wistrich's inci-sive analysis, will serve as a timely health warning.

The challenge throughout, in making the picture selection, has been how to reconcile the tension between choosing the best images (photographs that work on the page according to conventional criteria) and a desire to remain loyal to the feel of the original, mostly un-edited, pre-war footage. While trying to subvert the propa-gandist tone of the Nazi celebrations featured in the Munich footage and make a virtue of the novel qualities of this material, design conventions (to which the Nazi aesthetic made a not insubstantial contribution and to which we often unwittingly subscribe) prompt one, again and again, to choose the 'best' or 'most striking' image, frequently at the expense of one that is closer to the original feel of the sometimes quirky home movie of the amateur enthusiasts. The Third Reich has cast a long shadow.

In a project of this nature one cannot afford to be insensitive to the charge that one is cashing in on material that might, improperly handled, be described as 'Hitleriana'. These images are too important to be allowed to continue gathering archival dust. They might, as has been suggested, be as dangerous as an unexploded mine, but the instinct to ban or bury them may only render them even more dangerous.

Robert Wistrich was an important ally in helping to defuse and interpret the 1939 colour footage for its first television outing in the (1993) Channel Four documentary, *Good Morning, Mr Hitler!* He has returned to the material to dissect and deconstruct its multiplicity of meanings and make it marginally safer for the rest of us. I have enjoyed the privilege of working with him. This is also the opportunity to acknowledge my deep appreciation to my co-director Paul Yule and express again my relief that our friendship survived the traumas of our filmic collaboration.

Thanks also to Alexander van Dülmen, close collaborator and associate producer on the film project, who deserves much of the credit for bringing the Munich footage, properly, into the public domain. Every consultant needs a consultant and my special thanks go to my mother, who despite the enduring tragedy of her farewell, had the good sense and the good fortune to leave Vienna in time.

Luke Holland
LONDON, SEPTEMBER 1994

CHAPTER ONE

NAZISM: IMAGE, ICON AND MYTH

'Fascism is the aestheticization of politics.'

WALTER BENJAMIN

THE IMAGES in this book originate from a spectacular Nazi pageant called the Day of German Art, which was held in Munich during the weekend of 14–16 July 1939. It was to be the third and last time that this popular festival would be celebrated in the Bavarian capital, though the art exhibitions previously linked with it continued through most of the war years.

What makes this particular event so interesting is that a remarkable film record of it was recently recovered, made in 1939 by a talented amateur film-maker, Hans Feierabend. This film is in brilliant colour and the unique images it contains are reproduced here for the first time. They were not subjected to the usual stage management and manipulative techniques of the Nazi propaganda machine. Hence they provide us with a different angle of vision on the Third Reich, one which is deceptively normal, relaxed and disarming.

The effect of the colour is similar to being suddenly taken on a psychedelic trip into a sinister, traumatic past only to be confronted by unexpected visions of innocence and joy. It is a disconcerting and in some ways even a shocking experience.

In the Channel Four film *Good Morning, Mr Hitler!*, which is based on the original footage from 1939, this sense of dissonance is further sharpened by interviews with ordinary Germans who parti-

cipated in the original pageant. Their testimonies, which have been used selectively in this book, offer an interesting insight into everyday experience under National Socialism. They remind us that most 'normal' citizens (which in the Third Reich automatically excluded Jews, Communists, homosexuals, gypsies, the handicapped and mentally defective) could still live in comparative peace under a criminal regime.[1] This seeming innocuousness of National Socialism for so many Germans who lived through it raises serious methodological and ethical issues for the historian. How, if at all, can one reconcile *Alltagsgeschichte* (the history of everyday life) and its tendency to emphasize the blander, more private and banal aspects of life in the Hitler era with the public record of Nazi crimes? Is there any bridge between the German and Jewish memory of the Third Reich? Does not any attempt at 'normalizing' our historical consciousness of Nazism run the risk of eroding awareness of the *singular* evil embodied in Hitler's Reich? Such concerns have constantly echoed through the debates about the 'historicization' and relativization of National Socialism.[2]

Though this book is not intended to be a comprehensive social or cultural history of the Third Reich, I have been very much aware of these dilemmas, which are inherent in any responsible treatment of the Nazi period. The slices of daily life I have incorporated in the text generally tend to highlight aspects of the Third Reich which were *not* overtly criminal, ideological or political. They reflect the areas of 'normality' within a totalitarian system which, if not placed in context, can easily lead to a banalization of the Nazi past. At the same time, lived experience, despite its subjective bias and flawed memories, can sometimes offer a valuable supplement, even a corrective, to conventional historical interpretations. It can provide us with new insights into the vexed questions of how people within their concrete local and social environments could be caught up in the Nazi experience; how they reacted to specific events and how they recall them today – often with a revealing mixture of ambiguity, embarrassment, evasiveness and even self-induced amnesia. Provided that such memories, which invariably reflect the unpolitical 'normalcy' of everyday life under Nazism, are critically juxtaposed with the criminal dimensions of the political system, the danger of trivialization can be avoided.

There is, however, another ethical problem for the historian in dealing with the visual material in this book. There is an enormous suggestive power inherent in Nazi mythology, a seductiveness in the emotions, images and fantasies which it released, that should not be underestimated. The alacrity with which the mass entertainment industry since the 1970s has marketed this aspect of Nazism in sumptuous movie and TV treatments is a signal warning. While hard commercial considerations no doubt played as great a role in the Hitler boom as any sinister nostalgia for the Nazi past, this in itself is cold comfort. For it was already apparent forty years after Hitler's death that in the popular culture of the West Nazism was often no more than a

source of light-headed amusement, of distraction, perverse fascination and even sado-masochistic pornography. Clearly, any moral and political lessons to be drawn from Nazi terror and genocide are bound to be dulled by such mischievous and irresponsible approaches to the past.[3]

The role of pop art in this erosion of historical memory has not been negligible. It can be observed all around us in the way that Nazi insignia and emblems, the signs and symbols of the Third Reich from swastikas and 'Sieg Heil' salutes to high black leather boots, have become part of pop iconography. Stormtrooper or SS uniforms, Hitler T-shirts and the skinhead or neo-Nazi rock music glorifying violence still attract a part of the youth culture of both East and West. For some young people these symbols may simply be a fashionable expression of social or generational protest. For others, Nazi emblems might seem to be no more than interesting decorations, devoid of any political significance.

However, there is a lethal poison behind these artefacts which cannot be overlooked. For Hitler, even in the popular mind, is notorious (and in some cases perversely admired) for having been a great criminal. His name and the icons associated with it symbolize the sinister totality of nihilistic impulses in Western culture. Yet Nazism, which carried out crimes without precedent by releasing the darkest bloodlusts in mankind, has today become reduced to one more object of fashion, fiction and fun in contemporary mass culture.[4]

The politics of forgetting can also be found at a much more subtle level of historical understanding. Here is how historian Saul Friedländer records his critical impressions on watching Joachim Fest's visually striking film, *Hitler: A Career*, in a Munich movie house:

The dazzling rise, the titanic energy, the Luciferian fall: it is all there. As for the extermination of the Jews, a few words in passing, no more. An inconsequential shadow of this grandiose tableau. For anyone who does not know the facts, the power and the glory still remain, followed by a veritable vengeance of the gods … the mystical communion with the Brownshirt revolution and its martyrs still remains.[5]

The fact that even such an outstanding historian of the Third Reich as Joachim Fest could somehow be led astray by the fascination of the Nazi spectacle is troubling, though scarcely unique. This is only one of many examples, as Friedländer noted, of the aesthetic frisson generated by Nazism and its strange hold on our culture.[6] This impact probably has as much to do with the power of kitsch, of images and of modern myths as with the sadism and criminality of the Nazis which culminated in the mass murder of European Jewry. It is often difficult to avoid contamination by this debased aesthetic, but the effort must be made to deconstruct and neutralize its appeal.

There is an important contemporary resonance in all of this. We live in a culture which turns more than ever on the power of images to transform our view of objective reality. Politics itself has long since become part of the brave new world of image-making. No self-respecting candidate for high office in the Western world today will be found without his or her battery of press handlers, campaign strategists, pollsters, advertising gurus, scriptwriters and news-media consultants. No political campaign is conceivable without the familiar round of photo-opportunities, talk shows, intimate interviews, television ads, press conferences and endless briefings.

The political programme has become subordinate to the personality cult, the record of achievement to its perceived image, the real needs of

Manual !
Adolf Hitler rehearsing…

voters to the opinion polls. The art of rhetoric has been reduced to the sound-bite, the art of persuasion to public relations gimmickry, the reality of an action to its visual packaging and presentation. There seem to be no more great ideas or visions in politics, only the image and perception of the candidate and the way that he or she is sold to the public. In this art of selling, the distinction between reality and fantasy is gradually being lost; politics becomes a branch of advertising and media marketing. Form triumphs resoundingly over content.[7] Moreover, contemporary image-makers are only

political ideology or moral outlook. For the Nazis were masters of presentation, packaging, public relations and visual propaganda. From the beginning, they operated a political system which relied

Maniacal !
...for the 1,000-year Reich in the Munich studio...

Millennial !
...of his photographer friend, Heinrich Hoffman.

too aware of one of the golden rules of political propaganda – the need for constant repetition. There is almost no limit to the number of times that the same thing can be said by politicians over and over again.

In many respects the modern image-makers are the children of Hitler and Goebbels, without even realizing it and without in any way sharing their

on the meticulous organization of appearances, careful simulation, constant stimulation and the sophisticated stage management of huge public spectacles. Goebbels, in particular, was a virtuoso in the organization of the modern mass media and its instrumentalization for propaganda purposes. When it came to the choreography and dramaturgy of mass rallies, the Nazis learned a good deal from Hollywood. But in the marketing of Adolf Hitler and the creation of his 'myth' they surpassed the best that American advertising techniques of that time or even today could provide. Already then, they had taken the personalization of politics to new extremes – rarely if ever equalled.

Hitler himself, from the outset, grasped the nature of the new mass politics better than any of his bourgeois or Marxist opponents. Together with Goebbels, he was perhaps the first twentieth-century political leader to see clearly the similarity between selling a commercial product and market-ing a politician to the people;[8] to make a calculated and intense used of mass techniques of political agi-tation; to understand the value of shock tactics in grabbing media attention; and to perceive that the endless repetition of simple slogans was more important for winning the masses than a consistent doctrine or an inflexible Party programme. He shared with Goebbels the cynical view of human nature that appears to have become a platitude for many contemporary image-makers in politics. The only thing that ultimately counts, according to the old-new Machiavellians, is power and success. The means and the morality are altogether secondary.

Of course, for Hitler and the Nazis, propa-ganda was much more than simply a selling tech-nique and their radical methods included the kind of terrorism and systematic acts of intimidation that are rarely seen in our liberal democracies. Their views on propaganda, mass agitation and Party organization were far more comparable to the Bolsheviks than to Western bourgeois parlia-mentary parties. Their ruthless concept of politics as a Darwinian battle of wills involving coercion, violence, outright lies and manipulation, is not one generally shared by advertising people. Their frank, brutal contempt for democracy and their

openly fanatical anti-Semitism (which Hitler regarded as a deadly weapon in his propaganda arsenal) mark them off sharply from most current practitioners of image politics in the West. But these and other obvious differences with the present, which relate more to the social structure and instant electronic technologies of post-war Western society, should not induce excessive complacency.

Hitler and the Nazis excelled in using the tech-nology of their day and adapting their message accordingly. After 1929 they had the assistance of the conservative tycoon Alfred Hugenberg, whose press and film empire massively amplified the scope of their propaganda. They also enjoyed an increas-ing flow of money from heavy industry.[9] The devel-opment of microphones and loudspeakers further enabled the Nazis to organize vast meetings to expand their audience. In the 1932 election cam-paign Hitler was the first German politician to use an aircraft in order to conduct an unprecedented number of public rallies in German cities. The pro-paganda value of the 'Hitler over Germany' cam-paign in underlining the ubiquity, the energy, the speed and 'superhuman' reach of the Nazi move-ment, was huge. After 1933, when Joseph Goebbels achieved a monopoly over all the available means of mass communication, the hold of Nazi propaganda on the population and its ability to mould opinion were proportionately still greater. Hitler's domestic and foreign policy successes gave a new credence to their propaganda, which was futher reinforced by the impact of radio. It was Marshall McLuhan who, thirty years ago, first pointed out the tribal reso-nance of radio, 'its power to turn the psyche and society into a single echo chamber'.[10] Hitler, like no other leader of his time, knew how to play on this tribal drum to awaken profound, archaic forces and to stimulate more recent nationalist bonds by using a modern technology. The force of his message, according to McLuhan, was greatly enhanced because in Germany the tribal past had never ceased to be a reality for the national psyche.[11]

Other modern technologies were also adapted by the Nazis in pragmatic fashion despite their hate campaigns against so-called 'degenerate' modernism. In areas like industrial architecture, advertising, graphic design, functional furniture and consumer goods, modern forms were suited to the practical needs of mass production. Sometimes, as with the *Autobahnen* – in themselves a remarkable achievement of modern technology – their compatibility with National Socialist ideology was deliberately emphasized. Commentators pointed to their harmony with the German landscape and the linking together of the German 'living space'.[12] These highways were political symbols of 'the unity and authority of the new Reich' and at the same time a form of 'community architecture'.[13] The highways were called the 'Roads of Adolf Hitler' in tribute to the political master-builder who was personally remodelling the new Germany according to his own grandiose ideas.[14]

The engineer-artist Fritz Todt, who was most closely associated with the *Autobahnen* was often glorified as an ideal 'Aryan' type and liberator of German technology from outdated materialist thinking.[15] He was presented as a living embodiment of the happy marriage between technical rationality, National Socialist ideology and the German soul. His steel and concrete highways racing through the mountains and valleys of the Third Reich were eulogized as artworks that had rescued the German landscape from the blight of an urban, mechanical civilization! Thus the Nazis combined approval of technological advance with

rural nostalgia, anti-Semitism (before 1933 technology had allegedly been suffocated by 'Jewish plutocracy'), the rejection of Bolshevism and soulless 'Americanization'.[16]

Hitler embraced this romantic concept of technology since it supposedly embodied the 'Aryan' creative will and also served German military needs. Like Goebbels he pragmatically regarded modern technology as vital for mass propaganda, 'spiritual' mobilization and the extension of German power. In a speech of February 1939, Goebbels had summed up the dominant Nazi view when he maintained that 'National Socialism understood how to tackle the soulless framework of technology and fill it with the rhythm and hot impulses of our time.'[17] The production of the Volkswagen car – an impressive example of modern technology made accessible to the masses – was held up as an excellent paradigm for the new 'steel-like romanticism', fusing German soul and technical perfection.

But if technology could under certain circumstances be raised to the level of an art form, what about those exalted areas of 'true' art which the Nazis claimed as a repository of eternal values? Many of their ideas in this field were contradictory and confused, scarcely adding up to a coherent theory or practice of culture. Nevertheless, they did grant a central role to art and culture in the task of building a new 'Aryan' man and a new millennium. The lead was given by Hitler himself, as the self-proclaimed protector of the arts and of the common man. It was his view that cultural change was the key to a better way of life for the masses. However, Nazi culture had also to appeal to popular taste and prejudice. Hence artists and designers were expected to strike a proper balance between the functional and the beautiful, the useful and the traditional, while providing products that everyone could afford.

As with the 'People's Car', so with music, sculpture, painting and theatre. The Nazis always claimed to be taking art to the masses. Brahms, Beethoven and Wagner were no longer for an elite but for Mr Everyman. The 'Strength through Joy' organization sponsored theatre visits at cheap prices for the working classes. Its 'Beauty of Labour' department promised better lighting and working conditions in the factories as part of its seduction of the industrial workers. Sport, gymnastics and folk dancing were nationally promoted with a quasi-messianic enthusiasm, as healthy group activities which would encourage fitness, morality and the body beautiful. Love of nature and the simple life were advocated at every opportunity, not only for their intrinsic merits but also as a way of recapturing the link to an idyllic, traditional, pre-industrial way of life. Art, too, was generally expected to draw inspiration from the old customs, songs and oral traditions of what was presumed to be the Nordic, Germanic past. At the same time, impressive popular festivals were held to encourage the belief that Germans not only had a unique cultural heritage but that they now lived in momentous and happy times. National Socialism, it was suggested, would usher in the long-awaited cultural renaissance of a great new era.

On the face of it, much of this activity in the domain of popular culture seems neither original nor particularly sinister. It had precedents in the German past and parallels in other countries. Moreover, the Nazis were not the first or the only movement to believe that art should carry a political message or be mobilized in the service of the nation. Nor were they altogether innovatory in

their desire to subordinate all artistic endeavour to ideology and propaganda purposes. As the English writer George Orwell pointed out in 1941, the frontiers between art and propaganda had become increasingly blurred all over the Western world, as well as in the Soviet Union. Ever since the Great Slump of 1929 the old liberal doctrine of 'art for art's sake' had been redundant.[18] The emphasis on mannerism, technique and treating a work of art 'as a thing of value in itself', was better suited to an age of exceptional comfort and security. But in the harsher climate of the 1930s, life and politics had combined to destroy such pure aesthetic illusions. Literature, in particular, had become politicized, swamped by propaganda and didacticism. The arts in general had been invaded by partisanship. In a world where fascism and democracy were bitterly fighting each other, detachment was no longer possible. The 1930s had reminded people that 'propaganda in some form or other lurks in every book, that every work of art has a meaning and a purpose – a political, social and religious purpose – that our aesthetic judgements are always coloured by our prejudices and beliefs'.[19]

The integrity of the artist was seriously threatened by political rectitude even in Western democracies. But it was above all under totalitarian rule that all writing and art had been reduced to propaganda. The autonomous individual and freedom of thought had been the first victims of the totalitarian desire to control not only people's ideas but also their emotions. Everywhere the results of this policy were disastrous. As Orwell observed pessimistically, the most characteristic activity of the Nazis was burning books. But unless totalitarianism in general was defeated, there would be no future for literature and the arts anywhere on the planet.[20]

In the Third Reich there can be no doubt that

ABOVE : ***Tree-lined racism.*** *'Jews not welcome here.' A typical banner in the Bavarian village of Rosenheim, 1939.*
ABOVE RIGHT : ***After the fire.*** *A burnt-out synagogue, one of thousands throughout Germany destroyed on the night of 9 November 1938. Before 1939 there had been over 10,000 Jews in Munich. Just 200 would survive the Holocaust.*

the objective of the new rulers was to streamline all cultural life and seal it off as far as possible from outside influences. Everything defined as 'un-German', 'Jewish', 'Bolshevik' or decadently 'modern' was to be consigned to the flames. The very desire to question, criticize, evaluate or analyse art was seen as subversive. All aspects of culture were to submit to the aesthetic dictates of the Party and the State. In its turn, cultural life was mobilized in the service of racist stereotypes that could mean the difference between life and death.

There was a kind of mad logic in the hysterical Nazi onslaught against the modernist *avant-garde*. They were building here on well-established antitheses between a rooted Germanic *Kultur* and an alien Western *Zivilisation*; on *völkisch* myth, the conservative backlash against modernity and the basic philistinism of the German middle class. Nazi views of culture were saturated with the language of community, blood and race that had been promulgated in Germany and Austria for at least forty years before they came to power.[21] During the Weimar Republic, conservative right-wing intellectuals had further prepared the ground with their relentless cultural critique of liberal modernity. Walter Benjamin noted that Nazism attracted these intellectuals primarily as a possible resolution of cultural crisis: they mistakenly looked to it to provide a new creativity, beauty, aesthetic form and 'spiritual unity' of the nation in place of the formless, soulless chaos of liberalism and Marxist materialism.[22]

It was self-evident to most conservatives as well as the Nazis, that in Ernst Jünger's words, the ideal of form and beauty inherent in the *Volk* necessarily excluded the Jews from the national community.[23] Cultural anti-Semitism in Germany had consistently linked the Jews and Judaism to the rapacious materialism of modernity, to the iniquities of both capitalism and socialism, while slandering them as social parasites. The Jews embodied speculation, profit-seeking, rootless cosmopolitanism and corrosive intellectualism in the eyes of their enemies. They were the prime architects of big city corruption, of the venal press, of the dictatorship of money over the world of culture and politics. In their abstract rationalism, their over-refined intellectuality and urban restlessness, they were the living antithesis of the irrational mystique of 'blood and soil' espoused by *völkisch* ideologues, conservative romantics and Nazi idealists. The Jew as an archetype was synonymous with everything rootless, international, abstract and universal. Hence, by definition, he or she must be opposed to any *national* culture – expecially one dedicated to the 'Aryan' myth of a superior Germanic race.[24] Moreover, anti-Semites claimed that the 'Jewish spirit' ultimately reduced cultural activity to its exchange value, thereby stripping it of any authentic ideals. Hitler, Goebbels and Rosenberg converted such well-entrenched prejudices, so widely espoused by Germany's cultural elites, into immutable racist dogmas.

The traditional hostility to Jewish *Geist* (spirit) among the right-wing intellectuals was henceforth given a fanatical, biological grounding by the Nazis. This was the background to the relentless effort within Nazi culture after 1933 to expunge any trace of a Jewish presence from the arts, as well as from society, the economy and politics.

The term 'degenerate art' extended, in practice, far beyond the Jewish component, to include the whole of modern *avant-garde* culture, which was deemed unacceptable to the Third Reich. In persecuting everything that was experimental, innovative or deemed to be 'formless' in painting, sculpture and the applied arts, the Nazis were not always consistent. But they did have a deep horror of abstract complexity, ambiguity, the fragmentation of viewpoints and the dynamic view of reality evident in modern art. A movement like Cubism epitomized for Hitler this bold, threatening liberation from all static categories. He sensed its revolutionary quality, translating this immediately into political terms wholly alien to the Cubists themselves. In *Mein Kampf*, he wrote: 'If the creative spirit of the Periclean age be manifested in the Parthenon, then the Bolshevist era is manifested through its cubist grimace.'[25] It is surely significant that so-called Marxist critics in Moscow during the 1930s also denounced Cubism, along with Dadaism, Surrealism and Expressionism, as modern and decadent.[26] The denunciatory practices in Stalinist Russia in the realms of art and culture often echoed those of Nazi Germany during these black years. For both regimes, the modern movement in the arts – that is, virtually anything produced after 1870 – was unacceptable and liable to be branded as 'alien'. What the Nazis denounced as 'degenerate' was usually vilified by the Stalinists as 'formalist' art.

At the same time, art was assigned a key role in the propagation of ideology and of politics as a mass spectacle in the Third Reich. The importance of this topic was long ignored in the general literature on Nazism or else confined to highly specialized works on fascist and Nazi art.[27] Moreover, there was little attempt, until very recently, to analyse the paintings that appeared in the Great German Art Exhibitions in Munich between 1937 and 1944, on the grounds that this 'non-art' was inherently barbaric and repulsive. Access to this material, today stored in a customs and excise depot in Munich, is still greatly restricted. The question of whether these paintings should be publicly exhibited again in Germany remains controversial. But what seems clear is that without a free and critical scrutiny of *all* relevant art and artefacts, there can be no comprehensive understanding of National Socialism. Moreover, until one comes to grips with the undeniable mass appeal of the Nazi culture industry – which was not due to skilful propaganda alone – important facets of the regime's popularity will remain inexplicable.

Art and culture had many different functions in the Third Reich, which are elucidated in the following pages. At the simplest level the arts produced a decorative façade for a regime that sought popular consensus as well as ruling by terror and cynical propaganda. They were intended to provide uplift and consciousness of a higher destiny by focusing on a realm of 'eternal values' beyond the concerns of everyday life. Yet, at the same time, art was also supposed to be 'down to earth', 'matter of fact' and accessible to the plain man's understanding.

Architecture and sculpture, in particular, were designated to reflect the power and grandeur of the Third Reich. The Nazis attached great importance to their symbolic function and public role as vehicles of a 'heroic' ideology and will-to-power. It is in the visual arts, the main focus of this study for obvious reasons, that one can best see the megalomania, the monumentalism and the drive for domination

which animated Hitler's Reich. This trend did not exclude the selective adaptation of parts of the architectural heritage of modernism – technical rationality, economy, sobriety and functionalism – to the Nazi building programme. On the other hand, it is in sculpture that the best visual illustrations of the Nazi ideal of youth, beauty and 'Aryan' masculinity can be found. In its treatment of human form and its development of a new body perception, Nazism drew, however, on an *exclusionary* vision of superhuman perfection as oppressive as the monumentalism of its public architecture.

Painting, too, echoed this obsession with the perfection of the naked body and with purity of form, without attaining the same resonance or importance in Nazi eyes. In the officially approved style of painting, the anaesthetizing consequences of the purging of modern art are all too apparent. The deadening flatness in the depiction of idyllic landscapes, robust peasant families and 'blood and soil' pastoralism is glaringly obvious. Hitler's own provincial tastes in this field had a disastrous impact.

Inevitably, since this is a book about images and their relation to the Third Reich, literature, theatre and even music appear only in a minor key (with the exception of Richard Wagner). Nevertheless, a few points are worth noting. Hitler and the Nazis always attached far greater importance to the *spoken* than to the written word. The National Socialists despised and hated literary intellectuals, though their collaboration was deemed essential. The Nazis were well aware of the fact that the cream of German writers, including Thomas and Heinrich Mann, Bertolt Brecht, Jakob Wassermann, Franz Werfel and Stefan George, had left Germany after 1933. They also knew that the book burnings throughout the Reich had been subjected to a withering indictment abroad. True, there were a few important writers like the expressionist poet Gottfried Benn, whose aesthetic nihilism briefly led him to hail National Socialism as a great historic breakthrough. There was the extraordinary embrace of National Socialism by Germany's most charismatic philosopher, Martin Heidegger. Though he soon withdrew from all political involvement, the affinities between his thought and the Nazi project are undeniable.[28] Other important thinkers like Oswald Spengler, Carl Schmitt and Ernst Jünger could equally be described as fellow travellers, harbingers or literary accomplices of Nazism without ever espousing the movement as such. But they, too, were eventually disillusioned and usually retreated into some form of 'inner emigration'. As for the Nazi muse itself, even a passing acquaintance with the poems, plays and novels produced in the Third Reich reveals their drastic impoverishment and underlying sickliness.

Music, long regarded in the romantic tradition as the special preserve of the 'German soul', was a special case. The German (and Austrian-German) contribution to world music was second to none and the Nazis understood how important it was for the prestige and legitimacy of the regime to maintain this tradition. Hitler himself referred to music as the 'crown jewel' of the arts and his passion for opera needs no elaboration. For him, as for many of his countrymen, music best expressed the grandeur and eternity of the German 'spirit', its seriousness, its exaltation and *joie de vivre*, its majestic heights and its dizzying abysses. The Nazis therefore sought to appropriate the German classical music tradition while pompously adding a 'heroic' dimension. They secured the services of Richard Strauss (Germany's most famous living composer) as first president of the Reich Chamber of Music, and of the outstanding conductor Wilhelm Furtwängler – though both subsequently came into conflict with the regime.[29] The Bayreuth Festival was endowed by Hitler with a special subsidy and became an annual highlight in the Nazi calendar. Great efforts were made to popularize music and bring it to the masses. Their success was attested to by the impressive rise in attendances at concert and opera performances during the Nazi period.[30]

But while Nazi cultural policy was as popular in music as in the other arts, it contributed far more to the destruction of Germany's great musical tradition than to its regeneration. There was a vast exodus of musical talent as the Nazis denounced everything that was modern, atonal, jazz-influenced or 'Jewish' in inspiration. Such leading spokesmen of the musical *avant-garde* as the composers Arnold Schoenberg, Alban Berg, Anton von Webern, Hanns Eisler, Kurt Weill and Paul Hindemith were forced to emigrate along with many top conductors. Goebbels railed at Hindemith's atonal experiments as 'the most atrocious dissonance of musical impotence', while his henchmen foamed at the dangers of alien and 'Negro' influences threatening the integrity of the folk community.[31] American jazz, the product of 'blatant race mixing', was identified as a special danger and an example of the insidious Jewish subversion of German culture by opening it up to a 'barbarian' invasion.

In their struggle against the so-called 'Judaization' of German music, the Nazis drew on Richard Wagner's notorious anti-Semitic pamphlet of 1850. Mountains of paper were expended on vilifying leading musicians of Jewish descent and anyone associated with them.[32] They were invariably accused, from the time of Meyerbeer and

Offenbach, of having reduced music to an object of financial speculation. Jews in music were denied any creative ability (a favourite canard of Hitler's), their compositions were dismissed as 'Oriental' and certainly 'un-German', while their sympathies supposedly lay with 'cultural Bolshevism'.

The Wagnerian legacy to the Nazis extended beyond the great composer's obsessive anti-Semitism, his *völkisch* beliefs and love of Nordic myths. The artistic orchestration and *mise-en-scène* of the great Nazi festivals owed much to Wagner's sense of the communal function of art. His attraction to heroic virtues and to a mythical Germanic world, his skill in staging and dramatic effects, his ability to create a hypnotic, delusionary spell of suspended reality, were ideally suited to Nazi manipulation. Even Martin Heidegger was bewitched in the late 1930s with the Wagnerian ideal of the *Gesamtkunstwerk* (the 'total work of art'), finding the name itself highly suggestive:

> For one thing, it means that the arts should no longer be realized apart from one another, but that they should be conjoined in *one* work. But beyond such sheer quantitative unification, the artwork should be a celebration of the *Volksgemeinschaft*: it should be *the* religion.[33]

Heidegger's invocation of the 'collective work of art' as the new religion of the national community is highly relevant to our theme. Inspired by Wagner's romantic myth of a classless *Volksgemeinschaft* (community of the people), it held out the promise of a mystical communion and an organic unity between art and politics, the spirit and the senses, the rulers and the ruled. Through his music Wagner had tried to recapture this archaic sense of unity, permanence and timeless values. The contents of this aesthetic message were now said to be embodied in Hitler's persona, which combined the roles of a politician, priest, artist and Wagnerian mythic hero. The inauguration fanfares, flag songs and music composed for the Nazi pageantries, rallies and conventions reflected this Hitler cult.[34] Propaganda and organization soon transformed and perverted the Wagnerian dream into the deification of the first artist-politician of the Reich. The Nazis added their own obsessive fascination with destruction and a ritualized, stylized cult of death that also claimed its inspiration from Wagner.[35]

Joachim Fest, one of Hitler's most perceptive biographers, noted the fusing of these elements in the Führer's political style:

> The carefully developed artistic demagoguery had real high points, when he strode down the broad avenue between hundreds of thousands to honor the dead on the Königsplatz in Munich or on the grounds of the Nuremberg party congress with gloomy music in the background, for example. In such scenes out of a political Good Friday magic – 'magnificence is used to advertise death,' as Adorno said about Wagner's music – Hitler's idea of aesthetic politics matches the concept.[36]

But solemn ceremonies of death were only one side of the symbolic politics of Nazism. The aestheticization of social relations also involved the creation of an atmosphere of beauty, harmony and 'Strength through Joy'. Even during the Weimar era, the Nazis had always known how to put on a good show; their mass mobilization techniques had stood out against the drabness of everyday life during the Great Depression. After 1933 their mastery of the mass spectacle and of image-making created a world of illusion and standardized responses that greatly facilitated their hold on power.[37] The manipulation of the arts was an essential element in their ability to get the German public to identify with the regime and its Leader. Impressively choreographed festivals like the Day of German Art helped to reinforce their prestige at home and abroad as 'guardians of culture'.

In their cultural policy, the Nazis had an important advantage. They knew that many Germans shared their tastes and even approved of their defamatory onslaught against most of modern art. Moreover, at least until the outbreak of war in September 1939, they could count on a broad popular belief that Hitler had indeed restored 'normality', order and decent values to German society. This spurious impression reflected the extraordinary indifference of many Germans to the persecution of the Jews, left-wing political opponents, marginalized groups like homosexuals and gypsies or dissident artists and intellectuals.[38]

By the summer of 1939, when the colour film was shot from which many of the images in this book are drawn, Hitler could feel confident enough to cast off the earlier ambiguities in his politics, abandoning the hypocritical façade of peace. He had always regarded war as the natural state of man and the ultimate goal of politics. He also believed that it was the best way of hardening the German *Volk* for its historic task of ruling the world. He had in any case resolved to attack Poland – a fact carefully concealed from the mass of the German people. The pageant in Munich, like the music festival in Bayreuth at the end of July 1939, offered a welcome diversion from the war of nerves. It might further deceive and mislead the domestic and international audience.

When looking at the pictures in this book, it is therefore important to remember that we are seeing a *staged* cultural event. Nazism, more than perhaps any other regime, was literally obsessed by its own self-representation. Its leaders attached enormous importance to the production of images and were aware of the endless manipulative possibilities which they offered.[39] They knew the power of visual bombardment in overcoming the average person's resistance and critical resolve. They realized how easily the normal recipient can mistake the illusion he or she is being offered for an authentic experience. The Nazis were also very much the heirs to a peculiarly modern problem – the difficulty of articulating the past historically, 'the way it really was'. Their response to this fragmentation of historical objectivity was typically totalitarian – to transform the past to fit their image of the utopian future. History as myth and as propaganda!

Hans Feierabend's silent colour film from 1939 is not in this category, though it records an event that partakes of a manipulated collective representation of the German past. Its feeling for ordinary physical reality and the texture of everyday life, its small random moments alongside the set pieces of the Munich pageant and art exhibition, make it different. Unlike the black-and-white official Nazi version of the same event, there are no special dramatic effects, adulatory crowds or grand gestures in Feierabend's film. His Hitler is no horseman of the apocalypse madly evoking the end of humanity, nor is he the mythical Superman of Nazi legend. He seems more like a slightly edgy master of ceremonies concerned that his great show should go off without a hitch.

At the House of German Art, Hitler could indulge his daydreams. He could imagine that he was heir to the Greeks and their ideal of the *polis* as

'The evil that men do...'
William Shakespeare, Julius Caesar

Hitler was indeed one of those 'terrible simplifiers' who had the gift of reducing complex problems to their elemental foundations. Whether he was dealing with culture, economics or politics, his powerful if limited mind was able to grasp the broad sweep of history and analyse the available choices with ice-cold calculation. Rarely can so much mediocrity, vulgarity, cruelty and dogmatism have coincided in the same individual with such political skill and propagandist genius. Rarely can one find such self-consciously criminal barbarism mixed to the same degree with an obsessive concern for the state of the arts.

Nazi art cannot, however, be reduced solely to its propagandist element or dismissed as a crude advertisement for the regime. It was able to draw on, and at the same time it grossly distorted, the romantic and classical elements in the German cultural tradition. Ultimately, however, the Nazi 'aesthetic' was divorced from any anchor in reason, morality or humanistic aspirations. Its power lay in its appeal to an explosive mixture of archaic myths, irrational cravings and specifically modern anxieties. Hitler's uncanny ability to act as a screen or medium for the secret fears and desires of millions of Germans provided the psychological foundations for his initial appeal. The relentless barrage of propaganda, terror and symbolic artistry grafted on to the real achievements of the Nazi regime before 1939 consolidated his emotional hold over the masses. But when we look for some 'essential' core at the heart of the Nazi phenomenon, rational explanations begin to break down. It is like gazing into the nothingness of a disappearing black hole.

'a work of art'; that he had discovered the modern synthesis between 'form' and politics; that Nazism would create a new race of 'Aryan' heroes, rivalling the Greek gods.[40] The cartoonist David Low observed of Hitler: 'His political conceptions were the artist's conceptions, seen in shapes, laid on in wide sweeps, errors painted out and details left until later, the bold approach and no fumbling. Essentially a simple mind, uncomplicated by pity.'[41]

CHAPTER TWO

ADOLF HITLER: ART AND MEGALOMANIA

'Hitler was not some peripheral distorter of German Romantic ideas. He was, in many respects, their most extreme interpreter: the ultimate, because the maddest, of all the German Romantics. It is often said, because he dropped out of art school, that he was a failed artist who turned to politics, but Hitler was a monster, precisely because he always remained, at heart, more of an artist than a politician.'

ANDREW GRAHAM-DIXON, *INDEPENDENT*, 1994

ADOLF HITLER was born at Braunau-am-Inn on the Austrian border with Germany on 20 April 1889. The son of a Habsburg customs official and a doting mother, he was an average pupil, leaving his school in Linz at the age of fifteen. His great ambition was to become an artist but in his nineteenth year he failed the entrance examination to the Academy of Fine Arts of Vienna. Between 1907 and 1913 he led an aimless, drifting existence in the Habsburg capital, much of it among the *déclassé* low life of a men's hostel. He scrambled a living from copying postcards, while revelling in Vienna's architecture and the operas of Richard Wagner. Later, he claimed that Vienna gave him 'the granite basis' of his National Socialist worldview.

The ideology which he first developed there, and then polished in post-1918 Munich, was a bizarre mixture of Social Darwinism, pan-German nationalism (aspiring to the union of all Germans in one Reich), biological racism, Slavophobia and extreme anti-Semitism. For the young Hitler, life was a merciless struggle for existence of all against all; the Germans were a *Herrenvolk* (master race) who had a divine right to extend their living space to the east; the preservation of blood purity was the key to their great imperial future. Above all, the related perils of Marxism and Jewry would have to be eradicated by a mass movement of German rebirth. This could not be organized from a decaying Austria. Hence Hitler saw his own future in the neighbouring German Empire. It was to be in the artistic, south German city of Munich that he would discover his great oratorical gift for rousing the masses. Munich was the place where the Nazi movement was born and where it would experience its early triumphs and failures. Adolf Hitler had first arrived there in 1913 as a twenty-four-year-old bohemian dropout, to escape military service in his Austrian homeland. Initially he eked out an uncertain income from selling his sketches, posters and small watercolours of Munich buildings until the First World War rescued him from this lonely existence. During his four years of military service he proved to be an able and courageous soldier. Though never promoted beyond the rank of lance-

War celebrations. *The young Hitler joins a jubilant crowd in Munich's Odeonsplatz, to celebrate the announcement of the outbreak of the First World War, on 2 August 1914.*

corporal, he was given the Iron Cross (First Class) in August 1918. In 1919 he returned to Munich, briefly serving as a member of the Bavarian Reichswehr Propaganda Department before taking over a small sectarian racist movement which shortly afterwards became the nucleus of the Nazi Party.[1] In the city's seething, smoky beer cellars Hitler first made his reputation as a fanatical nationalist orator and local agitator. Through his mentor, the Bavarian poet Dietrich Eckart, he was introduced to Munich high society. It was also in Munich that he met the core of his closest followers, including Hermann Goering, Rudolf Hess, Alfred Rosenberg, Gottfried Feder, Hermann Esser, Max Amann and his personal photographer, Heinrich Hoffmann.[2]

Until the disastrous Munich *putsch* of 9 November 1923, the young Hitler was still a provincial beer-hall rabble-rouser rather than a national figure.[3] Certainly, in the eyes of some of his followers, he was already comparable to Benito Mussolini and a local reporter even described him as 'the only notable rarity in Munich besides the Hofbräuhaus'.[4] But Hitler at this stage still thought of himself as 'the drummer' who was to pave the way for Germany's coming Führer, as yet unknown.

His impressive speech before the Munich People's Court in March 1924 and his halo of martyrdom during his brief incarceration for treason (during which time he dictated *Mein Kampf*) helped to transform his image. The 'Führer myth' built up around Hitler became an important point of unity in a splintered Nazi Party after his release from prison in 1925. With the onset of the Great Depression and the swiftly growing Nazi vote, this personality cult began to assume nationwide proportions. Hitler-worship became a major factor in the Nazis' appeal to the broad public and assumed quasi-religious dimensions.[5] He was seen increasingly as the prophet, the political missionary, the redeemer and saviour of a Germany hopelessly sunk in the depths of economic crisis.

Following the Nazi seizure of power in 1933, Hitler's myth was consolidated and magnified to new heights by Joseph Goebbels's propaganda apparatus. Hitler was successfully marketed as a 'man of the people', a true 'People's Chancellor'.[6]

TOP : **New Nazi standards**. *The first SA parade, Munich, February 1923.* ABOVE : **Writers' block.** *Hitler, Rudolf Hess and his fellow-inmates pose for the camera in Landsberg prison, 1925.* Mein Kampf *was written here during Hitler's brief stay, following the abortive 1923 Munich putsch.*

Leader as a 'political genius' who had single-handedly brought life, honour and freedom to Germany. His iron will had liberated the nation from the 'yoke' of the Versailles system, his diplomacy had restored German power and prestige, his economic policy had solved the problems of mass unemployment. By 1936 Hitler's genuine popularity had been transformed by skilful Nazi propaganda into a ritual of deification.[7] At the 1936 Reich Party Rally in Nuremberg, Hitler himself now spoke in terms of the mystical bond between himself and the German people: 'That you have found me…among so many millions is the miracle of our time! And that I have found you, that is Germany's fortune!'[8] Hitler was not simply the embodiment of the Party and of the nation, he was not only

The simplicity, the modesty and bravery of the ordinary 'front-line soldier' who had risen to become Führer of the Reich was constantly underlined. He was presented as symbol and incarnation of the life-force of the German nation, the fighter for and creator of German unity, the architect and statesman of a new Reich.

Birthday eulogies invariably spoke of the

the infallible Leader of Germany: his own speeches would constantly invoke a special relationship with Providence itself.

Despite the street violence and the revolutionary aura of the Nazi movement, Hitler increasingly appeared to the German middle classes in the 1930s as the guardian of order, public morality and bourgeois virtues. His image as a protector and upholder of Christianity was maintained in many respectable circles before 1939, in spite of the strikingly pagan and atheistic elements of the Nazi creed. More surprisingly, he was regarded as a 'man of peace', notwithstanding his territorial claims, the *Lebensraum* (living space) ideology which he espoused and the bellicose rhetoric of some of his speeches.[9]

In the years between 1933 and 1938 Hitler would none the less succeed in convincing the German people and much of the international community that he sought nothing but domestic prosperity and a reasonable defence of German interests in Europe. But in March 1938, with the enforced 'return' of his native Austria to what was now Greater Germany, it was becoming clear that the Nazis were steering an expansionist course.

The break up of Czechoslovakia was the next stage. The British and French prime ministers were bludgeoned by Hitler at the Munich peace conference of 1938 into pressuring the Czechs to give up the Sudetenland. This region, which contained a three-million-strong German minority, also held the Czech frontier defences without which the country was extremely vulnerable. By March 1939 Hitler had occupied Prague and transformed Bohemia and Moravia into a German 'protectorate', while nominally independent Slovakia became a puppet state of Nazi Germany.

Internally, the pogrom of 9–10 November 1938 against the Jews of Germany and Austria was also a turning point in the history of the Third Reich. Ostensibly it had been 'provoked' by the murder of a German diplomat in Paris by Herschel Grynszpan, a seventeen-year-old Jewish boy distraught over his parents' abrupt deportation from Germany to Poland. After the shooting, the Nazi Party newspaper carried a menacing lead article containing the following piece of invective: 'It is an intolerable state of affairs that within our borders hundreds of thousands of Jews still control whole streets of shops, frequent places of entertainment, and as "foreign" landlords pocket the money of German tenants, while their racial comrades abroad agitate for war against Germany and shoot down German officials.'[10]

The news of the German diplomat's death reached Hitler on 9 November 1938 in the old Munich *Rathaus*, where he was presiding over the fifteenth anniversary of the 1923 *putsch*. He left early, but Goebbels made a rabble-rousing speech whose contents were tantamount to encouraging a 'spontaneous' pogrom across the country. As a result every synagogue in Germany was burnt down, desecrated, or demolished. In addition, some 7,500 Jewish businesses in Germany and Austria were destroyed, ninety-one Jews were killed and over 30,000 Jewish men over the age of sixteen were sent to Dachau, Buchenwald or Sachsenhausen concentration camps.[11]

This was the most violent public display of anti-Semitism hitherto seen in German history. Indeed, it was the first major pogrom in Germany since the late Middle Ages, albeit one which was centralized and controlled with modern communications techniques.[12] Its ferocity belied Hitler's promises to maintain law and order, while the open rituals of degradation and humiliation of Jews in various German cities were an ominous expression of sadistic anti-Semitism.[13] Organized Jewish life in Germany had been rendered impossible, and within the next few months a hail of draconian laws rained down on the helpless Jewish population.[14] The *Kristallnacht* (Night of the Broken Glass), as it was euphemistically called, proved that the Nazis were ready to use terror to enforce their racial goals. As far as they were concerned, the Jews were outcasts, subhuman pariahs to be degraded at will – enemies and outsiders who were 'beyond the law'. The German people too, while some responded with acts of private sympathy, were being conditioned to distance themselves sharply from the Jews.

Since 1933 official State propaganda in Nazi Germany had presented the Jews as corrupt, cowardly and sexually perverse. They were stigmatized as dangerous, scheming conspirators against the Reich with whom no honest German should have any dealings.[15] After the *Kristallnacht* these stereotypes became even more intense. Ian Kershaw's assessment seems pertinent:

Kristallnacht - the morning after.
10 November 1938. Clearing up after a night of terror, when thousands of Jewish shops and businesses were wrecked.

break out. The time had come, he warned, to 'settle the Jewish question' once and for all. His menacing 'prophecy' of annihilation was greeted with thunderous applause.

The *Kristallnacht* and verbal threats were not only ways of conditioning the German people to accept a complete dehumanization of the Jews, they also served to prepare the nation psychologically for a more bellicose policy of expansion. Hitler had been visibly disappointed by the lack of public enthusiasm for war during the Munich conference of 1938. The pogrom against the Jews offered 'an excellent opportunity to disabuse the German people of the growing illusion that the Munich agreement marked the end of crisis, and that the German ship of state was at last entering calmer waters'.[17]

The more the Jew was forced out of social life, the more he seemed to fit the stereotypes of a propaganda which intensified, paradoxically, its campaign against 'Jewry', the fewer actual Jews there were in Germany itself. Depersonalization increased the already existent widespread indifference of German popular opinion and formed a vital stage between the archaic violence of the pogrom and the rationalized 'assembly line' annihilation of the death camps.[16]

A chilling hint of what was to come appeared in a speech Hitler made to the Reichstag on 30 January 1939, which contained an unmistakable threat to 'exterminate' European Jewry if a world war should

Hitler was of course well aware that much of his popularity derived from the astounding series of triumphs without bloodshed which he had chalked up since 1933. The withdrawal from the League of Nations, German re-armament, the re-occupation of the Rhineland, the annexation of Austria and then of Czechoslovakia had cost no lives. The restored sense of German power and glory had been achieved at so small a price that public euphoria was understandable. But the frenzied acclaim for Hitler, which was again manifest during his fiftieth birthday celebrations in Berlin on 20 April 1939, was still no mandate for war. The spectacular military parade and the accompanying adulation could not remove a pervasive fear of armed conflict among the German population.[18]

In the summer of 1939 the 'Danzig question' was the main source of international tension. Nazi propaganda played cleverly on the alleged persecution of the German minority in Poland and on long-standing anti-Polish prejudices in Germany. The general public mood favoured incorporating Danzig within the Reich, but without war. The hope was that if anybody could, then Hitler might pull it off peacefully, as he had the previous annexations in the east. But despite the intensive propaganda efforts of the regime, there was no real understanding within the German population about the necessity of war.[19] What was striking, however, was the extraordinary trust that the German people still had in Hitler's charismatic leadership and their naïve belief that he wished to settle things peacefully.

By mid-July 1939 Hitler had unquestionably achieved a unique position of personal authority for himself. He was seen as the architect and creator of Germany's economic miracle, the defender of its sovereign national rights, the rebuilder of its military might and the guardian of public morals. He had crushed the Bolshevik danger, smashed the trade unions, disenfranchised the Jews and eliminated mass unemployment. In addition, as he reminded Germans in a speech on 28 April 1939, he had 'recreated the thousand-year historic unity of the German living-space…without spilling blood and without inflicting on my people or on others the suffering of war. I have managed this from my own strength, as one who twenty-one years ago was an unknown worker and soldier of my people.'[20]

Hitler's string of domestic and international successes had given him an apparently unassailable popular base, unmatched by any German leader before or since. His strength of will, his self-assurance and oratorical magnetism had turned him, in Albert Speer's words, into something like 'a hero of ancient myth who unhesitantly, in full consciousness of his strength, could enter and masterfully meet the test of the wildest undertakings'.[21] Moreover, this had not been achieved solely or even predominantly by terror, repression and intimidation. Such methods had, of course, been crucial in crushing any initial *opposition* to the Nazi regime. Nevertheless, Hitler knew full well that his myth could not be built simply on the widespread fear of the Gestapo. It had to be rooted in real achievements, in constant mobilization of the masses, in the shrewd use of his own unique demagogic talents and in the ingenuity of Nazi propaganda.[22]

In order to win the hearts of the masses, politics was not enough and even the best network of party organizations could not alone guarantee loyalty to the Führer and the Reich. A great movement needed a coherent world-view and an inspiring myth if it was to seize the popular imagination and give individual Germans a sense of belonging and community. In this *Weltanschauung*, artistic endeavours played a crucial role as part of Hitler's utopian vision of culture and of the 'good society'. The primacy of culture in his eyes derived from its rootedness in the *Volk* and its unchanging racial essence. One of the goals of the Nazi revolution was to recapture a mythical agrarian past and reconnect the present to Germanic traditions.[23] At the same time it was the task of culture to clarify, spread and popularize the Nazi ideology. In this endeavour it would have to build on popular tastes and prejudices, on the essentially conservative instincts of the masses.[24] The Nazi ideology of race, blood and soil would more effectively enter the mass consciousness if it could be shown to be consonant with familiar sentiments, conventions and bourgeois moral values. In these as in other policy matters, it was Hitler who set the tone. Already in *Mein Kampf*, he had indentified culture as being by definition an 'Aryan' product. The Aryan was:

the Prometheus of mankind, out of whose bright forehead springs the divine spark of genius at all times...Exclude him – and deep darkness will again fall upon the earth, perhaps even, after a few thousand years, human culture would perish and the world turn into a desert.'[25]

The Germans were to be assigned the task of cultural leadership among the Aryan peoples. Hitler saw them not only as the best stock for building a new *Pax Germanica* but as the harbingers of a new epoch of Aryan and world culture. But the absolute prerequisite for inaugurating the Aryan millennium was the maintenance of racial purity. History, he warned, 'shows with terrible clarity that with any mixing of the blood of the Aryan with lower races the result was the end of the culture-bearer'.[26] Petrification would set in, the master race would lose its cultural ability and begin 'to resemble more the subjected aborigines than his ancestors'.[27]

The Jews were the main danger to the Aryan world in this as in most domains. According to Hitler, they possessed 'no culture-creating energy whatsoever, as the idealism, without which there can never exist a genuine development of man towards a higher level, does not and never did exist in them'.[28] The Jew, whose intellect was essentially destructive, had transmitted his materialism to the German bourgeoisie. Through the influence of money and the press he consistently sought to undermine the race consciousness and national values of the 'Aryan' peoples. Moreover, as the inventor of Marxism the Jew was deliberately undermining the foundations of culture.[29] Even democracy, in Hitler's mind, was a weapon to subvert the national will of the Aryan peoples and to prepare the road for Jewish world domination.[30]

The extraordinary importance which Hitler and other leading Nazis attached to the 'Jewish question' was not thereof accidental. Germany was to be the pivot in the coming world struggle between Aryanism and Judaism.[31] The National Socialist movement saw its special mission as being to lead this universal war against 'Jewish Bolshevism' and international finance. This was to be a 'battle of destiny' in which no compromise was possible between two irreconcilable world-views. On its outcome would depend the future of Germany, of Europe and of 'Aryan' humanity.[32]

A crucial feature of Hitler's anti-Semitism was his assertion that the Jews had no true culture of their own; that there had never been any authentic Jewish art; and that, above all, 'the two queens of all arts, architecture and music, owe nothing original to Jewry'.[33] Whatever the Jew had achieved in the field of art was either 'bowdlerisation or intellectual theft'. There was, of course, nothing original in these racist assertions, which had been continually spouted by German and European anti-Semites since around 1850 when Hitler's cultural idol, Richard Wagner, wrote his notorious book *Jewry in Music*. What was novel was that after 1933 these warped racial theories and dull diatribes about art became official State policy in such a highly advanced and cultivated nation as Germany.

Already, at the Party Day of Victory in 1933, the pattern was set. The Nuremberg Congress was orchestrated with the familiar Nazi talent for theatrical effects, the morning session beginning with the overture to Wagner's *Die Meistersinger*, Hitler's favourite opera. Then after a hymn of thanksgiving, the blood flag of the Nazi 'martyrs' who had fallen in 1923 was carried to the front of the platform, to the sound of muffled drums. The SA chief, Ernst Röhm (himself to be assassinated a year later on Hitler's orders), read the roll of the Party dead. Later came the high point of the proceedings with Hitler's proclamation, predictably attacking Bolshevism, capitalism, foreign domination and the Jews. In the afternoon, he addressed the League of German Culture and emphasized that music, art and architecture would be kept strictly 'Aryan' in the new Reich.[34] The following day the chief Party ideologue, Alfred Rosenberg, echoed this theme, vapidly boasting that all the leading German poets and philosophers were of 'pure Aryan stock'. Goebbels, not to be outdone, quoted Richard Wagner's statement that the Jews were 'the plastic demons of civilisation' and affirmed that only Aryans could be creative.[35]

The culmination of this kind of cultural anti-Semitism and hysterical anti-modernism was the notorious purge of 'degenerate art' *(entartete Kunst)* in the Third Reich. In 1936 Hitler had ordered the prominent painter and president of the Reich Chamber of Visual Arts, Adolf Ziegler, to gather together all specimens of 'decadent' art from more than 100 museums in Germany. The purge tribunal collected more than 13,000 paintings, drawings, etchings and sculptures. Among them were 1,000 paintings by Emil Nolde (himself a Party member and leading German Expressionist), 500 by Max Beckmann, 400 by Oskar Kokoschka, and 200 by George Grosz. Many foreign artists such as Picasso, Matisse, Cézanne, Van Gogh, Dufy and

Braque suffered a similar fate.[36] The so-called 'Degenerates' were then displayed (for the last time) at a huge exhibition in Munich. This was, ironically, the most 'popular' art exhibition in the history of the Third Reich. Visitors were confronted with unframed paintings under such nauseating captions as: 'Thus did sick minds view Nature!' or 'German Peasants in the Yiddish Manner'.[37]

Of the 112 eminent artists whose work was publicly pilloried in this manner only six were of Jewish origin and very few were truly Marxist.[38] Nor were they 'decadent', 'immoral', 'subversive' or 'degenerate' as the Nazi press sought to suggest.[39] But for Hitler and the Nazis, all the main trends in modern art, including Dadaism, Cubism, Expressionism, Futurism, Surrealism and abstract painting, were by definition poisonous 'Jewish' and 'Marxist' products.[40]

The modernist, *avant-garde* movements that had flourished in the defunct Weimar Republic had sharply rejected traditional aesthetic standards. The painters, especially, appeared to be fascinated by ugliness, the composers by atonal dissonance, the poets and playwrights to be preoccupied with decadence and the madness of big city life. They seemed to find beauty in the loss of equilibrium and symmetry and in emphasizing the torments of the individual soul. Moreover, their aesthetic revolt against bourgeois existence was in some cases linked to a general movement of social and political revolution.

Dadaism, with its doctrine of anti-art *(Kunst ist Scheisse* – Art is Shit), reflected perhaps more than any other trend the prevailing post-war chaos and was the most obvious provocation against German petty-bourgeois *(Spiesser)* values.[41] Hitler had a special hatred for the Dadaists, who had mercilessly satirized him. Moreover, in his mind, like those of many inhabitants of Munich who had lived through the revolutionary period between November 1918 and May 1919, the artistic and political *avant-garde* represented identical evils.[42]

Expressionist and anarchist writers – some of them Jewish like Erich Mühsam, Ernst Toller and Gustav Landauer – had indeed been very prominent in the Munich revolutionary councils movement. This reinforced the tendency in right-wing circles to see modernist artists as the spearhead of chaos and anarchy. Long before the Nazis came to power, painters like Paul Klee, Wassily Kandinsky, George Grosz, Max Beckmann and the whole Expressionist movement had come under fierce attack. They were described as 'un-German', as Bolshevist and 'ferments of decomposition'. They had allegedly 'degraded' art to the 'level of primitive African or Oceanic tribes'. Moreover, it was suggested that their works bore a close resemblance to paintings by inmates of lunatic asylums.[43]

One of the most vocal and prestigious exponents of this opposition to modernist art in Weimar Germany was the prominent architect Paul Schultze-Naumburg. In his book *Kunst und Rasse* (Art and Race), published in 1928, he sought to prove the similarity between the figure-style of the Expressionists and the appearance of the physically deformed and the mentally deficient.[44] When the Nazis gained control of education in Thuringia in 1930, Schultze-Naumburg was briefly in charge of cultural policy. At his instigation, the modernist paintings of Kandinsky, Klee, Oskar Schlemmer, Karl Schmidt-Rottluff and the sculptures of Ernst Barlach were removed from public view in Weimar. They were deemed to be representative of 'eastern or otherwise racially inferior subhumanity'.[45]

Schultze-Naumburg also waged a relentless war against the Bauhaus as 'an infamous centre of art bolshevism'. This internationally renowned stronghold of modern architecture and design in Weimar Germany was little better than a 'synagogue' in his eyes, though its most prominent representatives were of impeccable 'Aryan' origin. Gradually, the leading Nazi newspaper, the *Völkischer Beobachter*, which had sometimes praised the Bauhaus in the past, came round to Schultze-Naumburg's position.[46] His fanatical anti-modernist and anti-urban diatribes were especially congenial to the most reactionary wing of the Nazi Party, which was organized around Alfred Rosenberg's Combat League (*Kampfbund*) for German Culture.

Rosenberg, who had originally trained as an architect, had established his *Kampfbund* to halt what he saw as the corruption of culture by 'Jewish' and left-wing influences. Unless these 'alien plants' were pulled up by the roots and replaced by an art based on heroic, 'Nordic' values, the desired regeneration of the German soul could not take place. These ideas were developed in turgid prose in his best-selling 'Blood and Soil' classic, *Der Mythos des XX Jahrhunderts* (Myth of the Twentieth Century), published in 1930. After the Nazis seized power, Rosenberg found himself in bitter conflict with Goebbels, who much to his chagrin had been given overall control of cultural policy in the Third Reich.

Goebbels was initially more sympathetic to modernist tendencies and tried to keep some Expressionist artists like Nolde, Barlach and Erich Heckel in the Nazi fold.[47] In this policy of encouraging a 'Nordic expressionism' he had the support of the more leftist National Socialist Students Union. He also defended the markedly critical position of *Die Kunstkammer* (the house organ of the Reich Chamber of Culture for the Visual Arts) towards *völkisch* art and frequently crossed swords with Rosenberg on this issue. Hitler appeared at first to incline more to Rosenberg's anti-modernism, declaring in September 1933 that there was no place for 'charlatans' and 'representatives of decadence' in the new Nazi order.[48] But while he continued to vituperate against the Cubists, Futurists and Dadaists, Hitler also upbraided those backward-looking *völkisch* enthusiasts like Rosenberg who had failed to keep pace with the times.

When it came to art and architecture, Hitler had never been deeply committed to the *völkisch* movement, though this continued to have a modest place in Nazi Germany. As a youth Hitler had been greatly impressed by the famous buildings of the Ringstrasse in Vienna with their predominantly neo-Baroque and Renaissance neo-classcist styles.[49] In *Mein Kampf* he described how he would stand for hours in front of the Vienna Opera, the Parliament building and the museums – 'the whole Ring boulevard seemed to me an enchantment out of the "Thousand and One Nights".' Despite his loathing for the Viennese, his love of this monumental architecture stayed with him for the rest of his life. Vienna, like Paris, was after all a city built 'with grand style', which expressed a sense of imperial glory. Berlin, by comparison, was 'nothing but an unregulated accumulation of buildings', as he

Arch of victory. Hitler's 1925 prison sketch for a triumphal arch in Berlin, designed to dwarf the Arc de Triomphe in Paris.

reminded Albert Speer, to whom he had entrusted the great task of its wholesale reconstruction.[50]

Highly impressed though he was with Vienna's architecture, Hitler always preferred the atmosphere of Munich, whose southern Baroque building style, conservative tastes and carnival mood greatly appealed to him.[51] Munich's artistic culture – more sensual than spiritual – suited his temperament. It was not a cosmopolitan multi-racial city like Vienna with a large Jewish or Slav population.[52] Nor did it have the restless, metropolitan brashness and mobility of Berlin, which he always distrusted.[53] It was in Munich during the late 1920s that Hitler became converted to the neo-classical building style of Paul Ludwig Troost, a Bavarian architect and interior designer of luxury liners.[54] Troost was commissioned by Hitler to design the new Party headquarters (Braunes Haus) located on the Königsplatz in Munich, which was to be overhauled and restructured.[55] This attractive square in the heart of Munich was already adorned with a series of neo-classical buildings, the creation of Bavaria's enlightened king, Ludwig I (1825–48). Hitler identified closely with this patron of the arts and saw himself as his heir in rebuilding the city.[56] Soon after taking power, he commissioned Troost to erect two temples of honour on the Königsplatz to the Nazi 'martyrs' in the 1923 *putsch*. Each temple displayed eight coffins, open to the sky, as a

Pupil and master*. Hitler and Paul Ludwig Troost with the model of his design for the House of German Art, Munich, 1933.*

A mausoleum for martyrs*. The shrine where the ornate caskets of the fallen 'heroes' of Hitler's abortive 1923 putsch were displayed. The classically inspired 'temple' set the architectural tone for all subsequent Nazi buildings.*

permanent reminder to the people of the National Socialist will to sacrifice for the cause of German renewal.

In 1933 Troost also designed two major new Party structures – the Führer Building and the Administration Building – as part of the Königsplatz complex. Then Hitler chose Troost to design a new art gallery, the House of German Art, which was intended to combine classical discipline and a cool sense of order with the 'Nordic' idea of race. Troost, who died in 1934, never lived to see the completion of this project, which was finished by his widow, Gerdy, together with the architect Leonhard Gall. Hitler, who had laid the foundation stone in October 1933, played an active role in its design, and had collaborated closely with Troost on other projects.[57] The Führer revered Troost's work, eulogizing him as 'one of the greatest German architects'.[58] He laid a wreath annually on Troost's grave at Munich's North Cemetery.[59]

Albert Speer, who was soon to be Troost's successor in implementing Hitler's architectural plans, had some interesting observations on his master's artistic passions. He believed that in architecture, painting and sculpture, Hitler had remained fixed in the world of 1880 to 1910 'which stamped its imprint on his artistic taste as on his political conceptions'.[60] Painting stopped for him at 'decadent' Impressionism, whereas he admired the glaringly anachronistic canvases of Hans Makart, the Viennese artist who specialized in decorative works of vast dimensions and glowing colours. By the time of the *fin de siècle*, this ornate, visually opulent style with decorous bunches of grapes flanking huge masses of languishing female flesh was already finished even in Vienna.[61] It had been replaced by the far more daring innovations of Gustav Klimt, Egon Schiele and Oskar Kokoschka – the Austrian Expressionist painter who was to be a prime target of philistine vilification in Nazi Germany. Klimt's motto for the Viennese Secession, 'To the era its proper art, to art its proper freedom', would of course, have also been anathema to the Nazis. Equally alien to Hitler were the new trends in painting initiated by Franz Marc, Paul Klee and Wassily Kandinsky in Munich, at the very time he arrived as a penniless vagabond in the city.

Nevertheless, in architecture, his attitudes were somewhat more liberal and the regime permitted modernists like Mies van der Rohe and Peter Behrens to work for a time in Nazi Germany.[62] Nor did Hitler appear to reject totally the innovations of the Bauhaus founder Walter Gropius and the modernist French architect Le Corbusier, despite the vehement attacks on them in most Nazi circles. These seeming anomalies underline Speer's point that there was no definitive 'Nazi style' in building. Troost's lean, Spartan approach, which was almost devoid of ornament, combining elements of traditionalism with modernity, came perhaps closest to a desired norm in public architecture. But this neo-classicism, as Speer noted, was 'multiplied, altered, exaggerated, and sometimes distorted to the point of ludicrousness'.[63]

Speer himself would, of course, eventually become the leading architect of Nazi Germany after Troost's death. An ambitious, well-educated technocrat, youthful and patriotic, he had first come to Hitler's attention as the organizer of the 1933 May Festival on the Tempelhof Field.[64] He

Pillars of art. *Hitler, accompanied by his architects Albert Speer and Professor Gall, views construction work on Munich's new 'Temple of Art'.*

greatly impressed Hitler with his innovative 'cathedral of light' effects, which became famous as backdrops for the Nuremburg Party rallies. He was put in charge of the Beauty of Labour office in the German Labour Front, which played an important part in providing a facelift for the German workplace. In this capacity, Speer showed himself to be a master of aesthetic illusion, finding new ways to give back to the German worker the sense of dignity in labour. Beauty of Labour was a microcosm of Nazi aesthetic politics in the area of technology and design, focusing on the need to sanitize and improve the environment.[65]

Speer and his assistants understood that the beautification of industrial plants could physically and psychologically transform the conditions of labour, leading to improved performance. It could contribute to strengthening the image of a people's community and thus help to implement Hitler's 'socialism of the deed'.[66] Beauty of Labour was intended to exemplify that there was only 'one culture and one life form, that of the German people'. The grey ugliness of industrialism was to give way to a new economy of technical form, order, symmetry and external cleanliness. Speer's concept was reminiscent in some respects of the *Neue Sachlichkeit* (new objectivity) of the 1920s (often execrated in Nazi literature) and pointed towards the increasing modernism of Nazi architecture and design after 1936.[67] This Nazified 'modern' approach based on a technical rationality divested of Bauhaus utopianism presaged a significant shift away from the *völkisch* anti-modernism still prevalent in other spheres of the Nazi State.

From 1933 Speer had also been artistic and technical organizer of Party rallies and his design of flags and standards was a key element in their extraordinary success. The brilliance of his theatrical backdrops and lighting effects was immediately acknowledged by Hitler and Goebbels. As a result he was commissioned by Hitler to redesign the Luitpold Arena and to build the Zeppelin Field Stadium at Nuremberg, to accommodate 340,000 spectators.[68]

Speer also designed the German Pavilion at the Paris World Fair in 1937, which was a monument to the growing sense of power and achievement in the Third Reich. But his most important assignment was the construction of the new Reich Chancellery in Berlin which was completed in record time by the beginning of 1939. Speer knew that Hitler had always insisted on an impressive, monumental, neo-classical style for representative State and public buildings. He was also aware of the Führer's megalomania, his desire to overwhelm his own people and, even more, visiting diplomats and dignitaries with German power.[69] Many times Hitler had told him that the purpose of building was to transmit one's own epoch and its spirit to posterity. Ultimately, he liked to philosophize, 'all that remained to remind men of the great epochs of history was their monumental architecture...'[70]

Speer's construction was designed to fulfil these requirements. The German media hailed it as a triumph of National Socialism, as a great communal labour, as a symbol of the new Greater German Reich and of its future glories.[71] Admiring writers stressed the clarity and symmetry of the building's lines and the sense of security and order which it exuded. They lauded its austere, Prussian 'soldierly character', so consonant with the tradition that Frederick the Great had stamped on Berlin. Some even saw the construction of the Chancellery as definitively marking the end of 'liberal chaos' in Germany and the return of genuine authority to the Reich. This was very much in keeping with a speech Hitler had made on culture in 1937, in which he had stated: 'Our opponents will come to realize it, but above all our followers must know it: our buildings are erected with the aim of strengthening... authority.'[72]

Hitler himself had declared that 'when one enters the Reich Chancellery, one should have the feeling that one is visiting the master of the world'.[73] Everything in the building was designed to evoke the sensation of loftiness and dignity, to impress the visitor and to induce a submissive mood. Dwarfed by giant decorations, large staircases, huge rooms and incredibly long marble galleries, those guests and visitors who came to meet Hitler had to be suitably overwhelmed by the grandeur of the Greater German Reich. Here is how Hermann Giesler, one of Germany's leading architects, compared Speer's *magnum opus* with Troost's Führerbau in Munich:

Two masterworks of the political rise to power...The Führer Building is a symbol of the newly found faith in a German Future... Troost's building with its Doric economy and severity shows the very image of the fighting Party... in Speer's Reich Chancellery speaks the eminence and richness of a Reich which has become a super-power.[74]

The contrast was particularly apt because

Berlin and Munich represented two different polarities in the Reich. If Berlin was indisputably the political capital and destined to be *the* metropolis of a new European order, Munich was both 'the capital of the movement' and 'the capital of art'. Hitler was determined to restore to it the predominant role which it had once occupied as the centre of German art in the nineteenth century. He hoped that the new monumental buildings erected there would revive its position as a *Kunststadt* (city of art). Troost's representative architecture was to serve as a model for all Germany, to create 'a community space for the *Volk*'. The newly reconstructed Königsplatz, with its granite slabs, was in the words of Werner Rittich, 'a stone symbol of the National Socialist ideology, its greatness, its struggle, and its victory'.[75]

On this granite square containing the roofless temples of the 'martyrs', surrounded by towering pillars and open to the elements, the Nazi movement had built its most important shrine. The victims of the failed *putsch* were no longer separate from the community for which they had fallen.[76] The temples expressed to contemporaries a sense of disciplined order, a classical design and a 'soldierly feeling for life'.[77]

Munich, the city which was so important in the history of the Nazi movement, remained therefore a point of commemoration and also of renewal. Its truly 'German' atmosphere, its neo-classical build-

Buildings for eternity*. Nazi architechture on the Königsplatz. The Führer Bau [left], in which the 1938 Munich peace conference took place, nears completion. Next to it stands the first Nazi building, Paul Ludwig Troost's shrine to the fallen 'martyrs' of 1923. Behind it is the Braunes Haus, the headquarters of the Nazi Party.*

ings and its artistic traditions assured it of Hitler's special favour. Above all, Troost's House of German Art on the Prinzregentenstrasse, officially opened on 18 July 1937, stood out in Hitler's words as a 'truly great and artistic' structure. He considered this 'temple of art' uniquely impressive in its beauty and functional in its layout and equipment.[78] Frau Gerdy Troost echoed this verdict, calling her husband's work a 'shrine' exemplifying the 'eternal values' to which National Socialism aspired.[79] It was a sign that Germanic traditions were being rescued from the chaos of destructive liberalism. For its admirers, the wonderful clarity and 'musical harmony' created by the contrast of pillars and columns with severe horizontal lines was reminiscent of Hellenism in the best sense.[80] The Nazis almost unanimously saw this gallery as standing for 'permanence' against the intrusion of unsettling change, modish caprice and dangerous foreign ideas. Yet, despite this broad chorus of praise, popular epithets for Troost's masterpiece like 'Palazzo Kitschi' or 'The White Sausage Terminal' (*Weisswurstbahnhof*) suggest that not all of Munich's citizens were so enamoured.

Nazi architecture cannot ultimately be separated from ideology, propaganda and politics, any more than the modernist style which preceded it. The dominant National Socialist motifs can best be seen as a backlash against revolutionary experimentation and the social ferment of the Weimar Republic. The obsessive quest for 'Germanness' was an answer to 'internationalism'; the drive for order was a reply to anarchy; the return to classicism and 'eternal' values a response to fears of innovation and transience. The Nazis mobilized tradition against modernity, heroic simplicity against bewildering complexity, *völkisch* rootedness against metropolitan nomadism. 'Cultural

Bolshevism' was a convenient if grossly misleading label with which to stigmatize those aspects of modernity that the Nazis vehemently opposed in art as in politics.

Hitler and the Nazi Party, from the outset, had attached great importance to architecture and the arts as an instrument of political propaganda.[81] Architecture, in particular, was seen as an index of national power and strength. Indeed, in 1929 Hitler had promised that 'out of our new ideology and our political will to power we will create stone documents'.[82] Moreover, to underline this commitment, his henchmen constantly referred to him as a 'political artist' or, in Goebbels's words, as 'that great masterbuilder', who had constructed a state of truly classical proportions.[83]

In the period before their seizure of power, the Nazis had flayed modern architecture as a symbol of the atomized mass society and the evils of urbanism. Modernist architects were constantly accused of helping to produce an 'uprooted people' who had lost touch with the soil. Conservative polemicists like Schultze-Naumburg, who were close to the Nazis, denounced the rampant 'materialism' of the new architecture in quasi-apocalyptic terms: 'For, just as in German politics, a battle of life and death rages in German art today.'[84] Walter Gropius and his Bauhaus school were especially vilified as 'salon Bolshevists' whose legacy would have to be extirpated once the Nazis came to power. Only National Socialism, it was asserted, would have the will to protect German cultural traditions against the international Jewish and Marxist conspiracy.

Once in power, the Nazi building programme showed more diversity than might have been expected, partly reflecting the varying stylistic preferences of different Nazi patrons. Nevertheless, Hitler did impose a certain unity with his dictum that both art and politics derived from the same creative force of an authoritarian 'will to form'. Architecture, above all, should awaken national consciousness and express national greatness. He saw it as a crucial element in giving the German people a sense of belonging and in transmitting to future generations the belief in their inalienable right to rule.[85]

Hitler's admiration for Greek art and architecture as a valid model emphasized both its beauty and its functionalism. But he also insisted that Nazi architecture must be of its time, utilizing the new technologies to 'build for eternity'.[86] Hence he did not oppose large-scale urban reform and planning. Nor did he interfere with the functional, efficient style of building favoured by architects employed within the German Labour Front. The Hitler Youth Movement was also permitted to use the most modern materials in its constructions. Moreover, some of the air force office buildings were unmistakably indebted to the modern movement in architecture. These anomalies could be justified by Hitler's own call for 'true practicality' and 'crystal-clear functionalism'. Thus, as Barbara Miller Lane has argued, Nazi building styles ultimately 'represented a compromise among contradictory ideas and purposes'.[87]

Hitler's building programme was also a good illustration of 'reactionary modernism', compounding worship of advanced technology with blood and soil romanticism.[88] But the 'final goals' were much more far-reaching than many of his contemporaries realized, involving nothing less than eventual world domination for the Reich. It is in this perspective that one needs to see Hitler's constant analogies with the Roman Empire, his preference for granite as a building material, his obsession with permanence and his gigantomania.[89]

The endless building projects could simultaneously serve different internal and external functions while at the same time remaining fixed on the ultimate expansionist purpose. Thus, they were used to raise German feelings of self-confidence, they helped to accelerate national productivity and they increased Hitler's own authority. They also lulled the outside world into believing in Hitler's peaceful intentions.[90]

Even more striking, however, was the sheer scale, extravagance and *folie de grandeur* of his plans. 'Berlin, the capital of the world' was to be comparable only to ancient Egypt, Babylon and Rome. The German eagle surmounting the Great Hall in Berlin was to be perched on a globe which would crown the dome of the tallest building in the world, dwarfing in size the Capitol building in Washington and St Peter's in Rome. The Central Station in Berlin must surpass New York's Grand Central Station; the engineer Todt's suspension bridge for Hamburg must be greater than San Francisco's Golden Gate Bridge.[91] The grand Stadium in Nuremberg was to be the largest in the world. Above all, Hitler's Arch of Triumph (which he designed as early as 1925) must be double the height of Napoleon's arch in Paris. 'That will at least be a worthy monument to our dead in the First World War,' he told Speer. 'The name of every one of our 1,800,000 casualties will be carved in granite!'[92] As Elias Canetti once pointed out, the feeling for this crowd of the dead was decisive in Hitler. They were his obsession, the source of his power, the ultimate reason for his existence.[93] They had helped him to rise, they were his first crowd. In their name he would avenge the defeat that never happened and the treason of November 1918. Those dead and the ones to come would be his 'victory' and his monument.

CHAPTER THREE

THE MASS SEDUCTION

'Propaganda, propaganda, propaganda. All that matters is propaganda.'

ADOLF HITLER, 1923

NATIONAL SOCIALISM had first emerged in Bavaria after the First World War as a backlash against economic crisis, social instability and the trauma of the Munich Soviet republic of 1919. The black swastika, which was its symbol on a flag designed by Hitler himself, represented, in his own words, the struggle for victory of 'Aryan' man 'and at the same time for the victory of the idea of creative work, which in itself always was and will be anti-Semitic'. The red background stood for the social idea of the movement and the white circle represented the nationalist idea. The National Socialists claimed to be a workers' party, adopting 'comrade' as an official form of address, but the bulk of their support initially came from lower middle class and *déclassé* elements. In the 1920s the movement was still split between its original, anti-industrial, racist-populist wing in south Germany and the more 'socialist' revolutionary pole led by the Strasser brothers in the north. Hitler provided the binding element and had indisputably established complete personal ascendancy over the movement by the end of the decade. His concept of the *Volksgemeinschaft* (the community of the people) was shrewdly designed to appeal across the profound class divisions in German society. Nazi propaganda constantly trumpeted its populist, social egalitarianism. Hitler, too, liked to describe himself as 'a son of the people', who had been a construction worker, a student, an artist and then a front-line soldier for four years, before entering politics.[1]

The experience of the First World War had been crucial for Hitler and his Stormtroopers (the early private army of the Party). Most of the Brownshirt leaders were former soldiers who had been unable to reintegrate themselves into civilian life.[2] Their commander, Ernst Röhm, was himself a military adventurer who believed in 'the socialism of the trenches'. His youthful, violent followers, drawn largely from the unemployed, were assigned the task of winning the battle of the streets against the Communists and Social Democrats. The brawling hooliganism and revolutionary élan of the SA were indispensable to Hitler before 1933, but thereafter it became an embarrassment. With the 'Night of the Long Knives' in 1934, its wings were brutally clipped.

The SA was the first uniformed, para-military organization of the Nazi Party. Its massed columns of marching men not only struck fear into opponents but exuded a sinister sense of power and uniform will. They called themselves 'political soldiers' and 'freedom fighters', though their nationalism was often little more than a mask for criminality and gratuitous violence.[3]

Hitler's followers, once in uniform, however, belonged to him alone, bound by an oath of personal loyalty and blind obedience. Whatever the particular Nazi Party organization of which they were members, they became part of a uniformed mass whose co-ordination did not fail to impress contemporary observers.[4] In the Third Reich, uniforms became, indeed, a central part of the visual backdrop to every public event. Their ubiquity and sheer variety was intended to create an overwhelming impression of power and authority. Through their extensive use of uniforms, the Nazis successfully repressed any individuality or personal freedom, thereby facilitating the co-ordination of the mass rallies for which they became famous.[5] As Baldur von Schirach, the Hitler Youth leader, told his adolescent following in 1939 – even their bodies 'belonged to the nation to whom they owed their existence'.

The body of the *Volk*, in its turn, belonged totally to the Führer. Organized in great marching columns, the disciplined but faceless ranks of the faithful became particles in a huge mass that had been welded into a single whole.[6] They exemplified the call of the Reich Organization Leader, Robert Ley, that in the future there would be 'no German without a uniform'.[7]

Hitler's own brown party uniform was an indispensable part of his public persona before the Second World War (when he assumed his soldier's coat), helping to distract attention from his somewhat ungainly, awkward body language. The decorations on his uniform were few – the swastika armband, the Iron Cross from the First World War and the golden Party emblem – but as Führer of the movement his pre-eminent rank was in any case assured. His real emblem and ornament were the masses that paraded before him in endless Party rallies.[8] Their serried ranks and their perfect formation provided Hitler with an ideal décor

for his new style of activist politics.

Hitler instinctively understood the importance of wartime camaraderie, a dramatic liturgy and colourful flags in mobilizing the masses.[9] Like D'Annunzio and Mussolini in Italy, he saw the value of the patriotic myth of battle and of the cult of fallen martyrs for his own nationalist movement. The blood of those who fell for the fatherland or for the Nazi movement helped to seal the covenant of a community of comrades. In this way, mass death in war could be integrated into Nazism and later, into the national community of the Third Reich.[10] It was as if these dead millions were being resurrected and reborn in the newly arisen masses, responding to the political call of National Socialism, 'Germany awaken!' (*Deutschland Erwache*).[11]

From his early years in Vienna, Hitler had grasped the central importance of mass politics. In *Mein Kampf* he recalled the impact made on him by the Austrian Social Democrats as a mass party: 'I gazed on the interminable ranks, four abreast, of Viennese workmen, parading at a mass demonstration. I stood dumbfounded for almost two hours, watching this enormous human dragon which slowly uncoiled itself before me.'[12] From the leader of the Christian Social Party in Vienna, Karl Lueger (whom he admired as one of the greatest 'German' mayors of all time), he would further learn how to use the 'social question' and populist anti-Semitism to arouse the masses. His own observations convinced him that the masses were essentially 'feminine'; they wanted and needed a strong and uncompromising ruler. In his cynically ruthless view, they felt 'very little shame at being terrorized intellectually and are scarcely conscious of the fact that their freedom as human beings is impudently abused'.[13] Hitler also became persuaded that physical intimidation would impress the masses greatly when it was successfully carried out.

Later, in Munich, when he first entered politics with the army's patronage, he applied these lessons with alacrity. As he wrote in *Mein Kampf*: 'Whoever wishes to win over the masses must know the key that will open the door to their hearts. It is not objectivity, which is a feckless attitude, but a determined will, backed up by power where necessary.'[14] Emotions, not abstract ideas, stereotyped formulas, not rational explanations, would best imprint themselves on the memory of a crowd. There was no room for hesitations, doubts, qualifications or concessions. The great magnetic forces which would alone compel a crowd were vehemence, passion and fanaticism. The masses would always respond 'to the compelling force which emanates from absolute faith in the ideas put forward, combined with an indomitable zest to fight and defend them…'[15] None of these notions were original in and of themselves.

The main insights had already been synthesized by the French writer Gustave Le Bon in his short, incisive exploration *Psychologie des Foules* (Crowd Psychology), first published in 1895. Le Bon, who had been influenced by the Boulangist mass movement in France and the crisis of the Third Republic in the 1890s, had prophesied that the twentieth century would be 'the era of crowds'. The future art of politics would consist in understanding their psychological laws and moulding them. The great leader would be the man who appreciated intuitively that 'crowds do not reason, that they do not accept or reject ideas as a whole', that they do not tolerate discussion or contradiction. Such a man would be the charismatic leader who knew how to organize a crowd politically by appealing to its soul (*âme*) and to the power of unquestioning faith.

Affirmation, repetition and contagion were the forces that moved the masses, who were infinitely 'suggestible'.[16] In their primitive hatred of 'natural' superiority, they tended to create a lower-class leadership in their own image which they would then blindly follow. Mussolini, as is well known, was profoundly influenced by Le Bon's 'excellent work', to which he frequently referred.[17] But Hitler, too, was very familiar with Le Bon's treatment of *Massenpsychologie* (mass psychology), which he found in the German translation of the book. It could only reinforce his own conviction that the masses are profoundly conservative and move forward primarily under the impulsion of myths, images, and feelings.[18]

The attribute that marked off Hitler from most ideologues and other rival politicians was what Alan Bullock once described as 'his unequalled grasp of what could be done by propaganda, and his flair for seeing how to do it'.[19] His own passion, verbal violence and carefully rehearsed oratorical gestures were a concrete illustration of his belief in 'the magic power of the spoken word'.[20] But propaganda involved much more than Hitler's uncanny ability to stir both hatred and exaltation in the hearts of his listeners. He turned Le Bon's advice about repetition into a deliberate technique.

The chief function of propaganda, Hitler explained in *Mein Kampf*, is:

to convince the masses, whose slowness of understanding needs to be given time in order that they may absorb information; and only constant repetition will finally succeed in imprinting an idea on their mind. Every digression in a propagandist message must always emphasize the same conclusions. The slogan must of course be illustrated in many ways and from several angles but in the end one must always return to the assertion of the same formula. Then one will be rewarded by the surprising and almost incredible results that such a persistent policy secures. The success of any advertisement, whether of a business or a political nature, depends on the consistency and perseverance with which it is employed.[21]

Propaganda was not limited to the spoken word alone. There was also the choreography of mass meetings and demonstrations which created a sense of power and belonging to the movement. The sea of Party flags and standards borne aloft by uniformed SA members, the militant songs of the movement, the military music and roll of drums, the tense expectation surrounding Hitler's entry before a speech and the loud chants of 'Sieg Heil' created a rousing atmosphere.[22] This political style, with its calculated sense of ceremonial, its fanfares and dense mass of uniforms, was unmatched by any other political party in the Weimar Republic. Only the Communists came close. But the organized Left (much less the bourgeois parties) had no prospect or intention of equalling the National Socialists in the use of violence and terror as political weapons.

Hitler understood perfectly the psychological impact of such brutality. He also saw that the isolated individual could be drawn into a mood of intoxication at well-organized mass meetings by feeling himself for the first time to be part of a larger community. Surrounded by thousands of people animated by a single conviction, by the noise, enthusiasm and hypnotic power of mass suggestion, his doubts and anxieties could by overcome. The 'community' which the Nazis aspired to forge explicitly renounced rational or intellectual persuasion in favour of emotions orchestrated by visual and aural décor. The 'truth' of their message was confirmed not by argument but through tangible success, the chorus of a thousand voices screaming in unison and the palpable unity of a densely packed crowd. This emotional frenzy of Nazi gatherings gave them a special character.[23]

At the same time, the ceremonial and liturgical aspects of the Nazi creed borrowed heavily from Christian forms while subverting them from within. The concepts, images and symbols were reminiscent of a caricatured version of Christianity. Nazism had its 'martyrs', its 'apostles', its 'dogmas' and sacraments. It was a *political* faith but one which drew on models like those of the Jesuit order or the hierarchical authoritarian structures of the Catholic Church.[24]

Hitler's feeling for ritual and liturgy may well have derived from his Austrian Catholic upbringing.[25] Like his fellow lapsed Catholics, the Bavarian Heinrich Himmler and the Rhinelander Goebbels, he had an intuitive sense of outward forms, of symbolism and the art of mass psychology. He believed that these were qualities that the Catholic Church had cultivated over the centuries and he fully intended to exploit them for his own Nazi 'religion'. In that sense, one could almost describe National Socialism as a politicized Catholicism stripped of any residues of Judeo-Christian ethics. Ironically enough, however, Protestants were to prove more susceptible than Catholics in Germany to the eschatological lure of Hitler's political messianism.

It is true that Hitler had little time for the 'cult places' or cult rituals, or for the obscure mysticism of some *völkisch* circles in the Party. At the Reich Party Congress of 1938 he had explicitly condemned such occultism.[26] But he had absorbed Le

Bon's lesson that the religious needs of the masses needed to be satisfied, by organizing ever larger infusions of ritual. Thus, eventually to supplant the Christian festivals, the Nazis instituted their own cycle of high holy days. These included the anniversary of the seizure of power, Hitler's birthday, National Labour Day, the Day of the Summer Solstice, the annual Party rally in Nuremberg and the anniversary of the November 1923 *putsch*. Here is one acidic description that perfectly captures the pseudo-religious significance of 9 November:

> the venerated cadre of the survivors of the Munich Putsch silently re-enacted their march through the crowd-lined streets of the Bavarian capital in a bombastic travesty of the Passion Play. Their march route to the *Feldherrnhalle* was an evocation of the Stations of the Cross – with one signal difference: the Saviour marched upright, grim-visaged and jack-booted, in the front rank of his disciples; Calvary and Resurrection had blended into one sombre, soul-stirring event.[27]

If this were not enough, each year Hitler would consecrate new Party colours by touching them with one hand while clutching in the other the cloth of the 'blood banner' (*Blutfahne*), riddled with bullets from the abortive *putsch*.[28] But it was above all Hitler's own person which was invested with special religious significance. He was the instrument of Providence, the source of all blessings, the omniscient guide endowed with supernatural powers. In a more sinister sense he was also the Sacred Executioner, the triumphant Germanic Christ-figure sent to carry out terrible judgement on Satan's people, the Jews.[29] The Nazis were ultimately the heirs to two millennia of Christian anti-Semitism, which they ruthlessly aggravated as a deliberate weapon of mass politics. But without the apocalyptic, pseudo-religious component in Hitler's own fanatical personality and the demonic attributes he projected on to the Jews, it is doubtful if a 'Final Solution' of the Jewish question could ever have been attempted.

Ideological myths and mass politics had not, of course, originated with the Nazis. Nor were they the first movement in modern Europe to use vivid nationalist imagery, rites and festivals to influence the masses. Since the French Revolution there had been many efforts to dramatize politics as a way of enthusing people about their own nation. The desire to create a sense of community and participation in the political process was part of the logic of popular sovereignty. In nineteenth-century Germany, Richard Wagner became one of the central figures in the revival of a particularly emotional, quasi-religious nationalism expressed through myth, symbol and festivals. His world of ancient Germanic myths and his belief in an unchanging Germanic *Volk*, his concept of the 'total work of art' and his efforts to bring it to the people, had an immense and lasting influence.[30] The Bayreuth theatre and festival, which he inaugurated, ensured that the Wagnerian tradition would carry through to the twentieth century. The carefully staged Wagnerian operas with their romantic and dream-like quality, had an intoxicating effect on spectators, inspired by the music, the settings and the atmosphere of Bayreuth. The creation of this festive and sacred mood was something that greatly impressed many imitators, including the Nazis.

Hitler, a passionate admirer of Wagnerian opera, was very much taken with his idol's construction of the festivals and his representation of the so-called 'Aryan' soul on stage and in his music.

In 1934 he would provide Hermann Rauschning with his own purely racist interpretation of *Parsifal* as a drama of the corruption of pure, noble blood. Hitler emphatically asserted that he had 'the most intimate familiarity with Wagner's mental processes', adding that at every stage of his life he had come back to him.[31] On another occasion, in 1936, listening to the prelude of *Parsifal* on his private train, he was overcome with euphoria: 'I have built up my religion out of *Parsifal*... One can serve God only in the garb of the hero.' Then listening to Siegfried's funeral march, he recollected the first time he had heard it at the Vienna opera house. 'And I still remember it as if it were today how madly excited I became on the way home over a few yammering Yids I had to pass. I cannot think of a more incompatible contrast. This glorious mystery of the dying hero and this Jewish crap!'[32]

In the Third Reich, Bayreuth would be *the* great cultural shrine and Hitler himself become the patron of the festival and doting friend of the Wagner family. As Albert Speer cryptically observed: 'On these festival days Hitler seemed more relaxed than usual.'[33] In January 1940 Thomas Mann, once one of the great defenders of Wagner's music, somewhat sadly admitted that it was indeed a progenitor of Hitlerism: 'With its...mixture of roots-in-the-soil and eyes-towards-the-future, its appeal for a classless society, its mythical-revolutionism, it is the exact spiritual forerunner of the "metapolitical" movement today

Swastikas and crosses. *The Nazis found enthusiastic supporters among the many German Protestants.*

terrorizing the world.'[34]

Nazi aesthetic politics took a great deal from the Wagnerian theatre of illusion and myth as a framework for its formation of the masses. In the pomp and circumstance surrounding its popular festivals as well as in its own cult of the Germanic *Volk*, Nazism could draw inspiration from Wagner's way of bringing myth to the people.[35] For Hitler, in particular, Wagnerian opera was *the* great spectacle. He had never forgotten the Vienna opera of his youth – the stage effects, the magic of the music and the ceremonial surrounding it. As George Mosse has written: 'Such taste was directly transferred to the liturgy of the Third Reich and made to symbolize romanticism and order, classical harmony and worship.'[36]

The new features from the 1920s, like massed flags and brilliant lighting effects, were simply grafted on to this basically conservative *fin-de-siècle* outlook. The traditional world of myth and symbol, too, had to be adjusted to a new age of mass movements and violent mass politics. Festivals, ceremonial and cultic rites – especially in the Third Reich – were now built into everyday life and the seasonal rhythms of the calendar. The Nazi liturgy, setting about the total organization of society, resolved to express the new feeling of community. Within this interlocking totality constructed out of sacred spaces, monumental structures, dazzling lighting effects, eternal flames and endless flags, Hitler stood at the centre of the Nazi cult as its living symbol. The *Aufmärsche*, the constant parades and processions, the flags, the uniforms, the slogans and the salutes created the desired atmosphere of shared worship and participation. But the entire ceremonial organization of these mass spectacles, whatever Hitler's own intentions, depended on the Leader and his myth, in order to weld the people together into a single unity.

The original function of the fascist ceremonies had been to bind the *movement* together and publicly display its sense of order and discipline. Like Mussolini before him, Hitler had seen in the meetings and parades an essential means of building and maintaining mass support. They were the primary way to establish a direct emotional contact with the crowds. But before his seizure of power in 1933, they retained an element of informality and even amateurism. Only afterwards did they acquire the elaborate theatricality, implacable precision and high stylization which we tend to associate with fascism in power.[37] Public ceremonies now assumed the role of representing the entire *nation* and its traditions. The glorification of the national past flattered the pride of the people and increased the prestige of the Leader and his regime. But ceremonial could also serve, as in the case of the Berlin Olympic Games in 1936, as a means of demonstrating to the entire world the concrete achievements and peaceful intentions of the new Germany. The glorification of sporting success and the cult of a healthy, vibrant youth were particularly suited to this goal.

What distinguished the Nazi regime from others was not its theatrical politics as such but rather the scale, intensity and frequency of the implementation. Not only the national and regional Party rallies but the many mass spectacles that coincided with anniversaries and the opening of public buildings were used to impress on the public at home and the world abroad the achievements of National Socialism. Meticulous attention on all such occasions was given by the Nazi leaders to the details of design, scale, colour and to symbolic representation. This preoccupation with visual elements was not merely decorative but a central feature in the propagation of fascist ideology and of mass politics as spectacle. In this respect, Nazism fundamentally differed from liberal and democratic societies while being more comparable to other fascist and Communist regimes.[38]

The Soviet Union, despite the ideological gulf which separated it from the Third Reich, did exhibit, under Stalinism, some striking similarities in artistic and cultural development to Nazi Germany.[39] Both societies were totalitarian dictatorships that had emerged out of a victorious revolution. They both deified their leaders and glorified the one-party State. In both cases, the Party exercised centralized control over all creative activity and subordinated it to ideological ends. Both regimes extolled the virtues of collectivism and execrated the liberal individualism of the Western democracies and their capitalist culture. Both States sought to mobilize the masses and claimed to speak in their name, on cultural as well as social and political issues. In both countries there was a drive to monumental architecture, heroic sculpture and officially correct painting, music and literature. Art was expected to conform but also to encourage positive attitudes to life, to reinforce the prevailing doctrines and to glorify the regime. Dissent and criticism were banned and those who did not toe the line found themselves persecuted not only by the State but often by their fellow artists. True, the dominant ideology in the USSR was Marxist and internationalist, which acted as a partial restraint on xenophobic tendencies. Racism was offically

No complaints, please ! *The placard reads: 'I am a Jew, but I will never again complain about the Nazis.' The true story behind this well-known image has only recently come to light. An eminent Jewish lawyer, Dr Michael Siegal, had lodged an official complaint with the Munich police, after the windows of a Jewish-owned store, Kaufhaus Uhlfelder, had been smashed in March 1933. At the police HQ he was beaten up by Nazi storm-troopers, had his front teeth knocked out, his ear-drum perforated and his trouser legs cut off. Dr Siegal is seen here being marched through the streets of Munich.*

banned, as was anti-Semitism until Stalin's last years. Moreover, art and culture were not consciously used to glorify military and imperialist aggression. But there were enough parallels to demonstrate that not everything in Nazi culture was a unique product of German history.

Two areas of special importance to both the Nazis and the Communists were the art and techniques of propaganda. Propaganda itself was regarded as an 'art' which had to be of service to politicians and to the consolidation of the regime. Its aim was to control public opinion through the media and to facilitate mass mobilization. During the years of struggle before 1933, verbal and visual propaganda had been one of the strong points of the Nazi movement.[40] After the Nazis' rise to power, propoganda came under the control of Joseph Goebbels, whose Ministry for Propaganda and Enlightenment was probably the largest apparatus of its kind in history. Goebbels in this role felt himself to be an artist, as he confessed to Germany's leading conductor, Wilhelm Furt-wängler, in 1933:

> Politics too is an art, perhaps the highest and most comprehensive there is, and we who shape modern German policy feel ourselves to be artists who have been given the responsible task of forming, out of the raw material of the mass, the firm concrete structure of the people.[41]

In his new role as a 'political artist', Goebbels established a near total control over the communications media – i.e. the radio, the press, publishing, literature, cinema and the other arts. He quickly achieved the 'co-ordination' (*Gleichschaltung*) of cultural life, 'cleansing the arts' in the name of the Nazi Revolution.[42] He subjected editors and journalists to State control, abolished all 'art criticism' and eliminated Jews and political opponents from any position of influence. He was a particularly venomous Jew-baiter, one of the most relentless in the Nazi Party. At the Party Day of Victory in 1933 he lashed out at what he called the 'Jewish penetration of the professions' (law, medicine, journalism, theatre and so on). Earlier in the same year, he staged the great ritual 'burning of the books' in Berlin as part of the struggle against the 'un-German spirit'. The works of Jewish, Marxist and other so-called 'subversive' authors were consigned to the flames in a huge bonfire. In November 1938 he was also the main instigator of the November pogrom (the *Kristallnacht*) and during the war years he was one of the chief secret abettors of the 'Final Solution', personally supervising the deportation of the Jews from Berlin in 1942.

Goebbels, who came from a strict Catholic, working-class background, had in the early 1920s been identified with the radical, more 'socialist' wing of the Nazi movement led by Gregor and Otto Strasser. He had switched his allegiance to Hitler in 1926 and in the same year was appointed Nazi district leader for Berlin-Brandenburg.

Within a short time he had become the most feared demagogue in Berlin. A relentless, tireless agitator endowed with a powerful voice, rhetorical fervour and complete lack of scruples, Goebbels had already emerged by the end of the 1920s as a master propagandist. With cynical, ice-cold calculation he transformed the Berlin student and pimp, Horst Wessel, into a 'Christlike socialist' and Nazi 'martyr'. In the years of the Great Depression he provided many of the images, the myths, the slogans, the outright lies and the telling aphorisms which spread the Nazi message.[43]

Goebbels also edited his own weekly newspaper *Der Angriff* (The Attack), founded in 1927, designed his own posters and organized his SA detachment for frequent street battles and beer-hall brawls in Berlin. Hitler quickly recognized Goebbels's verbal facility, intellect and organizational talents as being indispensable to the Nazi movement. After 1933 he also had cause to be deeply grateful to his propaganda minister for the flair with which he created the Führer myth, the image of a Messiah-redeemer of the German nation. Nobody else in Hitler's entourage could have matched Goebbels's skill in providing the requisite stage management, manipulation and theatrical effects.

Despite his proximity to Hitler and their shared radicalism, Goebbels was not loved in the Party by his more dull-witted comrades. The 'little doctor' was too much of the bourgeois intellectual and his physical deformity did not help. Though very few of the Nazi leaders were tall, blond and blue-eyed, none was further from the 'Nordic' ideal than the crippled little man with black hair. Bitterly conscious of these handicaps, Goebbels overcompensated through his ferocious ideological radicalism, and his burning hatred of the rich, the intellectuals and especially the Jews. Apart from Hitler, no other Nazi orator knew how to ignite in his listeners the same degree of rage, despair, hatred, fanatical determination and the need to destroy.[44]

If National Socialism was to a certain extent propaganda masquerading as ideology, then

Goebbels was its high priest. He shared with Hitler an underlying contempt for the masses and a similar ability to draw inspiration from their unconscious moods and feelings. But where Hitler's relationship to the masses was visionary, exalted and even ecstatic, Goebbels was more deliberately Machiavellian, calculated and theatrical. This extended to his view of propaganda, the task of which was not to be intelligent or well-bred, but only to lead to success.[45] Like Hitler, he recognized in the combination of propaganda, art and terror the essence of Nazi rule; all three elements were necessary to ensure its maximum effectiveness. By propaganda, he meant 'winning people over to an idea so sincerely, so vitally, that in the end they succumb to it utterly and can never again escape from it'.[46] At the same time, Goebbels understood that this could not happen unless the public was already receptive and the propaganda related to their real concerns and problems.[47] In other words, it was not simply a matter of manipulation and technique but also of focusing on and sharpening existing attitudes and beliefs. Propaganda had to canalize an already existing stream, giving direction and force to popular needs and feelings. Emotional elements alone would not achieve the desired goal of mass indoctrination. The public had to be convinced through an appeal to both rational calculation and to more irrational instincts.[48] Only in this way could the potential gulf between the Nazi regime and the people be overcome. The 'political will' of the nation could not be successfully co-ordinated unless the enthusiasm and commitment of the masses were maintained. The central task of propaganda after 1933 was to ensure this 'co-ordination', in order to cement the nation more firmly together.

As president of the Reich Chamber of Culture, Goebbels saw a special role for art in giving expression to this Nazi goal of *Volksgemeinschaft* and in creating a true people's culture. Initially, he was more moderate than other Nazi leaders in his cultural policy, partly out of concern for world opinion. He supported for a while those who wanted to fuse National Socialism with Expressionism. The Expressionist sculpture of Ernst Barlach and the work of the controversial painter Emil Nolde graced his home until Hitler denounced them as decadent artists. He tried unsuccessfully to persuade Stefan George to head the Reich Chamber of Literature, failed to convince Fritz Lang to take charge of the Nazi cinema and vainly sought to bring Thomas Mann back to Germany.[49] He was more successful in the musical field with the great composer, Richard Strauss, and the leading conductor, Wilhelm Furtwängler, both of whom remained in Germany and helped to maintain the Third Reich's cultural prestige.

In November 1936 the 'moderate' façade was abandoned and Goebbels banned all art criticism, having it replaced by mere description and reportage.[50] He glibly asserted that 'up to the Jewish *literati* from Heinrich Heine to [Alfred] Kerr', critics had been respectful of the achievements of others and not set themselves up as infallible judges. But Jewish cultural infiltration had led to 'a complete distortion of the the term "criticism"', by people who were not themselves creatively gifted. German critics had already been given four years to conform to National Socialist principles. Henceforth, they would confine themselves to commentary without evaluation.[51]

In a wide-ranging address to representatives of the press on 15 March 1933, Goebbels had adopted a considerably more subtle line, implying the freedom to criticize while ensuring that this would remain illusory. The role of the press and the media was to provide the link between the National Socialist government (which expressed the popular will) and the people.[52] Hence, the press had to *instruct* as well as inform, to win the people over to Nazi aims in an active way. Propaganda, Goebbels reminded his listeners, had unfairly become a much maligned term. In reality, a propagandist had to know men's minds, to understand 'the secret swings of the popular soul from one side to another'.[53] He had to speak to people from different social classes and regions, in a language they could grasp. The essence of propaganda was 'simplicity, force and concentration', to gather confused and complex ideas 'into a single catch slogan and then to instil this into the people as a whole'.[54] Even the lowliest man in the street must be able to understand what was expected of him. The Nazis expected the press to fulfil this didactic function. Objectivity was not the issue, since everything was in any case either overtly or covertly tendentious. Indeed, Goebbels said, impartiality was both sexless and worthless.

Ten days later, addressing the representatives of the radio, Goebbels had outlined his remarkably prescient vision of a new and topical broadcasting system, in tune with the *Zeitgeist* (spirit of the time) and national responsibilities. It was essential in an age of technical advance that national events should reach the whole people, offering them the possibility 'to participate directly in the great events of our time'.[55] There was no reason not to broadcast Reichstag (parliamentary) sessions; if television was one day developed, he declared, then the whole nation should be able to watch as events took place. But in the meantime radio, as the mass medium of the age, must be given a *modern* tempo. Indeed, the Nazi regime was extremely radio-conscious and

Hitler made no fewer than fifty broadcasts in his first year in office. His well-known dictum, 'Without motor-cars, sound films and wireless, no victory of National Socialism', showed an awareness similar to that of Goebbels concerning the importance of new technologies.[56] By 1939, about 70 per cent of all Germans were receiving radio programmes on their radio sets, popularly known as the Goebbels-blaster.

But the new instrument of mass communication was conceived in the early days more as an amplifier of the political rally or as a means to extend the number of listeners hanging on the Führer's words. Germans were always encouraged to listen to the radio in factories, barracks and other public places rather than in the privacy of their own homes. The radio was to provide them with a new sense that they were privileged to witness history in the making. However, when dealing with news reports, public events and international politics, every item was fitted by the Nazis into a preconceived, stereotypical and ultimately mythical perception of historical development.[57]

But it was the cinema rather than radio which really obsessed Hitler and Goebbels as being potentially the most powerful mass medium of the new age. Already in the 1920s the German cinema had enjoyed a kind of golden age. As Siegfried Kracauer pointed out long ago, there was a curious overlap between the dream world it had projected before Hitler and the Germany which actually emerged after 1933.

Self-appointed Caligaris hypnotised innumerable Cesares into murder. Raving Mabuses committed fantastic crimes with impunity, and mad Ivans devised unheard-of tortures. Along with this unholy procession, many motifs known from the screen turned into actual events. In Nuremberg, the ornamental pattern of NIBELUNGEN appeared on a gigantic scale: an ocean of flags and people artistically arranged. Souls were thoroughly manipulated so as to create the impression that the heart mediated between brain and hand. By day and night, millions of feet were marching over city streets and along highways. The blare of military bugles sounded unremittingly, and the philistines from the plush parlours felt very elated. Battles roared and victory followed victory. It was all as it had been on the screen.[58]

Fritz Lang's *Nibelungen* epic from the 1920s, which ends in an orgy of mutual extermination, fascinated both Hitler and Goebbels. Indeed, the propaganda minister's admiration for the half-Jewish Lang led to an offer that he should reorganize the German film industry – which was duly refused. Despite the massive exodus of screen talent (much of it Jewish) Goebbels did succeed in mitigating some of the damage after 1933. Recognizing that the public had little appetite for Brownshirt epics on the big screen, he developed the conviction that entertainment was the best film propaganda! Escapism became the favoured formula, especially during the Secoond World War when Germany's cities began to burn and the need to maintain morale became overriding.

Nevertheless, there were exceptions to this rule, including the three anti-Semitic films that were released in 1940 to convince the public that the 'Jewish question' required a radical solution. The first of these releases, *Jud Süss*, featured the rise and fall of a corrupt court Jew in eighteenth-century Württemberg, and its obvious parallels with the present were not overlooked. This relatively sophisticated feature film was a great box-office success and exactly the kind of perfidiously 'entertaining' material with a message which Goebbels favoured for the cinema. This was not the case with the much more explicitly propagandist approach in the documentary *Der ewige Jude* (The Eternal Jew). An extraordinarily vicious and obscene film which depicted the Jews as a criminal, parasitic race comparable to rats, it had been made even more bloodthirsty and aggressive by Hitler's personal intervention. There are horrific, distorted scenes of Jewish ritual slaughter of animals and many repulsive shots of Jews from the Warsaw and Lodz ghettos, whom the Nazis were already earmarking for extermination.[59] These eastern Jews, who had been deliberately herded by the Nazis into inhuman ghetto conditions in Poland, were depicted as if they represented the normal, everyday Jewish way of life. A significant indicator that this film was usable to justify a 'Final Solution' is the use of a film clip of Hitler's bloodcurdling 'prophecy' of 30 January 1939, threatening the extermination of European Jewry in the event of a Second World War. The film ends on an upbeat note, with blond, muscular 'Aryan' types set against a blue sky, Nazi salutes and flying banners: the unmistakable health warning is to keep the race pure and assure the future of the German people.

After 1940 Goebbels did not repeat such an anti-Semitic barrage in the cinema, presumably since the Nazis felt that the public had been sufficiently softened up for the planned 'solution' to the Jewish problem in Germany and the occupied territories.[60] The propaganda minister's doubts about *Der ewige Jude* were not, of course, grounded in principled dissent from its vitriolic anti-Semitism. (He knew instinctively that it was box-office poison but had to bow in this particular case to Hitler's

Another photo opportunity. *Staging* The Triumph of the Will. *From her aerial platform [high up between the swastikas] Leni Riefenstahl films her Führer. Nuremberg Party Rally, September 1934.*

intransigence on the matter.)

Seven years earlier, in a speech about the German film industry, Goebbels had already warned against concentrating the whole time on political correctness.[61] Films, so Goebbels insisted, needed to treat popular themes, if they were to fill the cinemas. The public rightfully demanded some distraction and amusement. Goebbels knew very well that an anti-Semitic horror film did not fit this need. Nor did some of the so-called National Socialist films, which reduced the movement to endless parade-ground marching and trumpet blowing. They unforgivably bored the viewers and 'made one inwardly shudder on seeing them'. What was crucial was the way in which such themes were treated. The three films Goebbels singled out for special praise as examples of the cinematic art were Sergei Eisenstein's *Battleship Potemkin* ('a marvellous film without equal in the cinema'), *Anna Karenina*, starring Greta Garbo, and Fritz Lang's *Nibelungen*. What had especially impressed Goebbels about *Potemkin* was its artistic brilliance and its 'power of conviction'.[62]

Goebbels, like Hitler, always regarded propaganda as the art of influencing the masses. His concept had little to do with advertising techniques. It was about political struggle and the need mentally and emotionally to conquer the German people for the Nazi Revolution. Power based on bayonets alone would, he warned, ultimately fail unless it invaded the hearts of a people and locked them into the system. Propaganda had a key role in this task, but to achieve its objective it had to find ways to keep mass enthusiasm alive.[63] Film art, Goebbels thought, could greatly contribute to this endeavour. Hence his admiration for Eisenstein's *Potemkin* as the cinematic myth legitimizing the Bolshevik Revolution in Russia.

The one German film-maker who came close to equalling that Communist feat was Leni Riefenstahl in her film of the 1934 Nuremberg Party Rally, *Triumph des Willens* (*The Triumph of the Will*). She had been commissioned by Hitler to produce an artistic film about the Party convention, after he had been suitably impressed by a number of her earlier mountain movies, especially *Blue Light*. In 1933 she had already made a film for Hitler of the Party Congress in Nuremberg, called *Sieg des Glaubens* (*Victory of Belief*), which she later disowned. (The assassination of Ernst Röhm, the head of the SA, who had featured in the film, no doubt explained its official withdrawal from circulation.) Almost casually, in her book on the 1934 film, she wrote: 'The preparations for the Party convention were made in concert with the preparations for the camera work.'[64] In effect, the rally was intended from the outset to be the stage for a spectacular piece of film propaganda glorifying Nazism.

The Triumph of the Will was indeed a film of the Nuremberg Party Congress, but the rally 'merely served as the set dressing for a film that was then to assume the character of an authentic documentary'.[65] The Nazis, under the supervision of Hitler, ably assisted by Albert Speer, meticulously laid the groundwork, with precise plans of the marches and parades. The grandiose building arrangements at Nuremberg were specially designed to encompass the mass movements. The speeches themselves played a secondary role, but the visual symbolism stimulated a mood of ecstasy and continual stimulation. The city of Nuremberg became a sea of waving swastika banners with the flames of bonfires and torches illuminating the night. The streets and squares echoed continuously with the rhythms of the march music.[66] In Riefenstahl's film, the overwhelming impact of the advancing standards, the

The Führer and the masses. *Nuremberg, 1935*

banners and flames, is captured by innovative cinematic techniques that emphasized endless, feverish movement.[67]

The opening sequence of *The Triumph of the Will* presents us with the Führer's aeroplane flying towards Nuremberg through banks of wonderful clouds, on noiseless engines. Before the descent into the city the inscriptions remind us that 5 September 1934 is twenty years after the outbreak of the First World War, fifteen years since the beginning of German suffering (Versailles, the Weimar Republic) and nineteen months after the German rebirth. Meanwhile, we view the scene of welcome through the Führer's eyes, an intimacy constantly repeated in the film through close-ups of his face interacting with the crowds. The descent of Hitler from the clouds had suggested the mission of a god or of a supernatural being. But once on earth, he is clearly a man of the people. This German people are depicted throughout Riefenstahl's film as being liberated through their amalgamation into the Nazi movement, as being made *whole* in the here and now. The one word they scream most frequently throughout the Party Rally is 'Heil!' (hail!), which also means 'whole' and carries the message of salvation.

It seems to me that Klaus Theweleit is right when he says that Hitler at this and other rallies was no mere demagogue or actor, but was offering the massed blocks of his listeners a new religion:

Raising the banner high, closing ranks and standing firm: all this replaces the 'foundations' of a God now abandoned. Once, when the world was populated by devils, God prevailed. Now the struggle has passed into the hands of the youth of Germany…They know God is dead. The Führer offers a new religion. Abjuring their faith in God, they become superior to the church as currently established.[68]

The Nazis filmed every phase and aspect of their rule in great detail in order to control their own image on celluloid, but no other documentary or full-length film ever matched *The Triumph of the Will* as propaganda. This was the supreme visualization in cinematic form of the Nazi political religion. Its artistry, reinforced by the grandeur and power of the Nuremberg décor, is designed to sweep us into empathetic identification with Hitler as a kind of human deity.[69] The massive spectacle of regimentation, unity and loyalty to the Führer powerfully conveys the message that the Nazi movement was the living symbol of the reborn German nation. There is the Leader, there are the *Volk*, the exaltation of community, the ecstatic faces of joy, faith in the ideal, the perfect geometric design of mass formations: the whole spectacle was reminiscent, in Kracauer's words, of the *Nibelungen*. 'Siegfried's theatrical trumpeters, showy steps and authoritarian human patterns reappear, extremely magnified, in the modern Nuremberg pageant.'[70]

Riefenstahl's subsequent efforts to separate her aesthetic conceptions from the propagandist intent are unconvincing. Her film of the Nuremberg Rally was not pure history, but history become theatre. In *The Triumph of the Will*, the film document is no longer simply a record of reality; in Susan Sontag's words, 'reality' has been constructed here to serve the image.[71] It is a construction that sympathetically reflects Nazi ideals of beauty, community, courage and heroic masculinity. The new Germany that passes across the screen in perfect marching formation and in an endless dynamic movement embodies the mass spectacle to perfection.

CHAPTER FOUR

THE CULTURE OF BARBARISM

*'Admittedly art has nothing to do with propaganda, but it is the profoundest expression
of a people's true soul. This soul has, however, been besmirched and led astray by Jewish
and Bolshevik propaganda, so that it has been cut off from its roots.
To that extent, the task of propaganda is to help the healthy perceptions
of the public back to freedom and truth.'*

HITLER TO GOEBBELS, 1932

THE DENUNCIATION of modern art as aesthetically repellent and politically subversive was not an invention of the Nazis. Already in the second half of the nineteenth century concepts like decadence and 'degeneration' had begun to flourish as part of the general critique of European culture and society.[1] Perhaps the most forceful and certainly the most controversial assault on *fin-de-siècle* artistic decadence came from the pen of Max Nordau, a German-speaking Jewish physician and *littérateur* from Budapest who later settled in Paris. In his book *Degeneration* (1892) he had denounced the restlessness of modernity and the shattering of men's nerves induced by urban life for their disastrous effects on body and mind. He dealt at length in his best-selling book with artistic decadence, linking it directly to bodily degeneration, sexual deviancy, criminality and insanity.[2] Among the nineteenth-century artists whom he singled out as 'degenerates' were Baudelaire, Wagner, Ibsen, Tolstoy, Rimbaud, Verlaine, Zola, Oscar Wilde and many of their followers. Few, if any of the modernists, could escape his morbid diagnosis.

In early twentieth-century Munich and Vienna, experimental art was tarred with the same brush. In 1909 the painter Oskar Kokoschka was execrated in the leading liberal middle-class newspaper of Vienna as 'mentally sick', a 'degenerate artist' and an *Untermensch*.[3] The Dresden Expressionists were accused of *Meschuggismus* ('fostering a cult of insanity') and a respectable Munich paper around 1910 called for the arrest of the *Blaue Reiter* painters, Marc, Klee, Kandinsky and Macke.[4]

After the First World War this fear of modern art reflected more than simply the deeply ingrained philistinism, conservative traditions and popular taste of bourgeois society. In Germany, in particular, the lost war provoked a vehement animus on the Right against the pacifism of Expressionists like the sculptor Ernst Barlach, the painters Otto Dix and Georg Grosz, or the mocking satire of the Dadaists. The Bauhaus design school was also seen as an 'enemy fortress', guided from Moscow, in the very heart of the fatherland.[5] Above all, there was Berlin, which in the eyes of the *völkisch* Right, had taken over from Paris as the world capital of lasciv-

56

iousness, obscenity and decadent modern art.[6] The culture of the Weimar Republic which was centred on this 'corrupt' metropolis, was by definition rootless, sensation-mongering, ugly, blasphemous, shameless and even criminal. As Alfred Rosenberg delicately phrased it: 'German post-war art is that of *mestizos* laying claim to the licence of depicting bastard excrescences, the product of syphilitic minds and painterly infantilism…'[7] Hitler, too, in *Mein Kampf*, was no less contemptuous about modern art, warning that the State must intervene to prevent people 'being driven into the arms of spiritual lunacy'.[8]

Once the Nazis came to power, they lost no time in showing that they intended to reshape Germany's cultural life. At the Party Day of Unity in 1934, held in Nuremberg, Hitler proclaimed that 'the nervous nineteenth century has reached its end'.[9] The German nation would have to be re-educated through a purification of the race to new cultural goals. He violently assailed 'Jewish intellectualism' for allegedly sowing the seeds of spiritual confusion and anarchy that had penetrated Europe since the Middle Ages. As the guardian and custodian of German art he solemnly promised to put an end to this morbid state of affairs.

A year later, at a rally in Nuremberg, Hitler again vituperated against the Dadaists, the Cubists, Futurists and Expressionists. They were either fools, cheats or 'Jewish Bolshevists', he thundered, if they thought that artists must draw cretins 'as a symbol of motherhood' or hunchbacked idiots as 'representatives of manly strength'.[10] Such pronouncements signalled that the funeral obsequies of modern art would not be long in coming to the Third Reich. The mediocre though fanatical Nazi painter Wolf Willrich, with his call for 'Cleansing the Art Temple' in a book published in the spring

of 1937, echoed Hitler's words and helped to set the tone for the greatest purge in art history.[11] He was one of a four-man purge-tribunal which toured museums and galleries across Germany, ordering the removal of drawings, paintings and sculptures that appeared to be 'degenerate'.

Apart from Willrich, the other members included the indefatigable Professor Adolf Ziegler (aptly described as the Third Reich's 'aesthetic Torquemada'), Hans Schweitzer-Mjölnir and Count Baudissin.[12] The count, who was director of the Volkswang Museum in Essen, appropriately considered the steel helmet to be 'the sublimest image that has recently been created in Germany'.[13] The result of their combined efforts was a display of some 650 works by the cream of Dadaist, Cubist and Expressionist painters, deliberately presented as a mocking horror show.[14] It was officially opened in Munich at the old gallery in the Hofgarten on 19 July 1937, exactly one day after the inauguration of the first Great German Art Exhibition.

The intentions of the organizers were to demonstrate to ordinary, honest Germans from what perverse, distorted and loathsome monstrosities they had been delivered. The representatives of 'cultural Bolshevism' were accused of having traitorously blasphemed against the German fatherland and its army, mocked religion, perfidiously raised prostitution to a moral ideal and insulted German motherhood.[15] 'What you see here are the crippled products of madness, insolence, lack of ability and degeneration,' Professor Adolf Ziegler declared in his opening address, which lauded Hitler's infallible aesthetic judgement.[16] Only the Führer, he added, could show German art the path on which it must proceed in order to express the German racial character.

The guide to the exhibition explained its goals

'Degenerate music'. From the exhibition guide by Dr Hans Severus Ziegler, Düsseldorf, 1938. A racist image, vilifying jazz music as 'Jewish', 'Negro' and sexually deviant.

with brutal conciseness. The organizers wished to demonstrate 'the degeneration of culture' from the beginning of the twentieth century until the great political change of National Socialism. They aimed to show that this decadence was not the work of isolated artists but that cultural and political anarchy have common roots; they hoped to expose 'cultural degeneration' as 'cultural Bolshevism' in the full sense of the word; to prove that artists without conscience, character or scruples had thereby become 'the allies of the Jews and Bolsheviks'; and to warn the German people against the 'dangerous artistic activity' of Jewish and Bolshevik ringleaders and those who mendaciously denied any association with them. Finally, they appealed to the

healthy common sense of the German people, reminding them that this hideous pseudo-art had only been overcome as a result of the Nazi Revolution.[17]

The German media enthusiastically hailed this exhibition as a final clarification of National Socialist cultural goals and a decisive break with the past. Hitler's call for a 'merciless cleansing war against elements of cultural decomposition' had been answered. Everything 'modern' in German painting and sculpture since the founding of the *Blaue Reiter* group in 1906 had been comprehensively negated. Documents exhibiting 'the profoundest decay of our people and its culture' had been exposed to the judgement of the people.[18] Germans had been given an unprecedented glimpse into the depths of complete disintegration and the loss of all faith and ideals immediately after 1918 – revealing a world of cynicism and madness peopled by sick minds.[19] It was, according to one critic, a terrible warning against the dangers of chaos in the visual arts, which had been inspired by the 'intellectualism of racially alien elements'.[20] According to another observer, the exhibition had the great merit of showing to the German people from what morass of perversity they had been released. Artists could now finally create according to 'the eternal laws of their blood and aesthetic sensibility'.[21] Having expunged the decadent horrors of a barbaric age, art under National Socialism could now turn to its true task – depicting the beautiful, the sublime and the transcendent.

In an address to the Reich Chamber of Culture in Berlin on 26 November 1937, Goebbels picked up these and related themes, welcoming the 'healthy purging action' in Munich. Contemptuously, he dismissed foreign complaints about infringements of artistic freedom and mod-

'For Jews only.'

ern progress. The pillorying of botched works by decadent artists 'whose monstrous, degenerate creations still haunt the field of plastic arts of our time', had been fully justified. It was in line with the taste of the broad masses, 'which has always remained the same'.[22]

The terrible cultural devastations of the past had been largely due to the boredom and snobbery of the idle rich.

Had the representatives of decadence and decline turned their attention to the masses of the people, they would have come up against icy contempt and cold mockery. For the people have no fear of being scorned as out of step with the times and as reactionary by enraged Jewish literati. Only the wealthy have this fear, when it is combined with insecurity in matters of taste.[23]

Injecting an even more venomous anti-Semitic slant, Goebbels added: 'How deeply the perverse Jewish spirit had penetrated German culture is shown in the frightening and horrifying forms of "Exhibition of Degenerate Art" in Munich, arranged as an admonitory example.'[24]

Having lambasted the Jews and the 'empty and hollow culture lackeys', responsible in his opinion for the decline of art, Goebbels effusively praised the healthy taste of ordinary Germans who had attended the Munich exhibition. By the million they had shown their disdain for 'this insolent arrogance'. Equally, he lauded Hitler for having again

So it was

When mornings on your way to work
You tread the dark-worn cobblestones
And every corner whispers at you
Do not forget, you are a Jew.

And when you seek a quiet spot
To eat your bread, a bench to rest,
The bench cries out: Get up you Jew!
And up you start and steal away.

And when the children in their play
Turn to catch your shadow's shadow,
You see in their bright features glaring
Nothing but the Devil's grin.

And when a lightning sideways glance
Senses and sees just who you are,
The pavement arches up towards you
Your heart stands still, your soles on fire.

And if your tired evening hour
Is broken by a strident ring
Your chair hurls you from its embrace:
Now, here they are! They've come for you!

You seek the woods. The trees there rustle,
'Jew' they whisper after you.
The echo swells, the mountains call
Jew, Jew, Jew, at you!

You're hunted over far-flung fields
And quiet hamlets see you flee.
Alone, alone, you run! An inner voice cries out,
Oh curse, that I'm a Jew!

To the dead dumb stones you cling,
Listening to their deepest sound.
Will they too wake, only to shout,
A shame on your claim to innocence.

What of hunger's gnawing pangs,
What of the streams of refugees!
Who suffered torment as we did
My heart is torn and heals no more.

GERTY SPIES, 1945

'established order and a sure footing in this chaos'. Hitler and National Socialism would guarantee the economic security of German artists, their social status and appreciation by the broad community, encouraging their total integration in the *Volk*. The Führer, Goebbels promised, regarded art as 'a sacred mission and a lofty task, the ultimate and highest documentation of human life'.[25]

Hitler's own views on art had been articulated in considerable detail on 18 July 1937, the day he opened the House of German Art in Munich. His speech was a familiar mixture of well-worn clichés, dogmatic prejudice and utopian, visionary rhetoric. He began by attacking the phrase-mongers in the cultural field, who under Jewish influence had declared art to be 'an international experience'.[26] By speaking about 'modern art' as a time-bound phenomenon, they reduced it to the trivial level of fashion. Under the motto 'Every year something fresh', they had decried the great masters of the past, forgetting that 'true art is and remains eternal'.[27] This 'Jewish discovery' that art was merely the affair of a period was, according to Hitler, 'a conspiracy of incapacity and mediocrity against better work of any age'. It was to counter such folly that the House of German Art had been created, as an eternal monument to contain 'that which is abiding and permanent'. The building was designed to hold a truly 'German' art, faithful to the character, life and feeling of the German people. It was to complete 'the cultural cleansing of the people's life' as a step towards the German cultural renascence.[28] The National Socialist State had now created the conditions for a new, vigorous flowering of art. The new age was at work on 'a new human type'. Men and women were healthier and stronger, they exuded a new joy in life. Hitler extolled, in this context, the Olympic Games, sport in general and the radiant, proud, bodily vigour of youth. 'Never was humanity in its external appearance and in its frame of mind nearer to the ancient world than it is today.'[29]

But against this glowing ideal of health, Hitler juxtaposed the products of so-called 'modern' art. 'Misformed cripples and cretins, women who inspire only disgust, men who are more like wild beasts, children who, were they alive, must be regarded as cursed of God.' He deplored the fact that there were painters who on principle 'feel meadows to be blue, the heaven green, clouds sulphur-yellow – or as they perhaps prefer to say "experience" them thus'.[30] It was clearly his duty, as the Leader of the German people, 'to prevent these pitiable unfortunates who clearly suffer from defects of vision' from presenting their failure of observation as 'art'. Hitler's brutal solution for such maladies ominously presaged his future way of dealing with all those he considered outsiders – whether Jews, gypsies, homosexuals, criminals, the insane or the permanently sick. If these artists believed in what they represented and their defect of vision was hereditary then, he announced, 'the Minister of the Interior will have to see to it that so ghastly a defect of vision shall not be allowed to perpetuate itself – or if they do not *believe* in the reality of such impressions but seek on other grounds to impose upon the nation by this humbug, then it is a matter for a criminal court.'[31]

Hitler suggested that the 'art-stutterers' who claimed to be modern, were in fact in the highest degree 'archaic, far older probably than the Stone Age'. What characterized their work above all was its shameless insolence and 'shocking lack of skill'. This was something the people had always instinctively grasped. For instance, they had understood the genius of a Richard Wagner long before the snobbish critics. The same was true with the modern art fraud. He concluded his speech with the hope that before too long, 'the Almighty will once more raise up individuals to the eternal starry heaven of the imperishable God-favoured artists of the great periods'.[32]

The two art exhibitions held simultaneously in Munich in mid-July 1937 in order to contrast 'Germanic' with 'degenerate' art were a decisive symbolic confrontation for the regime. After four years of trial and error, hesitation and occasional ambiguity, so-called modern art was irrevocably equated with abnormality and degeneracy. In the field of painting and sculpture, organicist theories of racial superiority, the *völkisch* ideology and the Aryan myth had decisively triumphed.[33] 'Modern' art was defined as nothing but a putrid excrescence, a source of cultural decomposition, an alien body to be thoroughly cleansed from the German national organism. It was a prime symptom of that internal poisoning associated with Jewish influence, Marxism, parliamentary democracy and the Weimar Republic: the most vivid exemplar of the degeneration of the modern world.[34]

For the Nazis, Expressionist, Cubist and abstract painting exemplified the break-up of coherent form, the fragmentation of the body and the disintegration of the social organism. In their eyes, such artistic incoherence, alienation and disorientation was the inevitable reflection of a chaotic society that had lost its 'racial purity': hence the loss of all idealism, heroism, cohesion or sense of identity. National Socialist art, once cleansed of this poison, would undoubtedly be able to reconstruct a hierarchical, ordered society with a coherent vision of man, with a 'heroic' ideal and the ability to totally reintegrate the individual into the community.

The role of politics and the State was crucial in the implementation of this utopian Nazi vision. Goebbels, who had frequently described Hitler as an artist-politician, saw in the shaping of the people out of a primitive inchoate mass the supreme exemplar of art. Nazi politics, at its highest level, was nothing if not this 'giving of form' (*Gestaltung*), an act of creation which would sanitize the sick body of the State and a decaying culture. Hence the intervention of the State in cultural affairs was a crucial part of a wide-ranging utopian Nazi vision of politics as a *Gesamtkunstwerk* (total work of art). Similarly, there was no such thing as *l'art pour l'art* (art for its own sake), since all creative activity was conditioned by a larger totality. This total culture could not tolerate anything chaotic, unhealthy or dissonant in its midst.[35]

The two Munich exhibitions juxtaposing 'healthy' and 'degenerate' art dialectically illustrated these ideological imperatives. They presented the German public with two antithetical visions, two opposing discourses and modes of representation. The House of German Art stood out with its monumental contours, its regular and symmetrical forms and impressive columns, as a new form of imposing State architecture. Its design as a sanctuary of art, aspiring towards order, permanence and 'eternal values', exactly corresponded to Hitler's vision.[36] The display of paintings and sculptures, arranged with perfect military precision inside the

Cleansing the culture. *Official visitors at the 'Degenerate Art' Exhibition, Munich, 1937.*

spacious rooms, had a similarly ordered structure. By contrast, the disposition in the 'Degenerate Art' Exhibition across the way seemed deliberately chaotic and was intended to render 'modern' art as obnoxious as possible. Aggressive, inflammatory captions like 'The Niggerizing of the Visual Arts', 'Total Madness' or 'The Prostitute Raised to a Moral Ideal', were more like obscene jokes or graffiti than informative statements.[37] The pictures, some without frames, were crowded together in long, narrow and claustrophobic rooms to accentuate the sense of anarchy and disorder. In contrast to the new Aryan supermen in the House of German Art, bursting with health, the 'degenerate' painters were accused of representing on canvas nothing but the dregs of humanity. For the Nazis, this antithesis was a visual consecration of their racial myth and proof of their final victory over the forces of disintegration.

The exhibits were organized into nine groups, beginning with 'the progressive destruction of sensibility for form and colour' in the works of painters like Otto Dix, Oskar Schlemmer and Ernst-Ludwig Kirchner. Group two included works by Emil Nolde, in particular, presenting unflattering 'revelations of German religiosity'. A defamatory slogan above Nolde's *The Life of Jesus* dismissed it as 'painted hocus-pocus'. Group three focused reprobation on paintings with a critical message about hunger, want and misery. They 'proved' the link between artistic and political anarchy. The next section attacked Otto Dix and Georg Grosz for their 'Marxist propaganda against military service'. Their 'art' had been misused to defame German soldiers as 'idiots, sexual degenerates, and drunks'. Group five mainly lambasted Expressionists who saw the whole world as 'one huge whorehouse', who had idealized the prostitute and obsessively depicted pimps and libertines. In group six the 'Negro and the South Sea Islander' were sarcastically shown to have become 'the racial ideal of modern art'. Expressionist sculpture was explicitly pilloried here. Group seven presented the 'spiritual ideal' of modern art as being the idiot, the cretin and the paralytic. This linked up with the ghastly final section in this group, comparing the works of the mentally ill with those of modern artists. There were also two other groups representing the 'height of degeneracy'. One group, which was captioned 'Total Madness', primarily featured abstract and Constructivist pictures. The other, group eight, represented 'the endless supply of Jewish trash' which could not be adequately described in words.[38]

The Nazi attempt to equate artistic 'degeneracy' with Jewishness was in ludicrous defiance of the facts. There were relatively few Jews working in the visual arts, though they had been somewhat more numerous and prominent on the commercial side or in promoting the *avant-garde*. In style and outlook, German Jewish artists were far more obviously German than Jewish.

Similarly, there was little sense to the 'cultural Bolshevist' label except as a time-honoured method of striking fear into the hearts of neurotic conservatives and obtuse petty-bourgeois philistines. But it was effective emotionally as a catch-all concept which could encapsulate the widespread popular

TOP: ***The Matchseller*** *by Otto Dix, whose work was condemned by the Nazis as 'Marxist propaganda'.*

ABOVE: ***Framing Jesus.*** *John Heartfield's graphic critique of the Nazification of Germany's Protestant churches during the Third Reich.*

animosity towards many aspects of Weimar culture and politics. By constantly repeating that modern art was 'Bolshevik', 'Jewish' or 'international', the Nazis were attacking a mythical *principle* more than individual artists. They were also staking their claim to be a populist mass movement which, even when in power, sought to exploit the resentments of ordinary people against cultural elitism, snobbery and the experimental character of modern art.[39]

The exhibition of 'Degenerate Art' (the last time such pictures were shown to the German public in the Third Reich) was in fact a great success. There were over two million visitors, more than three times as many as saw the Great German Art Exhibition. But it is doubtful if more than a minority came to say farewell to works of art that they loved. Paul Rave, who witnessed the droves of people attending day after day, later wrote: 'It is clear that the propagandistic purpose of dealing a death blow to the genuine art of the present had essentially been accomplished.'[40]

The official art exhibitions in Munich continued to attract good attendances after 1937. In 1939 there were 400,000 visitors and the number increased during the war years, approaching 850,000 in 1942.[41] But how far was the claim of a new and authentic 'German' art, made by the Nazis, actually justified? At the 1937 exhibition all German artists in the Reich who were 'Aryan' were invited to participate. In the end about 900 out of the 15,000 works submitted were exhibited. Hitler angrily rejected many of the submissions as being 'unfinished' and a year later, opening the same exhibition, he declared pointedly: 'In the case of many pictures it was obvious that the artist had confused the two exhibitions, the 1937 exhibition of "German" art and the concurrent one of

"degenerate art".'[42] The problem was that the call made by Adolf Wagner at the 1937 Munich opening ceremony for 'only the best and most perfect products of German art' conflicted with the basic idea of an *annual* exhibition. As Berthold Hinz has noted, all eight of the Great German Art exhibitions were essentially displays of works for sale at reasonable prices. This market structure was not easily compatible with Hitler's demand for a 'timeless' art, worthy of the great cultural shrine on the Prinzregentenstrasse.[43]

Moreover, the Nazi claim to have created a new style was especially dubious in painting, though less so in sculpture. This was pointed out by a shrewd observer at the time, Bruno E. Werner.

Most of the painting shows the closest possible ties to the Munich school at the turn of the century. Leibl and his circle and, in some cases, Defregger are the major influences on many paintings portraying peasants and their wives, woodcutters, shepherds etc., and on the interiors that lovingly depict many small and charming events of country life. Then one finds an extraordinarily large number of landscapes that also continue the old traditions…We also find a full display of portraits, especially likenesses of state and party leaders. While themes taken from the National Socialist movement are relatively few, there is nonetheless a larger group of paintings with symbolic and allegorical themes. The Führer is seen as a mounted knight in silver armour, carrying a fluttering flag…the female nude is also strongly represented in this exhibit, which is full of joy in the healthy body.[44]

At the same time, Werner pointed out that the more than 200 sculptures, primarily busts and figures of the naked human body, displayed a good level of achievement and were clearly in advance of the paintings.

The conventionality of the 'new' painting undoubtedly echoed Hitler's own taste for minor German and Austrian provincial artists of the late nineteenth century. The subjects which were generally favoured until the outbreak of the Second World War were traditional and close to nature. They depicted the landscape and the virtues of honest labour on the land. Alongside many figures of farmers, fishermen or artisans, the painters in the Third Reich stressed the themes of motherhood, of families and their domestic animals, of rootedness in the earth. The endless portrayals of the female nude also had an obvious ideological slant. The artist usually focused on 'the healthy physical being, the biological value of the individual as a precondition of all folkish and spiritual rebirth'.[45] The Nazi view of painting insisted that artists must combine perfect forms, harmony of movement, health and vitality in a Germanic version of the classical athletic ideal.

After the outbreak of war in 1939, a greater emphasis was laid on pictures of marching columns, battle scenes, heroic workers, factory complexes and ships putting out to sea. The farmer, the worker and the soldier were now singled out as select callings, as emblems of the 'national community' and the Germanic race. But it is apparent that workers were considered little more than soldiers of production in the folk community.

The iconography of women, with its emphasis on motherhood, the family, social hygiene and sanctioned sexual domination, was no less stereotypical. Even in the more sensual canvases, women exist solely to satisfy the desires of men, with a strong voyeuristic element involved. They are generally shown in passive or submissive postures, offering themselves to the gaze of the male spectator. At a more ideological level, the visual arts underlined the role of women as a 'life source' of the *Volk* and a pillar of the 'natural' order. Drawing on traditional bourgeois concepts as well as *völkisch* values, the Nazis expected women to provide a reassuring family image of fertility and robust strength.[46] They had, after all, a moral as well as a social role as 'guardians of the race'. When translated into symbolic sculpture this produced female nudes who supposedly represented a classically Nordic racial essence. They were the counterparts to male heroism; their athletic bodies devoid of any hint of eroticism and no doubt intended as a Nazi answer to modernist art.[47]

As bearers of children women were assigned a special mission in the Nazi State. As future mothers they were expected to take care of their bodies through physical training and sporting activity. The *Bund deutscher Mädel* (Association of German Girls), with its emphasis on hiking, camping and the outdoor life, reflected these priorities. Girls were taught to be 'clean', 'pure' and 'natural' and as far removed as possible from the stereotype of the 'emancipated woman' of the Weimar Republic. Lipstick, powder, smoking and 'decadent' dress were frowned upon. Modern dancing was seen as an open incitement to sexual promiscuity, especially swing and the 'Negro music' of jazz.

Both in art and in life, Nazi attitudes to women reflected their petty-bourgeois traditionalism and their conservative values.[48] From the outset they had rejected the women's emancipation movement and had insisted that the woman's sphere must be the family. Indeed, the Nazi philosopher, Alfred Rosenberg, in his inimitably clumsy, obscurantist prose, claimed that this was exactly what women themselves wanted:

> Emancipation of woman from the women's emancipation movement is the first demand of a generation of women which would like to save the Volk and the race, the Eternal-Unconscious, the foundation of all culture, from decline and fall.[49]

While returning women to the sphere of the family, at the same time the Nazis totally excluded them from any leading positions of power and responsibility. As Engelbert Huber, the Nazi political theorist, bluntly summed it up: 'The German resurrection is a male event.'[50] The 'political woman' in Nazi eyes had always been as much a symbol of degeneracy as Bolshevism, the Jews, democracy or modern art. Indeed, unhealthy female preoccupation with politics as with sexuality was denounced as a deliberate conspiracy to subvert the moral values of the Christian German people. The Nazi theorist Gottfried Feder, blaming the 'insane dogma of equality', even claimed that the Jews had 'stolen the woman from us…we must kill the dragon to restore her to her holy position as servant and maid'. For Feder, the emancipation of women and Jews were twin evils of liberal modernity, both related to one another and to the wider social and cultural crisis. The hidden link between misogyny and anti-Semitism was clearly an important subterranean theme in the neurotic masculine fears that drove Nazi culture.

Yet, despite their obsessive anti-feminism, the Nazis won substantial support from women during their rise to power.[51] Many women believed that they would regain lost dignity as defenders of spiritual values and family life. Some welcomed the idea of having a well-defined separate sphere of child care, education and welfare work.[52] The Nazi slogan of 'different, but not inferior' (*nicht gleichartig sondern gleichwertig*) had a certain crude appeal.

After they came to power, the Nazis built on this support by giving special privileges to 'prolific mothers' and establishing a Medal of Honour for them at the Party Day of Labour. On the German Mother's Day in 1939, three million German women were for the first time to be awarded the new badge of honour.[53] Adolf Hitler, in this as in so many other areas, had set the tone. In a speech on 15 September 1935 to the National Socialist Women's Congress, he announced: 'The woman has her own battlefield. With every child that she brings into the world, she fights her battle for the nation.'[54]

What were the implications for Nazified popular culture of such extraordinarily Spartan and puritanical views? And how did morality and aesthetics relate to each other in this cleansed culture? A wonderful illustration of the social reality behind Nazi rhetoric can be found in the diatribe against five o'clock tea which appeared in a Stormtrooper paper. It began by praising the Führer's speech at the Munich art festival of 1937 as 'undoubtedly the most important cultural-political document of modern times'.[55] The Nazi writer approvingly compared the recent cleansing of 'the most hideous creations of a degenerate humanity' with the burning of the books in 1933. There was a direct link between 'artistic impotence' and 'the most evil products of Jewish scribblers', as there was a connection to 'the glorifiers of Negro music'. But tea and dancing were no less of a danger to the *Volk*! This was a custom which had come to Germany from a decadent England, but in reality it was shaped by the 'Jewish spirit'.

Five o'clock tea encouraged chatter, not conversation; restless 'Jewish vagabondage', rather than 'community-conscious' German sociability. Worst of all, young people would be dancing swing (another 'Jewish impulse'!) against which the Führer and all healthy-minded Germans had declared a war to the death. The nation of Beethoven, Bach, Mozart and Haydn could not allow one of the noblest forms of its cultural life to fall victim to the 'monstrous degeneration' and nihilism of contemporary music. This noisy, meaningless swing music was the product of jaded, diseased nerves, a symptom of decay, 'the mark of the Western Asiatic racial and cultural expression'.[56]

Such wild vituperations against any fashions or customs which were deemed international rather than authentically German were standard fare in the Nazi press. So, too, was the grotesque attempt to vilify modern music and dancing as 'Asiatic', 'Jewish' or 'Negro'. This so-called degenerate music was, however, especially dangerous because of the puritanical fear that it might encourage sexual licence and be harmful to the Nazi ideal of womanhood. The themes of cultural degeneracy, sexual immorality, Jewish and alien influences and the collapse of structured form converge together in a miasma of primitive racism.

In the Nazi vision of 'degenerate art' the contours of the enemy were more sharply etched than the positive ideal which was to take its place. It was easier to point to the 'disease' of modern culture than to find convincing, concrete alternatives that could translate into authentically creative art. The National Socialists endlessly pontificated about culture as *the* goal of human life and about art as 'the supreme expression of national existence'.[57] But their 'guided culture' proved remarkably sterile, once they killed off alternative options. We have already seen how they blocked the possibility

of co-opting Expressionism into their service.[58] Nothing comparable to the 'revolutionary' and dynamic character of Futurist art in Italy or Constructivism in the USSR was permitted to flourish in Nazi Germany. Goebbels, who might conceivably have moved in this direction, adapted himself opportunistically to Hitler's wishes. The systematic defamation of modernist painters and sculptors in 1937 revealed just how deeply the Nazis feared what they represented. It is also worth noting that the entire cultural cleansing operation was actually carried out by artists, art critics, teachers and academics – driven by a curious mixture of envy, hatred and cultural mission. These were members of the educated middle classes who evidently shared the reactionary Nazi conceptions about formlessness, chaos and decadence.[59]

Hitler was able to articulate their sense of anxiety and rage, and to assuage it with the aggressiveness with which he put modern art beyond the pale. (While delivering his speech at the opening of the House of Art, he apparently frothed at the mouth.) But the vehemence of the assault and the ritualized pillorying and exorcism in which the Nazis indulged betrayed their deep fear of freedom. They were incapable of seeing in the open-endedness of modernity anything but an expression of derangement. Modernist sensibility, experimentation and playfulness were met with a murderous seriousness that literally sought to extirpate the possibility of innovation or change.

Like the book burnings of 1933, the purging of 'degenerate art' was a spectacular act on the public stage in which the whole nation participated.[60] Furthermore, it was genuinely popular, for never in the history of art had so many people attended an exhibition of painting and sculpture. The regime had received a further vote of confidence in its

Nazi book-burning. Opernplatz, Berlin, 10 May 1933.

cultural policy and Hitler could feel that he had been politically strengthened.

In order to project more effectively their positive alternative, the Nazi regime spared no expense in playing up the visual arts in all their forms and attributing a quasi-sacred significance to their cultivation. There were huge headlines, celebrations, countless 'cultural speeches', parades and newsreels about the major artistic events. The black and white film of the 1937 Great German Art Exhibition was even accompanied by the first movement of Beethoven's Second Symphony. The Nazi Party newspaper wrote breathlessly of 'the historical greatness of this moment' and the 'sublime ceremony with national hymns that resoun-

ded like a pledge from the people and its artists to the Führer'.[61]

The climax of all this ceremony and publicity was the pageant in historical costumes and fancy dress around the theme of the Day of German Art.[62] This giant parade in 1937 was intended to embody everything that was permanent and immutable in German history, to present its 'greatness' in a striking visual form. The images, figures and symbols of that history were to be distilled in a beautiful, awe-inspiring spectacle. It was a history that proclaimed *German* cultural identity and continuity in aesthetic categories.

The correspondent of the *Völkischer Beobachter* was suitably ecstatic:

68

Germanic warriors, Germanic women, Germanic priests and seers pass before us...Even these mere imitations of mighty symbols drawn from the mythical world of our ancestors have the power to overwhelm our modern sensibility. The sun, the symbol of day, the moon, the goddess of the night, are convincing and impressive in their brilliant colours. Figures from our forefathers' sagas are suddenly among us...The stirring tones of trumpeters and drummers on horseback rouse us from our ecstatic meditation.[63]

This was followed by a visual representation of the deeds of Charlemagne, Henry II, Frederick Barbarossa and Henry the Lion (the great colonizer). Then came the Gothic period with its knights and ladies, its choir stalls, altar pieces and carvings – symbols 'bringing a whole world to life in our imagination'.

Mercenaries, accompanied by pipers and drummers, led the German Renaissance parade. The tableaux from the High Baroque, then the classic and romantic periods followed in their train, climaxing in the modern age. Rhetorically, the report asked whether it was necessary or even possible to portray this last era of German history. Predictably, the answer was an unequivocal identification with the present. 'Today we sat as spectators in the theatre of our own time and saw greatness...'[64] To drive home the point to any numbed spectator who had failed to grasp the seamless web of past and present, the reporter concluded:

At the end of this pageant celebrating 2,000 years of German culture, soldiers appeared again, soldiers in grey, soldiers in brown, soldiers in black...The Wehrmacht and the SA marched down lanes of cheering spectators. The National Socialist Motorized Units, the Labour Corps and the SS reaped the final waves of applause.[65]

CHAPTER FIVE

A GLITTERING FAÇADE

*'The success of the day [of German Art] was testimony to the power of Nazi
mythology. This was gift-wrapped National Socialism, its victims out of sight,
its appeal apparently uncontaminated by the existence of a concentration camp in the
picturesque town of Dachau, only a twenty-minute train ride from Munich.'*

ISABEL HILTON, 1993

BY THE summer of 1939, the Day of German Art was one of the established high points of the festive calendar in the Third Reich. On the morning of 16 July Adolf Hitler came to Munich to open the third annual German Art Exhibition, which was part of this spectacular three-day event. In the afternoon the familiar pageant entitled 'Two Thousand Years of German Culture' braved sometimes torrential rain to wind through the streets, passing by Hitler's review stand. In the evening, he

Art guards. *An official image of the Führer inspecting his SS battalions at the House of German Art.*

attended a performance of his favourite operetta, *The Merry Widow*. In honour of the festivities, all traffic in Munich was stopped, to permit the public and the artists to dance in the squares to the music of Germany's best orchestras.

The festive atmosphere was given a political flavour by the participation not only of Hitler, but of nearly all the senior Nazi officials.

Those present included Heinrich Himmler, Joseph Goebbels, Robert Ley, Albert Speer, Rudolf Hess, Julius Streicher and Adolf Wagner, the Nazi district leader for Upper Bavaria, who gave the initial welcoming speech. The most prominent absentees from the event were Field-Marshal Hermann Goering, who was on a yacht trip through the German canals and rivers, the foreign minister Joachim von Ribbentrop and Wilhelm Frick, the interior minister. However, a large delegation from fascist Italy, and some 300 members of the foreign press (out of a total of 650 journalists) were also present at the opening reception.

The international press corps was eager to hear Hitler's remarks in the light of growing diplomatic tension over Danzig, though it was known that his speech was unlikely to be political. As the correspondent of the *Manchester Guardian* put it laconi-

Unease in Munich. *Chamberlain, Daladier, Hitler, Mussolini and Count Ciano, posing for peace. 30 September 1938.*

cally: 'Uncomplimentary references to the Jews and to the democracies will almost certainly appear, but no announcements of international importance are to be expected.'[1] Hitler's speech was indeed confined to art, without a single reference to politics, not even to international Jewry, Bolshevism or the Western democracies. By his standards, it was a remarkably moderate and economical performance – lasting a mere fifteen minutes. Unknown to any of those present, it was to be the last 'cultural speech' of his life.

Hitler's main point was to justify once more the need for artistic guidance and regulation from the top in times of rapid revolutionary development. Only in this way could the separation of art from the people (and the isolation of the artists themselves) be prevented. In the past, when the Second German Reich had been founded in 1870–71, its leaders – according to Hitler – were not interested in art. The most successful statesmen and soldiers of that period did not personally know the 'immortal' artists of the time. National Socialism, by contrast, recognized its cultural tasks as 'a significant part of its mission'.[2]

The Nazi regime, which had not hesitated two years earlier to purge Germany of the 'sickening, decadent swindle' of fashionable, modernist 'daubings', would do everything to provide respectable artists with commissions and working possibilities. Hitler solemnly declared that 'a decent general average of achievement had already been secured'. But he lamented that no artist had thus far recorded the great events in Nazi Germany with a talent and force comparable to the artistic record of earlier periods. The Führer expressed the hope that individual artists would henceforth turn to the experiences of the present, drawing their inspiration from the splendour of their own time 'which need not fear comparison with the grandest epochs in our German history'.[3]

Later that morning Hitler lunched privately with Himmler, who was Reichsführer of the SS and chief of police, Goebbels and other members of the government. The Italian minister of propaganda, Dino Alfieri, was also present. The Nazi district leader of Danzig, Albert Forster, attended a separate lunch given by the mayor of Munich, sitting next to the Sudeten German leader, Konrad Henlein. The acting Soviet ambassador to Berlin, George Astachov, was seated between two German generals. A week later his country would begin trade talks with Nazi Germany. In under a month, Hitler and Stalin initiated serious discussions that would lead to the Nazi–Soviet Pact and the partition of Poland. The diplomatic coup of the century, which would free Hitler's hands for war, was only weeks away.

In the afternoon a five-mile-long procession symbolizing two millennia of German culture snaked past the Führer's reviewing stand. Watched by a million spectators in the streets of Munich, it took two and a half hours to pass Hitler's immense golden canopy. It was a stupendous show, intended to put the Nazi seal on German art and history as a whole, to display the 'living eternity of the people'.[4]

On the previous two days the weather had been glorious, but the parade itself took place on a rainy Sunday afternoon. A British correspondent noted that thunder and a cloudburst had greeted Hitler's arrival 'and a cascade of water from the canopy forced him and Dr Goebbels to retreat a few steps'.[5] What particularly caught the British reporter's eye were the floats symbolizing Austria, the Sudetenland, Bohemia, Moravia and Memelland, which were included in the parade.

One of them represented a silver German eagle on top of Germany's new frontier fortifications, while the next showed two Bohemian lions holding wide open the 'gate to the East', behind which could be seen Slavic architecture symbolising Slovak and Ukraine cities.[6]

These reminders of the German annexation of Austria, the brutal dismantling of Czechoslovakia and hints of a continuing *Drang nach Osten* (drive to the east) were of obvious concern to the Western media. The British press was full of news stories about Nazi pressure on Poland. Then there were the Polish statements on Danzig, news of German troops on the Czech borders and the angry reply by Goebbels to a 'wave of British incitements'.[7]

Only two days before the climax of the Munich cultural extravaganza, on 14 July 1939, the British war minister, Leslie Hore-Belisha, had been in Paris to watch the military parade. It was 150 years to the day after the storming of the Bastille. Before leaving Paris he said: 'The review which we witnessed was without question a magnificent spectacle which has left in my mind a deep impression of the calmness and strength of France.'[8] The French prime minister, Edouard Daladier, was more cautious, emphasizing the 'heavy sacrifices' and the 'immense effort' needed to ensure safety, peace and liberty.

The headlines in the London *Daily Telegraph* were not particularly encouraging. They included such items as 'Last Foreign Tourists Leave South Tyrol. Briton Searched at Frontier', 'French Reports of Germans in Italy', and 'Without Gas

Technical progress! *The new gas mask for the German family.*

Masks' – a correspondence about their apparent unavailability to local residents in Clapham.[9] The government-controlled German press eagerly pointed up the contrast between the allegedly belligerent talk abroad and the festive mood in Germany. The French were busy organizing noisy military parades, the Poles had become obsessed with their Danzig 'fever', while the British parliament sought to 'encircle' Germany by organizing new alliances against Hitler. Prime minister Neville Chamberlain spoke only of increasing the numbers of bombers, fighters and destroyers. But the German Führer in complete tranquillity prepared his new designs for buildings that would last for centuries.[10] Great Britain, it was alleged, sought to drive a wedge between the German government and its people.

According to the Nazi media the best demonstration of German intentions was the spectacular festival of joy, creativity and inner edification being held in Munich. The Nazi media stressed that the task of German art was to go beyond the familiar, everyday sense of community (*Gemeinschaft*) and give to it a higher meaning.[11] As if to illustrate the point, Hitler attended the opening of the Bayreuth festival on 25 July, watched a performance of Wagner's *Tristan and Isolde* the following day, and gave a reception for the artists on 1 August at Haus Wahnfried.

The official media admitted that the quiet self-confidence of Germans was ultimately based on faith in their powerful Wehrmacht. The rearmament of the past few years was the necessary prerequisite and justification for the gaiety and rejoicing of the Day of German Art. But Germany had not rearmed in order to conquer new territories. It simply wished to enjoy itself in peace and to create new cultural values![12] Its political unity would now enable *all* the talents of the German nation – especially its cultural abilities – to blossom freely.

In his address to the assembled guests, Munich *Gauleiter* Adolf Wagner (the host of the ceremonies) placed the strongest emphasis on the pace of Germany's 'peaceful' reconstruction and cultural activity.[13] Before introducing Hitler, Wagner said that the art celebration 'grows in the same measure and tempo with which the Führer augments the Reich'. Pointing to the exhibits of Vienna, the Sudetenland, Prague, Bohemia, Moravia and Memel, he added: 'We do not need to project German culture into these lands. It has been there for centuries. The Führer has brought it home again with land and men.'[14] The territories annexed or incorporated into the Greater German Reich (Wagner ominously added to the list 'our German Danzig', which had not yet suffered this fate) were not 'colonies' or overseas countries to be materially exploited. They were 'German *Kulturgüter* [cultural properties] in the highest sense of the word'.[15]

The Reich press chief, Dr Otto Dietrich, at a press conference in the Nymphenburg Park,

Munich tea party. *Reich Press chief Dr Otto Dietrich hosts representatives of the German and foreign press corps in the gardens of the Nymphenburg Palace, Munich, 14 July 1939.*

indulged in a more subtle apologia. He implied that it was no coincidence that the Third Day of German Art had opened on the 150th anniversary of the French Revolution.

> This [French] Revolution wrote, as it were, the word freedom on its banner but, in truth it placed freedom in the arbitrary will and licentiousness of the individual…This idol of 1789, which was the enemy of freedom and personality, has been destroyed by us and replaced by a monument of true freedom.[16]

The German Revolution, said Dr Dietrich, had effected 'a complete change from the concept of "I" to the concept of "we", from the individual to the whole'. It had not only provided millions with work and bread, constructing great buildings and highways, but it has also 'created new temples of the spirit' and a new cultural basis. The Nazi Revolution had not renounced freedom but had stripped it of a false phraseology which encouraged irresponsibility to the community.

Nazism had corrected the decadent abuses of liberal individualism, replacing them with an ideal of 'service to the community'.[17] The Führer himself had declared that the aim of German art was to appeal to the whole of the German community, not just to a handful of intellectuals. Art had to draw its sustenance from the life of the German people, 'whose most glamorous, beautiful and honourable expression it is'.[18] To those who claimed that National Socialism robbed the individual of his creativity, Dr Dietrich boldly replied: 'How could an artistic nature like that of the Führer have created this national community if it were antagonistic to individuality? No, a genius created this community in order to breed geniuses from it!'[19]

Like other top Nazis, Goebbels pointed to the fact that in the Third Reich art had been restored to the mass of the people. It was no longer 'only for the upper ten-thousand' but had been brought once again into the everyday life of the average German. According to Goebbels's speech at the second session of the annual Congress of German Art, exhibitions and artists had in the past been 'so completely under Jewish control that no artistic development was possible'.[20] German art had been degraded by the Jews, first in the sphere of art criticism (where they prevented honourable work from achieving recognition while they praised 'dishonourable', so-called modern art to the skies). Jewish art dealers, who dominated the market, had offered for sale only 'degenerate art' which ordinary people could not understand. National Socialism had swept away this 'Jewish art salon snare', restoring 'a sense of natural beauty and harmony which is always very vibrant in the people'.[21]

Goebbels boastfully claimed that in the House of German Art, 'only the beautiful, the honourable, in short, art itself, enters. But more than that, an attempt is being made to instil art itself into the people's perspective.' The Reich Chamber of Culture, over which he presided, was supposedly an attempt to balance individual creative freedom with obligations to the wider community. Its task was not to find genius or talent itself, but 'to remove all the obstacles and hindrances standing in the way of the organic development of the artistic potentialities of our people'.[22] Ultimately, however, Goebbels believed that the arts must immortalize the contribution of Adolf Hitler to German history; they should praise and glorify Nazi deeds 'so that through song, word, melody, colour or stone they will be carried into the most distant centuries'.[23]

Goebbels naturally did not mention that any practising artist had to belong to his Chamber of Culture if he wished publicly to sell or exhibit his work or demonstrate his talent. The price of membership was conformity and the effect of regimentation was generally to produce a deadening atrophy. Only that art which was officially sanctioned and permitted could appear and it was virtually beyond criticism by virtue of being exhibited. After all, had not Goebbels himself decreed that art criticism was superfluous?

The many prizes and subsidies offered to creative artists for works embodying 'the spirit of our times' as well as the honorary titles and emoluments available to those who glorified Hitler and the Nazi State, could not disguise their hollow uniformity.[24] Even Hitler himself had half-recognized the problem in his address in Munich, bewailing the fact that 'individual artists of true ability' had not yet inwardly turned to the Nazi Revolution as their source. The difficulty did not only lie in the authoritarian, paternalist attitudes at the top, but in the very nature of Party ideology as it related to the artistic domain. Hitler and his followers regarded art as 'timeless' and biologically conditioned, as the highest expression of the genius of each race. Hence the arts in the Third Reich had to express pure German racial consciousness, as defined by the Nazi world-view.[25]

The arts were supposedly to be founded on a 'beautiful simplicity' accessible to all, on the principles of strength, clarity and logic. In practice, however, artistic creation was largely subordinated to the needs of propaganda and became an important vehicle for popularizing the ideology of the regime. Indeed *Kultur* was a vital component of the ethos of the Third Reich, alongside the development of its material, military and political power. The militarization of the Reich was often defended by its apologists as a necessary means for nurturing the cultural goals which the Nazi regime had set for itself. It was the sword, which had allegedly provided Germans with the 'opportunity to be creative'. The other side of *Kultur* was the Nazis' desire to refute constant accusations of barbarism which were made against them abroad. If National Socialism could point to an authentic cultural renaissance and provide substance for far-reaching claims about Germanic *Kultur* as the heir of Hellenism, it would then have acquired a formidable propaganda argument for both domestic and foreign consumption.

The Day of German Art in Munich showed, if nothing else, just how seriously the regime took its mission as patron of the arts. But more discerning foreign observers were not readily convinced by bombastic Nazi assertions. There seemed little evidence, for example, that artistic masterpieces would necessarily evolve from the 'superior' type of man supposedly developed in the Third Reich. C. Brook Peters, reporting to New York a week after the great show in Munich, was openly sceptical.

Literature, music, the theatre and the graphic arts have produced little meriting praise. Most modern literature in Germany today is translation from foreign language – mostly American and British. In music and the theatre most effort appears to be directed toward reproducing the classics – and the revivals are usually superb. But there is little which is new and good.[26]

Turning to painting, the reporter noted the gap between the pronouncements on German art regularly made in Munich and the mediocre quality of the exhibits in the annual exposition.

Most difficulties between the artists and the government in painting are met in the realms of subject matter and conception rather than composition and technique – although extravagant brush work is taboo because the Führer does not like it. The result as illustrated in the current Munich exhibit, is an abundance of neutral subjects such as nudes and an inexhaustible array of 'blood and soil' subjects – animal life, farmyard motifs, peasants in picturesque costumes, landscapes, and the old theme of mother and child.[27]

According to one breakdown, at the Great German Art Exhibitions after 1937, 40 per cent of the entries were landscapes, 30 per cent depicted ordinary people, 11 per cent were portraits of historical figures, 10 per cent showed animals and 7 per cent still lifes.[28] The style of painting was traditional, often reminiscent of Bavarian art shows in the pre-Nazi period. This was scarcely surprising, given the large number of painters and sculptors approved by the regime who had exhibited their

Rural bliss. *Adolf Wissel's idealized portrait of a farming family in the Third Reich. Great German Art Exhibition, Munich, 1939.*

work in Munich academy exhibitions before 1933. Many of these artists had been members of the old Munich Secession who simply accommodated themselves to the new order. Some, like Franz Eichhorst and Fritz Erler, had been painters of German peasants who turned to depictions of heroic soldiers or steely SS and SA men. Elk Eber was another artist who specialized in war themes. Then there was Conrad Hommel, the most popular portrait painter of the Party, who churned out innumerable pictures of the Führer, Goebbels and lesser Party leaders. Adolf Wissel was the acknowledged master of peasant rusticity, while Julius Paul Junghanns became Germany's best-known painter of animals. The Nazi art magazine *Die Kunst im Dritten Reich* described his animal paintings, which Hitler had personally selected for the first Great German Art Exhibition, as 'monuments of a speechless, heroic attitude and strength, the most dignified witnesses of our time'.[29] The genre of earthy peasant painting, celebrating the simple country life on canvas and emphasizing its uncomplicated virtues of strength and rootedness,

76

obviously fitted well into the Nazi 'Blood and Soil' ideology. So, too, did the depiction of the family, especially the peasant family as the healthy core of the nation, living close to nature and to the landscape. In books and films, as well as paintings, the family was eulogized as a source of stability, morality and racial purity.

The ideal woman was assigned a similarly eugenic function as the guardian of the Germanic race, proud to bring healthy children into the world as part of her 'battle for the nation'.[30] Her image as mother or Madonna with child was paramount. Women had to have healthy bodies and preferably were represented as tall, blonde and blue-eyed. Woman was the incarnation of the beauty of nature, its ripeness, fertility and playfulness. But her depiction in painting and sculpture was invariably stereotypical. Peter Adam puts it well:

> The surface was smooth, with no bulging flesh, no natural folds of skin, no wrinkles. Woman was described with soft lines and gentle contours, the image of devotion and co-operation. Woman was an object; her role was subservient, to be looked at, to be

fertilised. Her own sexuality was denied.[31]

TOP: ***The Peasant Venus***. *The painter Sepp Hilz and his woolly-stockinged pin-up.* ABOVE: ***Beerotic art.*** *Leda and the Swan by Paul Mathias Padua. The sensation of the 1939 Great German Art Exhibition, it caused a scandal, but was snapped up by the Führer.*

The nudes painted by such leading Nazi artists as Adolf Ziegler, president of the Reich Chamber of Arts (and organizer of the notorious Exhibition of Degenerate Art in Munich), were particularly slick, cold and impersonal.

A mediocre painter, if technically accomplished, Ziegler's prim, pseudo-classical, waxwork nudes left nothing to the imagination – not for nothing was he popularly known as 'Reich Master of German pubic hair'.[32] His *Judgement of Paris*, displayed at the 1939 German Art Exhibition, has an obviously voyeuristic aspect. As in all his paintings, the photorealistic representation of perfect bodies and 'Aryan' types is monotonously celebrated, which doubtless explains Hitler's passion for his work.

Another painter of more titillating nudes, verging at times on the pornographic, was Sepp Hilz, known as 'the Master of the Rustic Venus'.[33] His painting of a 'Peasant Venus' as a woolly-stockinged pin-up was one of the main attractions of the 1939 exhibition.

But the most controversial picture in the Munich show was undoubtedly Paul Mathias

Padua's *Leda and the Swan*, which *Time* magazine in its July 1939 issue described as 'beerotic'.[34] Padua was one of the younger, more talented artists favoured by the Nazis; his earlier paintings of Bavarian peasants had been very popular. *Leda and the Swan* was so obviously lascivious that only one German newspaper carried a reproduction of the painting.[35] Its daring and almost photographic execution provoked a scandal but it was none the less bought by Hitler himself.

The offerings of nudes multiplied over the years and provided the Munich art exhibitions with a healthy surfeit of 'Aryan' flesh. Like the farmers, the bucolic families and the soldiers readying themselves for the fight, these female nudes were embarrassingly artificial expressions of a racial type. But offical Nazi critics who like to echo Hitler's thundering words that 'Art is a mighty and fanatical mission', were convinced that the paintings hung on the walls of the House of German Art represented a genuine breakthrough. Writing about the 1939 German Art Exhibition, Walter Horn emphasized that this was a true 'harvest of the artistic will' and not merely an art display. Art had returned from its solitude to the German race and people, 'mirroring the richness of the German soul in pictures which reflect the political changes'.[36] Horn insisted that Nazi painting and sculpture in their simplicity and directness were no Biedermeier idyll, but the expression of a new manly, heroic ethos whose clear rendering of beauty was akin to Greek antiquity.[37]

Such Nazi didacticism could not, however, disguise the almost total divorce from reality in this genre painting. There was no hint of suffering or sickness, no references to the cruelties or crimes of the regime, no allusions to the horrors of war. As one contemporary critic recently put it: 'Nazi art was a gigantic visual lie about a clean, moral, better Germany which Hitler pretended to have created, but which in reality never existed.'[38]

Nowhere was the Nazi myth of the 'new man' and its essential divorce from reality more apparent than in sculpture. As in painting, many of the leading sculptors such as Georg Kolbe, Fritz Klimsch and Richard Scheibe, had done their best work before 1933. But there were also official State artists like Arno Breker and Josef Thorak who became prominent exponents of a distinctive National Socialist style. Their public honours and commissions were an index of the importance which the Nazis attached to sculpture as an expression of their ideology and as a vehicle for political messages. Their huge sculptures, closely related to the monumental public building style favoured by the regime, conveyed the grandeur of form that was considered appropriate to the new era. In the idealized male nude, National Socialism seemed to have found its desired image of physical strength, classical beauty, order, masculine courage and heroic will.[39] The 'eternal German art' which the politicians constantly proclaimed as their aspiration, could best reconnect to the 'pure forms' of ancient Greece through the medium of sculpture.

The Nordic version of the Hellenic ideal emphasized the beautiful and harmonious body, the heroic athlete in his 'naturalness', as standing in the sharpest contrast to the alleged chaos and distortions of modern art. Hitler, Rosenberg and other Nazi leaders based this attachment to the Graeco-Roman model on both racial and political affinities. In a speech in Munich on 22 January 1938, Hitler had pompously proclaimed: 'Each politically heroic period will immediately build a bridge to another equally heroic past. Greeks and Romans will suddenly become near to the Germans, because their roots lie in the race.'[40] In her cinematic masterpiece, *Olympia–Festival of the Nations* (1938), Leni Riefenstahl captured the National Socialist ideal of beauty by dissolving shots between images of contemporary Nordic-looking Olympic sportsmen and ancient Greek statues.

The Greek model in sculpture was assumed to correspond to the Nazi postulate of a 'timeless' art and the need to lift man above himself into a transformed, ennobled reality. Sculpture was of course intended to convey such 'eternal' values. But in the Third Reich this essentially meant the visual depiction of a strong, healthy master-race. As the Nazi aesthetic hardened after 1936, sculpture became ever more obviously monumental, propagandist and subservient to those virtues of obedience, discipline and steely courage promoted by the regime. Monumental sculptures now adorned public buildings and squares, new stadiums and arenas, with their god-like figures trumpeting the Nazi ideal of the heroic Aryan.

Arno Breker, Hitler's favourite sculptor and an artist of considerable talent, perfectly expressed what the regime expected from its creative artists. The two bronze figures, *The Army* and *The Party*, which he sculpted in 1939 for the Reich Chancellery inner courtyard in Berlin, were obviously intended to legitimize and arouse admiration for the twin pillars of National Socialism. They

Readiness. *Arno Breker's image of Aryan manhood, for the Great German Art Exhibition of 1939, combines classical allusions with muscular belligerence.*

represent aesthetically perfect, noble, idealized images of man, but they lack the breath of life. Like much of Breker's work, these images of masculinity and power ultimately leave the spectator feeling numbed. But they echo all too well the aura of brutality, strength and overbearing dominance that Nazism self-consciously embodied.[41] At the 1939 Great German Art Exhibition in Munich, Breker's sculpture *Readiness*, depicting a man with a half-drawn sword, ready for battle seems all too appropriate. The forceful hand ready to seize an adversary, the tension and aggressiveness in the pose, the exaggerated muscularity of the arms and legs, convey an image of intimidating power. For Nazi critics, Breker had admirably captured in his sculptures a new political ideal of human form and racial beauty in his striving for impersonal monumentality.[42] He had truly achieved the goal of ennobling reality and lifting people into a higher sphere of myth. But in retrospect, Breker's synthetic, metallic-looking musclemen, like Thorak's plastic monuments of a gigantic and heroic humanity, seem more like unconscious anticipations of the coming Nazi war of aggression.

At the time, however, the new art canon invoked by the regime seemed popular enough. The banishment of ugliness, of human anguish, distress and pain in favour of the idyllic, the beautiful and the heroic aroused little protest. The conscious elimination by artists of the stresses and strains of modern industrial and urban life was welcomed by many ordinary people with enthusiasm. From the outset, Hitler had declared himself the arbiter of popular taste, insisting that all art works exhibited in the House of German Art must be clear, comprehensible and accessible. Speaking in Munich in July 1937, he had quoted the well-known dictum 'To be German is to be clear' as his own guiding star – 'and that means that to be German is to be logical and true'.[43] It was this spirit, he insisted, that henceforth had to direct German painters, sculptors, architects, thinkers, poets and musicians. Above all, they had to create for the people and 'we will see to it that henceforth the people will be called in to judge its art'.[44] Hitler was convinced that:

> the people when it passes through these galleries will recognise in me its own spokesman and counsellor: it will draw a sigh of relief and express its glad agreement with this purification of art. And that is decisive: an art which cannot count on the readiest and most intimate agreement of the mass of the people, an art which must rely upon the support of small cliques is intolerable.[45]

The Munich exhibitions of art which Hitler always opened, of which he was often the best client (in 1938 he bought over 200 works), and where he frequently determined what was to be shown, were undeniably popular. The opening exhibition of 1937 had attracted 60,000 visitors, prompting Goebbels to call it 'a national event' in which 'after years of terrible defeat German art has found itself again'.[46] Part of its fascination undoubtedly derived from the impressive pageantry which accompanied and celebrated the openings of these

exhibitions, with their brilliant displays of banners and colours.[47] Before the huge, cheering crowds in the streets of Munich passed the exemplars of the art of different times (covering two millennia of Reich history from the early Germanic to the contemporary period) as well as models of the new Nazi architecture in the city. Everything could be found here from ox-drawn wagons symbolizing the 'Blood and Soil' mystique to models of Viking vessels; from medieval knights on horseback with swastika banners fluttering in the breeze to figures of Pallas Athene, Father Rhine or huge busts of Adolf Hitler himself.[48] This was not only lavish entertainment, a kind of modern 'bread and circuses' for the masses, but a public statement by the regime, expressing its self-confidence that the new Reich would be there for the next millennium. It was also National Socialism's way of appropriating and scavenging everything of value to itself from the German past, in order to bolster its own 'civilized' credentials.

The Day of German Art parade of 1939 cast an interesting light on how the Nazis sought to portray different eras of German history. What was called 'the Germanic' (as opposed to German) period was obviously of crucial importance, since here were to be found the roots of German culture and the 'original' German character.[49] The Germanic tribes were naturally assumed to have been brave, warlike, generous and noble-minded; their pagan religion was based on the natural cycle and worship of the sun as a symbol of ever-renewed life (one of the meanings of the swastika); loyalty to the family and clan, heroism in the face of death, readiness for battle and closeness to the soil were among their cardinal virtues. These warrior values of the Nordic spirit found symbolic expression in the *Nibelungen* and other sagas; in the cult of

Valhalla and in the Viking ships which expressed the fearlessness, love of adventure, of booty, and the freedom residing in the ancestral spirit. These primitive Nordic sagas were to be seen in Alfred Rosenberg's words, as 'the Old Testament of the German people' and a reminder of its unbroken racial continuity and strength.[50]

The Romanesque period was valued for its architecture, sculpture and heroic songs but even more for the emergence of a Germanic Reich and its consolidation. Beginning under Charlemagne (expropriated for German history), continuing with Henry I and culminating in Frederick Barbarossa and the Hohenstaufens, this period was taken to exemplify the warlike virtues of racial nobility. Since 1937 it had been well represented in the pageants. The Gothic period, which witnessed the disintegration of the First Reich, was more problematic for the Nazis, despite the soaring cathedrals which Oswald Spengler had once described as supreme expressions of the 'Faustian' Germanic soul. For example, the chief ideologue of the Party, Alfred Rosenberg, who passionately reproved the influence of Roman Catholicism, bluntly asserted that the Gothic style was a dead end for the German will to expression. At the same time he did not deny a certain grandeur and 'Germanic' quality to the Gothic.[51] The Gothic emphasis in the Munich parades was, however, on the medieval knightly orders, the Crusaders, the town halls, the emergence of a solid burgher class and the quality of German craftsmanship.

The Renaissance, with its revival of classical motifs, of the arts and sciences and of German humanism, was adequately represented but not given special attention. Its architecture had left relatively few monuments in Germany, its concern with classical learning was seen as being elitist

and some influential racist critics like Schultze-Naumburg regarded it as a 'foreign body' on the German scene.[52]

The Baroque was another period that received a mixed response, partly because its origins also lay south of the Alps and its links with Catholicism made it seem suspect to many Nazis. Rosenberg thought it was a 'Jesuit style', Schultze-Naumburg and others called it 'un-German', though Hitler actually liked Baroque architecture, of which there were many fine examples in Bavaria.[53] Its theatricality, with which he was familiar from his adolescent years in Austria, was one striking feature that the Baroque shared with the masters of mass festivals in the Third Reich. In a category of his own came Frederick the Great, the only German political and military hero of modern times with whom Hitler and the Nazis consistently identified. In the Munich pageants, Frederick the Great is the sole *Führergestalt* (leadership figure) to grace German history between the Hohenstaufens and Hitler himself.[54]

Late eighteenth-century neo-classicism (especially the Greek revival) was generally well received. Goethe, Schiller, Mozart and Beethoven had their honoured place in the festivities of the Day of German Art and they were seen as an integral part of this historical period. Early nineteenth-century Prussian neo-classicist architects like Friedrich Gilly and Karl Friedrich Schinkel had left an enduring influence on Hitler's architectural mentor, Paul Ludwig Troost, and on Albert Speer. Indeed, the House of German Art built by Troost in Munich in the early 1930s owed much to Schinkel's Berlin Museum, constructed almost a century earlier.[55]

The Romantic period, with return to the Middle Ages and its emphasis on the Germanic past, its *Sturm and Drang* fervour and its Wars of Liberation against Napoleon, was no less important. Here, for the first time, the *Volk* (nation) appeared on the stage of history as a semi-independent actor. The Romantic age had also brought forth Richard Wagner, whom Hitler and the Nazis unmistakably regarded as the greatest herald of Germandom in music before their own time.

Significantly, the pageants sharply downplayed the modern period between 1850 and the Third Reich, despite the centrality in modern German history of such events as the Franco-Prussian war and German unification, or the roles of Bismarck and Kaiser Wilhelm II. Politically, this only seems explicable as a deliberate effort by Hitler to aggrandize his national role and that of the Third Reich at the expense of his immediate predecessors.

Artistically, German cultural history since Wagner was presented as a desert, or what the Nazis often liked to call 'the time of decay'. The pageants, which focused exclusively on the positive, had no interest in showing this era of 'decadence' in which rapid industrialization and modernization had destroyed the inner bonds of the *Volk*. Decline was interpreted as the inevitable consequence of the prevailing individualism, liberalism and materialistic ideology which had dominated both the middle and working classes. The sense of German community had vanished under the impact of big industry, profit-seeking, unhealthy urbanism and sinister 'Jewish' influences. Here is how Gerdy Troost (Paul Ludwig Troost's widow) described the *fin-de-siècle* German bourgeoisie before Nazism: 'indifferent to race, un-*völkisch*, unsocial, devoid of any deep connection with the community, wedded to money and machines, misled by Jews, and driven closer and closer to destruction'.[56] The Weimar Republic (which was totally erased from the cele-

brations) was merely the culmination of this social, cultural and political degeneration. But with the advent of the Third Reich, the German *Volk* and its *Kultur* had been rescued at the last moment from self-destruction.

Skilfully using all the visual devices of a parade that combined elements of carnival, costume ball, history lesson and kitsch, the Munich pageant was therefore very much a medium with a message. This message climaxed with the representation of the contemporary period (*Die neue Zeit*) with its symbolic figures of faith, loyalty and sacrifice; with its parades of youth; its models of the Führer buildings; its glorification of peasants close to the soil; its flags, swastikas and marching columns of the Wehrmacht, the SA, the SS and other Nazi formations.

The Day of German Art was intended to be a celebration of the *Volk* in all its glory, its greatness and its purity; basking in the achievements of its history and in the continuity of its culture. From the Germanic tribal chieftains, the Crusader knights and the Gothic cathedrals to the giants of German music (Bach, Beethoven, Mozart), from Prussian soldiery to the Wehrmacht, from the *Nibelungen* to Wagner and Hitler – it was essentially one past, one *Volk*, one Reich. The same pristine virtues of heroism, courage and will-power, the same racial purity and superior *Kultur* visible throughout German history would help the Third Reich to triumph again over its enemies and expand towards the east.[57] All these threads had come together in National Socialism, which was not only intended to be the heir to but also the culmination and salvation of two millennia of German history. One Nazi commentator felt fully confident in claiming that 'the Day of German Art demonstrates how much art is the concern of the whole nation and the people in which it is anchored'.[58]

Taking refreshment. *Participants in Munich's annual parade take a break.*

The sheer scale of the pageantry undoubtedly contributed much to its impact on the masses. In 1937, the first year of the parade, there had been twenty-six floats, 426 animals and 6,000 people decked out in period costumes.[59] The Nazis triumphantly published statistics to show that 33,821 people had been involved in the preparations and that 690,000 labour hours had been expended. Such figures were designed to illustrate not only their successful organization of such events and value in providing work but also to highlight the economic importance to Munich of the *Feste*.[60]

As with all their mass spectacles, great attention was paid by the Nazis to choreography, design, symbolism and street decoration. Overall responsibility for the organization of the pageant was put in the hands of two distinguished Munich art professors, Richard Knecht and Hermann Kaspar, who were assisted with street decorations by Professor Georg Buchner (also from Munich) and by a costume designer, Otto Reigbert. Care was taken to include all the most important streets, squares, gates and buildings (especially those constructed by the Nazi regime) in the parade route. The procession began in the Prinzregentenstrasse and wound its way over several kilometres to the Maximilian Monument. The rhythm of the parade, the costumes, the flags with eagles and the fluttering swastikas were designed for maximum effect, to draw spectators into the event. Participants and spectators were, after all, part of the same *Volksgemeinschaft* (community of the people).

The street decoration with its brilliant colours was also carried out on a monumental scale, to create the desired visual unity of expression.[61] The classical buildings of Munich were carefully chosen for their suitability as an impressive backdrop to the great parade and to the marching columns in their black and brown uniforms who brought up the rear. Though the Day of German Art was clearly intended to be a happy occasion, celebrating the joy of the people in artistic life, its apotheosis in Nazi eyes was undoubtedly the perfect military precision of the Wehrmacht, the SA and the SS.

The historical pageant and the art exhibition were not only seen as a legitimation of the regime, they were also a necessary diversion from social and economic problems and a triumphant assertion of popular mass culture. Above all, they were a fusion of all the dominant myths of the Third Reich: the *Volksgemeinschaft*, the 'living eternity of the German people', the heroic continuities in its past, its warrior virtues and racial purity, the cultural community of the German nation and its final, mystical resurrection.[62] Munich, the city of festivals and birthplace of the Nazi movement, was chosen to herald the new German renaissance and to provide the elaborate cultural façade for the coming expansion of the Reich. Hitler had designated it the artistic *Via Triumphalis* of the new Reich, but the elaborately constructed façade of *Kultur* heralded only a brutal will to power and conquest

CHAPTER SIX

BROWN SHIRTS, BLUE SKIES

*'The colour had an uncanny effect, transforming evil back into its original semblance
of innocence…days of innocence and hope rendered vile by knowledge…
The programme emerged as a cautionary tale against the attractions and perils of naivety…
the naivety of simplifying life by exterminating an entire people.'*

CRAIG BROWN, *THE SUNDAY TIMES*, 23 MAY 1993

WHAT WAS the source of the Nazi appeal to the masses? How did a regime which was responsible for war, devastation and mass murder on an unprecedented scale seduce a civilized nation and lead it to disaster? Was there a secret charm to German fascism that we ignore at our peril if we are to understand the fascination it exerted on millions of people? What were the deeper wellsprings on which the Nazis drew in deluding even decent, honourable, intelligent people as to their true intentions?

We have attempted an answer to these difficult and troubling questions by engaging with Nazism on a terrain in which it was a proven master. It is doubtful if any other political movement ever matched Nazism in its visual orchestration of power, its manipulation of myth and illusion or its finesse in political propaganda and mystification. To obtain an insight into this world of fantasy and imagination we have been

Hans Feierabend

aided by some unique images, shot by a highly skilled amateur film-maker on the Day of German Art held in Munich between 14 and 16 July 1939.

These images are troubling in their power to evoke a past that seems carefree, naïvely joyful, full of hope and even innocence. The azure blue Bavarian skies, the colourful costumes, the German eagles, the swastikas and brown shirts blend into what looks like a beguiling, peaceful harmony. Yet, as we have seen, there was a dark, chilling reality behind that spectacular façade. Not only was the Third Reich about to invade Poland (the act which launched the Second World War), but in less than two years it would embark on a terrible 'war of annihilation' against the USSR that culminated in the Holocaust of European Jewry.

Our text and the images which accompany it have dealt with Nazi Germany on the eve of this tremendous upheaval. We have analysed the background to the glittering pageant, celebrating 2,000 years of German art and culture. The event had brought virtually all the top Nazi leaders to Munich. It was widely publicized in the German and international media, especially since Hitler was due to speak during the festival at the opening of the German Art Exhibition in the House of German Art. But the Nazi propaganda machine, already feverishly oriented to preparations for war, overlooked one record of the event which the Munich *Gauleiter* Adolf Wagner had himself commissioned to record the festivities. This ravishing colour film was shot by an unknown amateur called Hans Feierabend (and members of Munich's Amateur Film Society) with a 16mm Bolex camera. It would resurface publicly more than fifty years after the event.

The film was re-discovered by a young German researcher, Alexander van Dülmen, working for the Munich film archive. He had been intrigued by the existence of a Munich Amateur Film Society in the late 1930s, of which Hans Feierabend had been a pillar. Feierabend, an artificial limb manufacturer by trade, had won a prize at the Munich Amateur Film Festival in 1940 for a short black-and-white film, appropriately entitled *Wooden Leg*. Although Hans was no longer alive, van Dülmen managed to trace his two sons, Berndt and Peter, who still lived in Munich.

It was Peter Feierabend who subsequently brought the previously unknown colour footage, shot by his father, to the Munich film archive. The thirty minutes of loosely assembled footage, originally shot on Kodachrome, was in remarkably good condition. The colour remains sharp and brilliant, bringing to life a city in festive mood. The beautifully decorated streets and squares of Munich, some of its historic buildings, the dancing troupes

in the English Garden, the preparations for the procession and the excitement of the parade itself are all recorded. We see some of the huge floats, the Teutonic knights, their shields and caparisons emblazoned with swastikas, the flaxen-haired Rhine maidens, the beautiful young girls decked out like Greek nymphs and children carrying flowers. There are smartly dressed women in summer attire and elegant hats, ordinary citizens peacefully going about their business in the streets and parks as well as precious glimpses of the Munich crowds as they view the parade. Above all we are shown Hitler and other Nazi leaders, looking unusually relaxed and informal, for once unrehearsed. Hitler, in stinging colour close-up with his brown party uniform, his Iron Cross First Class and sandy moustache, has a somewhat dreamy, Chaplinesque quality. He and the other Nazi bigwigs seem well content with the proceedings and at ease with the crowds. Except for the rain-affected Sunday afternoon parade, the Bavarian skies are resonantly blue, the atmosphere festive and the Brownshirts march in impeccable formation.

All this visual detail, heightened by the still-vivid colour which is mesmerizing in its effects and unusual in its quality, gives Feierabend's short film its engaging freshness. It is also unique because in the entire visual record of the Third Reich there is nothing of this length, in colour, which offers comparable access to a major event. There are, it is true, a number of grainy colour sequences showing Hitler in his mountain retreat at Berchtesgaden and some snippets survive from other amateur film-makers, but that material is comparatively trivial. It must be remembered that colour, like television itself, was still in its infancy at the time. The Nazi propaganda machine relied on black and white, in more senses than one, up until the

Art guardian. *Adolf Hitler opens the Great German Art Exhibition in the House of German Art, 1939. The event is being recorded by a member of Munich's Amateur Film Society.*

end of the Second World War.

Hans Feierabend's original film has no commentary and it was never manipulated by Party authorities or used for propaganda purposes. The contrast between its detached unideological approach to the event it depicts and the official Nazi film version of the Day of German Art is striking. The black-and-white record has Hitler purposefully striding through adoring, anonymous masses to the sound of martial music and fanfares: the German Art Exhibition, which he opens, leads us to a huge, overbearing portrait of the Führer and the exhibits singled out for attention by the camera are powerful, muscular, sculpted figures of 'Aryan' manhood. The cultural construct which Goebbels and his assistants normally relied on for filming such occasions was replete with hysterical adulation, Wagnerian pomp, the rhythmic marching of the Wehrmacht, the SA and the SS.

Feierabend's Führer is, by comparison, almost user-friendly: determined, but also hesitant, confident yet strangely diffident, exuding power but not without a certain comic awkwardness and even shyness. The interaction between the Nazi elite and the crowds comes over as more complicit and easygoing than we are used to seeing in German propaganda material. Not only Hitler, but Himmler, Goebbels, Hess, Ley, Speer, Streicher, Wagner and the other Nazi leaders seem almost at home among the people. The crowds, too, judging by their faces, scarcely seem intimidated. They do not appear troubled by fears of an approaching world war, nor are they likely to be thinking either about the persecuted Jews or the dissident artists banned from the Great German Art Exhibition. If anything, they seem more preoccupied by the sudden change in the weather which threatened to dampen the parade with a torrential downpour on Sunday afternoon. The amateur cameramen catch this apparently carefree innocence, which is the more uncanny given the stark European realities of the summer of 1939.

In his film there is none of the orchestrated mass hysteria, the elaborate theatricality and stage management which characterized a normal Goebbels propaganda production. There is no attempt to overwhelm the spectator with a sense of Hitler's power or the grandeur of the Third Reich. The dimensions are everyday, almost human, and given an unexpected immediacy and contemporaneity by the effect of colour. The shock value of the film lies in seeing Adolf Hitler and his Brownshirts, Himmler and his SS, the rapturous spectators, the elegant women and the laughing German youth, literally walking into our living rooms. Yet this unexpected, unnerving intimacy

Soldiers and children line the route of Munich's 1939 pageant of Nazi art and culture.

with the Nazis, stripped of its usual propaganda trappings, is no less seductive in its potential appeal. Feierabend was of course filming a Nazi-orchestrated event and even if his approach was wholly unpolitical, we can still sense something of the magnetism of these mass festivals. It becomes easier to understand how ordinary people could be drawn into National Socialism and how its magical manipulation spellbound the German masses into complicity with the regime.

Hans Feierabend's footage, suitably edited, was eventually incorporated in a Channel Four documentary titled *Good Morning, Mr Hitler!* (1993). The directors, Luke Holland and Paul Yule, having acquired the rights to the original material, travelled to Munich to search for living participants in the 1939 parade. Following advertisements in the local press, they managed to assemble a number for a group screening of Feierabend's home movie, at which they elicited some spontaneous reactions. Among those people interviewed were the two sons of the film-maker, Berndt and Peter Feierabend, who have carried on their father's artificial limb manufacturing business in Munich; Martin Summer, an eighty-year-old optical engineer who still lives and works in Munich and who was a close associate of Hans Feierabend in the pre-war Munich Amateur Film Society; Else Peitz, a

*Hitler and Goebbels at the 1939 exhibition
in Munich.*

friend of Hitler's and the daughter of his publisher, Adolf Müller, the man who first printed *Mein Kampf*; and a horsewoman, Inge Ungewitter, who as a young girl rode through the streets of Munich in 1939 dressed as a Valkyrie. Another young participant in the pageant, Josefa Hammann, who was only eighteen at the time, was also interviewed; as was the landscape painter and designer Günther Grassmann, who had been an eye-witness of Hitler's failed Munich *putsch* of 1923. He had designed some standards for the Day of German Art. By the time of the interview he was ninety-two years old and blind, but his memory was remarkably keen.

Last, but not least, an interview with Charlotte Knobloch, the president of the Jewish community in Munich, was included in the documentary. She lived in Munich as a young girl, until the mass deportation of Jews began in 1942. Her father, a wealthy Jewish lawyer and war hero in 1914, had been forced to choose between sacrificing his mother or his daughter to an earlier death transport. Charlotte only survived the Holocaust because her father hid her with a local Bavarian

farming family, and she was subsequently liberated in 1945. Not surprisingly, her memories of this period are rather different from those of the other German interviewees.

The Channel Four film was mainly constructed out of the interplay between Feierabend's silent images and the reminiscences of the survivors. My own role had been first to identify and describe the Nazi leaders in the original footage, and then to contextualize and analyse the significance of the pageant itself. This involved asking wider questions concerning the nature of Nazism. What was its relation to the masses? What was the link between art and politics in the Third Reich? What was the connection between propaganda, myth and image-making? Why was the Hitler myth so powerful in Nazi Germany? What was the position of the Jews and why was historical amnesia still so strong in post-war Germany regarding this and other aspects of the Nazi past? What indeed was the relationship between history and memory in contemporary German discourse?

These were issues that could only be sketched in the briefest manner in the commentary, essentially an unmediated reaction to the silent images on the screen. The strength of the film as a visual medium lay, after all, in the sinister and irresistible quality of the images themselves; in the 'unreal' vividness of the colours and their uncanny effect of 'transforming evil back into its original semblance of innocence'.[1] Is there not something dangerous as well as unnerving about the casual, unremarkable, banal look of the Nazi leadership as it is conveyed in Feieraband's film? Is there not a risk of humanizing rather than simply deflating Hitler, Hess, Goebbels, Streicher and other Nazi criminals, by watching them enjoying themselves at a summer art festival? Was one not inadvertently trivializing

Nazism by focusing on splendid parades, fluttering flags, coloured decorations, happy faces, 'friendly' swastikas and gaudy costumes that looked about as threatening as a village funfair?[2]

If this was indeed a cautionary tale about how masses of people can be drawn into a totalitarian movement – if it was warning about 'the naivety of simplifying life by exterminating an entire people' – then a deeper analysis was surely required of the content behind the beautiful façade. It is not enought to speak with Hannah Arendt of 'the banality of evil', though that too is part of the Nazi phenomenon. It is patently unacceptable to enjoy a psychedelic trip back into the Nazi past to consume pleasurably its 'strength through joy', unless we aim critically to confront its appalling legacy. The potency of the visual orchestration, even at this remove in time, should not be underestimated. As Isabel Hilton has perceptively put it:

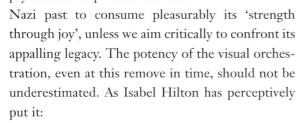

Charlotte Knobloch

> The success of the day [of German Art] was testimony to the power of Nazi mythology. This was gift-wrapped National Socialism, its victims out of sight, its appeal apparently uncontaminated by the existence of a concentration camp in the picturesque town of Dachau, only a twenty-minute train ride from Munich.[3]

In the documentary, Charlotte Knobloch, the Jewish survivor watching the glorious pageant on screen, makes a similarly telling point: 'It's completely unbelievable to me that people can be so happy here, when twenty kilometres away there's a concentration camp in Dachau, already overflowing with people, who hadn't broken any laws and who, just because of their race or because of the way they looked, were put behind barbed wire and tortured.'[4]

But what did Hans Feierabend know of Dachau and its inmates? According to his son Berndt, he *did* know something because he was friendly with another amateur film-maker, a Mr Bielmayer, who was the baker of Dachau.[5] Bielmayer, who was in the Nazi Party and 'always very well organized', made a jolly though mediocre home movie in 1943 about the film society's picnic in Dachau and its environs, which has survived. Hans Feierabend was one of the twenty or so participants in that outing. At one point, the group is joined by a passing SS officer, who leaves them, in the final shot, waving cheerfully from his Mercedes.[6]

Feierabend's own film of that day in Dachau has not been preserved, but that same year he went cycling in the mountains and made a short black-and-white film about the sources of the River Isar, which runs through Munich. There is, however, no direct evidence of his concern with what was happening to the Jews or to political prisoners in Dachau, though his sons vigorously maintain that he had strong reservations about the regime. His friend Martin Summer insists that 'in the Film Club we never did anything political' and 'one would never talk about politics'.[7] As 'normal, young people' they had never thought about international issues. People simply wanted to live and work, enjoy their hobbies and stay out of trouble. Looking back nearly fifty years after the war, Summer observed: 'We didn't know it was so extreme. We knew there were concentration camps but it was simply political opponents that were locked up there. But what happened there, nobody knew that. We never knew. It didn't interest me. I mean…nothing happened to us. And if nothing happens to you, then you don't really bother about it.'[8]

It is difficult to know whether Hans Feierabend shared this somewhat complacent if commonplace indifference or whether, as his family insist, he was an opponent of the Nazi regime. Certainly it seems clear that, whatever his politics, Hans Feierabend was probably commissioned by Adolf Wagner, the *Gauleiter* of Munich, to make a film of the Day of German Art. It was Wagner who may have supplied the rare and expensive Kodachrome film and arranged the security pass that allowed Feierabend and his associates to film Hitler and the Nazi leadership close up. This was among the first 16mm colour film available in Germany and if Feierabend was provided with it, this surely meant he was trusted by Adolf Wagner and other Party members.

According to his son Peter, Hans Feierabend was given special access because he was 'well respected', a 'very good cameraman' and a 'real technician'. He suggests, plausibly enough, that what motivated his father to accept the commission was a passion for film rather than any political identification with Nazism.[9] But if Hans

Martin Summer

Feierabend was *not* very politically oriented, then one is bound to wonder why he hated Hitler and was so much 'against these brown hordes of National Socialists'?[10]

According to his sons, the love of his hobby ultimately outweighed Hans Feierabend's anti-Nazism. Later, he was able to stay in Munich during the war, thanks to his much-needed professional expertise in making wooden legs for wounded German soldiers. This also permitted him to continue with his film hobby and to edit the colour footage with its unique close-ups of Hitler. It was projected at home in family film shows during the war years, but hidden under a woodpile in the cellar when the Americans and Russians came in 1945.[11] Later, he did show the film to some visiting American officers and generals with whom he had a good relationship and 'they were very excited about it'. But he had no desire to go public with it, for fear of being tainted with the Nazi brush.

At this distance in time Hans Feierabend's motivations, feelings and intentions in shooting the film must remain something of an enigma. One point in his favour is that before 1939 he did employ a German Jew in his orthopaedic workshop, at a time when this must have been considered a dangerous act. His employee, Ernst Eisenmann, subsequently emigrated to British Mandatory Palestine and became a doctor. He remained on good terms with the family and personally confirmed to me in Israel that Hans Feierabend was a very decent man. But he had no idea how and why he came to make this colour film.[12] What is clear enough is that Mr Feierabend was an unusually dynamic individual who took great pride in his professional orthopaedic skills as well as being a gifted amateur film-maker. He probably did dislike the Nazi regime, without ever being an active opponent or becoming overtly political. His visual record leaves open this and other questions and that, too, is part of its fascination.

Berndt Feierabend rightly sees his father's film as an important historical document and as a warning that remains relevant for a reunited Germany. In the end, he observes, 'it was Nazi propaganda to display this power and this beauty...that made it so impressive and so many went and worked for the Führer and became enthusiastic about the whole thing. It was all a pretence and, sadly, people keep falling for it.'[13] His brother, Peter, admits that 'it is still a puzzle why so many people worshipped this crazy dictator', but ultimately he too puts it down to Goebbels's skill in 'cretinizing the masses'. Goebbels, he adds, was one 'of the greatest public relations managers ever' and knew how to exploit mass psychoses and the mass media of the age to perfection.[14] This aspect of image-making is still with us today, as he shrewdly points out.

Peter Feierabend believes that his father's film can show people 'with what finesse the population can be enveloped into jubilant enthusiasm for a dictator'. What comes over very dramatically is 'that the packaging was so very exciting and people allowed themselves to be blinded by it. They were

Berndt Feierabend

simply enthused and things did actually improve at that time; unemployment was reduced; there were so many things that people saw as positive and of course, they did not see that Hitler wanted nothing else apart from conquering more land, and that was wrong.'[15]

Interestingly, the Feierabend family has no fear that today this kind of representation of the Nazi era might be viewed negatively. Though neo-Nazis could use such material for their own purposes, Peter Feierabend is convinced that the German people today are simply too educated and sensible to be endangered by exposure to such beguiling images of the past.[16]

Professor Winfried Nerdinger, an expert on Nazi architecture who teaches in Munich, is much less certain about this point. He notes the extraordinary ignorance that prevails among ordinary Munich citizens and even among his own students concerning the Nazi era. Few, if any, are aware that the 'Temples of Honour' which the Nazis built in the centre of Munich for their movement's martyrs were their most important shrine. Many do not even know that Munich was 'the capital of the movement', the place where it all began.[17] The architecture, he claims, is not seriously discussed, nor are its connections with the Nazi system of repression and terror properly examined. The context of Nazi art in general, whether painting, sculpture or architecture, is largely ignored and therefore its links with a racist ideology and a totalitarian political system are blurred. The result is that the memory of the past is not kept alive in a pedagogically useful way. This, he thinks, has made it easier for a new racism to revive in Germany, calling into question the effectiveness of post-war re-education for democracy.

Charlotte Knobloch, with her vivid childhood memories of the Gestapo terror against the Jews in Munich, is also sceptical, for different reasons. Her personal opinion is that 'the Jews who after this terrible period again sought to have a future here [in Germany] are still just guests'.[18] True, younger German Jews, born after 1945, did not experience the Nazi era as a personal trauma. They went to

Inge Ungewitter

German schools and were integrated into the language, the culture, the surrounding society and the workplace. But even so, though not openly treated as 'aliens', they remain separate and distinct 'Jewish fellow citizens'. They have the same rights as others but they are not fully part of the country. Jews, she notes, can still be attacked in Germany simply because they look like Jews. Admittedly, two years ago there was a large demonstration by candlelight in Munich, directed against racism. But that was an anti-racist rally on behalf of foreigners. 'If there had been a call to go out on the streets on behalf of Jews,' she asks, 'how many lights would there have been on the streets?'[19]

Looking at Hans Feierabend's film, Frau Knobloch was struck by how shiny and glowing the city had looked in 1939 and by the glossy splendour with which the Nazis presented themselves. She felt that these pictures would give encouragement

to the neo-Nazis today, in Germany and elsewhere. 'You wouldn't believe that fifty-five or sixty years ago people were so excited, were taken in by all this grandeur; and this is something that can really motivate the neo-Nazis in their fanaticism. It is unbelievable how this shows itself. One would think it was yesterday when you see these people there. Unbelievable. They did this perfectly; they are really perfectionist people, the Germans, I have to say that: whatever they do, they do it perfectly. They also annihilated the Jews perfectly.'[20]

Frau Knobloch felt, despite some reservations, that it was important for young Jews to see this film, simply to understand how it was possible to convince a population 'to be so jubilant about such a murderer'.

For Munich Jews like the Knobloch family, the 1939 celebrations were a nightmare. After the Nazis came to power in 1933, they lived a very secluded life, full of fear, never knowing what the next day might bring. 'Everyone was scared. If a Jew was seen anywhere, he was immediately taken away. That also happened to us when we went for a walk; they immediately took my father away to the Gestapo…the Jews were, after all, free game, they could do with them whatever they wished. There was not a single judge who would take a stand for them.'[21] Naturally, in these circumstances, Jews kept well away from any public festivities.

Good Morning, Mr Hitler! sharply brings out the gulf between German and Jewish memories. For Munich's Jewish citizens the Day of German Art, like any other Nazi celebration, was a bitter reminder of their total exclusion from the national community. They were pariahs who had been robbed of their rights, humiliated and persecuted, who were afraid even to show their faces in public.

For most of the German survivors, on the other hand, the prevailing memory of these expensive parades was pleasurable. It was all good, clean fun which cheered them up no end. Inge Ungewitter recalls that, as a fifteen-year-old, she rode her thoroughbred horse through the Munich streets, carrying a spear and a shield. 'It was a wonderful day. If you give Bavarians something like that…all that glitter and gold, they love it.'[22] Interviewed in her splendid apartment situated on the Grillparzerstrasse, near Hitler's old Munich flat, Frau Ungewitter remembered above all the bright costumes, the music, the noise and the typically boisterous Munich atmosphere of festivity. A painter and a keen horsewoman, lacking any interest in politics, she had no inkling about the intentions of Hitler and the Nazi leaders. Nor did she have the slightest idea of the fate of the Jews at that time. But like many Germans she did have a vivid memory of the destruction of buildings and homes during the war.[23]

Josefa Hammann, who was a young girl at the time, participating in the parade, recalls 16 July 1939 as 'a really beautiful day, a sunny day with a blue Bavarian sky, which later ended with a rainstorm'.[24] She had been chosen for her height and blonde 'Aryan' looks ('the Nordic race was sup-

Josefa Hammann

posed to be shown off here', as she ironically recalls) and was sent off to dance school, to learn how to walk properly. She remembers marching through the streets to the House of German Art, then on through the city to the Odeon Square where Hitler and the top Nazis were waiting. Then, in the evening, there was dancing and merriment in all the open areas of Munich and even in the Nymphenburg Castle. As an innocent eighteen-year-old she had paid little attention to the presence of Hitler and his henchmen (many of them with their smartly dressed wives) or of the Bavarian top brass. At that time, she emphasizes, young people were uninterested in politics and 'it did not have anything to do with politics for us'. It was essentially a wonderful day, an opportunity to meet people, have fun and show oneself off in different sorts of costumes.[25]

Frau Hammann vividly recalled the dancing troupes, the theatres and concerts which were part of the festival. Coming herself from a modest background, such entertainment was 'much too expensive and inaccessible for us, so these kinds of festivities were really something great – you could experience all of this for free'.[26] In the midst of all this rejoicing, she had paid little attention to Munich's Jews, having virtually no contact with them. However, she did recollect having seen Jewish shops with broken windows at the Gärtnerplatz and then again at the Marienplatz during the *Kristallnacht* pogrom of November 1938. It was the first time she had ever seen shops smashed to pieces

Dressing up for the Führer. *Josefa Hammann (far right) and friends. Munich, 1939.*

and she could not understand what had happened. There were people standing around and 'everyone said that the SA people had done it and that Jews lived in these shops and their businesses had been destroyed'.[27] At the time she was bewildered. Nobody, she says, 'had any idea or even thought about any of these things. What was the matter with the Jews? What did they want with the Jews, you know?'[28]

Frau Hammann's memories of Adolf Wagner and of Hitler are also interesting. Wagner, one of Hitler's old Munich comrades and previously Bavarian minister of education and culture, was the host for the Day of German Art. He was also Frau Hammann's old boss and a 'sadistic, self-righteous person…He always shouted terribly when something was up and if he didn't understand it immediately. He once told me to hit someone, you know.'[29] If everything did not run perfectly, 'then there was absolute mayhem in the place. It was really bad,' she recalls. Wagner was also a notorious womanizer, who would simply take any girl he wanted, whether in the office or on the streets. This coarse Bavarian with a wooden leg and a thick scar from his student fencing days often behaved

'like a savage'. Yet he liked to make bombastic speeches about the Nazi cultural renaissance and Munich's great artistic traditions!

Frau Hammann was struck by the near panic whenever Hitler came to visit the building organization where she worked, to check on sketches and architectural plans. 'There was always a big brouhaha, you know, because they all had to fly, all the doors had to be open when Hitler came, and then the house was stirred up like a bees' nest. And often, well Hitler was also very easily upset, and when everything did not function perfectly the way that he imagined it should, or whenever someone argued with him, then in less than ten minutes all the doors were slamming and they were off again.'[30] Frau Hammann's general impression of Hitler was of a basically insecure, irritable, and power-crazed individual with an overwhelming craving to be admired and feared.

This was not at all the feeling he aroused in Else Peitz, who knew him rather well. The Führer was a regular guest at the family house on the Tegernsee, outside Munich, where he came to visit her father, Adolf Muller – publisher of *Mein Kampf* and of the leading Nazi newspaper, the *Völkischer Beobachter*. Looking back fifty-five years later, she still thinks of Hitler as a real gentleman – 'privately he was very attentive and gallant'.[31] On learning of her engagement, he had come with flowers specially to congratulate her. Later, he had agreed to be a witness at her wedding. He had the highest respect for women – ('He always thought that every woman was sacred') – and 'to go into a room in front of a woman was unthinkable for him'.[32] According to Frau Peitz, he never married because he did not want to make his spouse unhappy in view of the great commitment and dangers he had taken upon himself. He considered himself 'married to the German people'. But that did not diminish his chivalrous regard for women and for 'all things of beauty'. Frau Peitz emphasized Hitler's great love of art. He enjoyed painting, the theatre (especially comedy) and architecture. He was always enthusiastic about being in the company of artists. Hitler really liked the House of German Art and admired great architects such as Troost. His taste, whether in architecture or painting and music, was for classical things 'because they were far more eternal than these modern ideas'. He was above all a 'passionate opera fan' and insisted that the performers should be physically fit for the role. He demanded, for example, that even big stars with great voices 'should slim down for the opera performances'.[33] Hitler, of course, 'loved Wagner and he also understood something about music'.

Else Peitz

Frau Peitz strongly underlined Hitler's personal modesty and fondly reminisced about his summer visits to Tegernsee: 'He would come with six or eight people, like Goebbels and many others from the Party… and they would drink coffee with us, or watch while all of us young women were swimming around the lake…it was fun somehow. It was a good laugh. But then, of course, when Hitler came to power, it was a bit more difficult because a lot of National Socialists also wanted to come and see the Führer. "Where is my Führer?" they would say. And of course, he didn't want that… he wanted things to be much more private. So we would never say "Heil, mein Führer!" but we would greet him: "Good Morning, Mr Hitler!" '[34]

In *Good Morning, Mr Hitler!*, Frau Peitz's memories of July 1939 are no less idyllic. She recalls that at the time 'everyone really liked to join in, everyone was activated and all this enjoyment triggered something off… we thought we were going towards a better future, rather than what actually came afterwards.'[35]

People thought in a positive way and found joy in their personal involvement. Also, since there was no television and everyone had a more modest lifestyle, they 'looked forward to these kind of festivals much more'. Moreover, industry was thriving, the autobahns and other public works had greatly decreased unemployment, giving the population hope that they were moving forward economically. The prestige of the Third Reich had also increased greatly. Frau Peitz remembers the big diplomatic reception in Berlin at the beginning of 1939 when representatives of many foreign countries came to see Hitler. The public festivals, too, 'made an enormous impression on the rest of the world'.[36]

On the other hand, 'the Jewish question was always kept very quiet'. According to Frau Peitz, this was handled 'very discreetly' by the Nazis. 'They would always say that you were not allowed to buy things in a Jewish shop. And there were lovely big shops in the Kaufingerstrasse, and almost all of them belonged to Jewish people. And at the hospital, for instance, the top doctor was a Jew. Jewish people really stick together and they have a real sense of family… and there were a lot of civil servants who were Jewish too, and they would look after each other, you know.'[37]

Asked whether in 1939 she or other Germans knew what was happening to the Jews, she insists that this knowledge only came *after* the war. 'Now and then you would hear that they had connections with other countries, and that some were locked up. And if you asked "Well, why?" this was very much kept a secret…People would just say they wanted nothing to do with them, and they would make sure that none of them held public office… Perhaps we were all too indifferent about it all, because of course there were some very, very respectable Jews, you know.'[38]

Frau Peitz admits that she knew there was a concentration camp called Dachau but thought it was solely for political people. She was amazed to learn later of the terrible things that had been done to the Jews. As with so many Germans of her generation, she maintains: 'we hadn't known at the time. And even if they said something about it, we didn't really know. No one believed it, no one would believe it.'[39] To this day she does not believe that Hitler was an anti-Semite! The following anecdote which she recounts is surely priceless. 'For example, his [Hitler's] flat on the Prinz-regentenplatz had belonged to a Jew and the Jew lived on the first floor and Hitler on the second, you know. And when Hitler received a big crate of wine for Christmas, he would always send it down to the Jews. No, he wouldn't send it down – I said that wrong – he would get a crate of wine from the Jews, and he would then give it to the SA or the SS, because he was an anti-alcoholic. But that man [the Jew] who lived on the first floor, they weren't

allowed to touch a single hair on his head. Of course, the Party would have said they should look for a different flat for him, but that wasn't possible at all. Personally, he never went against the Jews. Perhaps he ordered it – I don't know – but that's the way it was.'[40]

Frau Peitz confesses that the news of the death camps appeared completely unbelievable to her when it was revealed after 1945. Like so many people, she had always thought that Hitler 'had a blameless character, and then it turned out that this was not the case'. Nevertheless, she still believes that Germany was not solely responsible for launching the Second World War. The British and French were also responsible because they had wanted to keep Germany economically, technologically and militarily backward.

Looking at the images in Hans Feierabend's film, she still remembers 1939 nostalgically as a high point in her life. She watched the procession in a mood of optimism and national pride. She went to the House of German Art regularly during that summer. It was so beautiful, it made her feel so clean that she wanted to go home and tidy her house! There was something uplifting there which gave her a sense of strength and order, quite unlike the modern art which she could never understand. It was 'very consoling', 'impressive' and 'constructive' to look at these 'massive masterpieces' on the walls of the Great German Art Exhibition.

Such a reaction was, of course, exactly what the Nazis had hoped to achieve with their great pageants and art exhibitions. When Hitler purged the German art galleries and museums of what he took to be decadent modern rubbish, he was confident of meeting with mass approval. Whether the German people agreed with him that modern art was literally a sign of cultural and biological

The Nazi eagle adorns Munich's main railway station on the eve of the 1939 Day of German Art.

Hitler considered that the German nation, cleansed of its decadent influences, had become the standard-bearer for the new artistic vision.

degeneracy is perhaps an open question. But the goal of making the nation healthy and sound by ridding it of Jewish, Bolshevik and other artistic 'impurities' was a popular programme. After 1937, as we have seen, this resulted in a style of painting that was resolutely anti-modern, banishing from Germany the works of Picasso, Chagall, Paul Klee, the Impressionists and even the leading German Expressionists. The work of these and many other modern painters was branded as 'degenerate art' and confiscated or even burned in some cases. In its place came the anodyne landscapes, glowing nudes and rustic idylls that could appeal to a lower-middle-class Austrian teetotaller like Adolf Hitler, with plain, Spartan tastes.

Günther Grassmann

The Munich painter Günther Grassmann, (himself a minor victim of the purge), when interviewed for the Channel Four film, was understandably caustic about this Nazi 'non-art'. In his view, once the more liberal, 'modernist' trend was crushed in the Third Reich, art became reduced to Nazi kitsch, over-the-top 'heroic' propaganda and pastoral fantasy. He recalled Hitler in 1937 having one of his famous fits of rage when visiting a preview of the first exhibition in the House of German Art. '"Where are the great German artists?" Hitler said furiously. "Yes, well, they are in the cellar." "And why are they there?" And Frau Gerdy Troost still had the courage – well, she said, "Because it's kitsch." Well that didn't impress Hitler very much, and he got up on a little buggy and was driven through the various rooms, shouting in every direction, "Raus! Raus! Raus!" [Out! Out! Out!]. And so the whole jury was dismissed, and he employed the photographer Heinrich Hoffmann instead as the real curator of the exhibition.'[41]

Grassmann's own role in the Day of German Art pageant was apparently confined to painting a few flags and coats of arms for Professor Hermann Kaspar, a close personal friend and one of the two main organizers of the event. But he had not a shred of sympathy for the way other more opportunistic artists had adapted themselves to the so-called 'Nazi' art, which was merely tasteless propaganda subordinated to a repressive State ideology. Even seemingly 'neutral' themes like landscapes and still lifes, if painted for the sake of money, position or prestige, were inwardly 'a lie and a false compromise' with a rotten system. Grassmann, who reports that already in 1931 he had been beaten senseless by the SA for protesting at the racist art doctrines of Alfred Rosenberg and Schultze-Naumburg, did not have any illusions about Nazism. On the other hand, he conceded that the ordinary German citizen living under a controlled press did not often grasp in the 1930s the 'worst aspects of National Socialism'.[42] Those who did have more insight mistakenly hoped that perhaps more moderate politicians might come to power in the Nazi Party.

Grassmann's dismissal today of all Nazi art is only too understandable, given its corrupt role as a vital element in the propaganda apparatus of the Third Reich. Nevertheless, such blanket condem-

Decorative flags, liberally interspersed with the Nazi swastika, were festooned throughout Munich.

nation is ultimately unhelpful if we are to understand why the Nazi brand of aesthetic politics proved so successful. Hitler may have been a failed artist and a provincial petty-bourgeois by origin, but when it came to the visual organization of mass politics, his mediocrity was raised to the level of genius. In the staging of mass events as a constant, remorseless assault on the senses, 'explicitly intended to hypnotize the public by ersatz moods of exaltation', Hitler and Goebbels had few, if any, equals.[43] The blend of marching columns, flags, emblems, uniforms and rousing music – combining the vulgar and the aesthetic, the barbaric and the idyllic, the violent and the sentimental – was one of the most striking hallmarks of Nazism.

The Nazi mass aesthetic with its theatrical Wagnerian *mise en scène* could be experienced as one gigantic happening. It was consciously designed to engender a pseudo-religious state of submission and a feeling of mystical communion with the *Volksgemeinschaft* (community of the peo-

ple) – aims which were largely attained. Through parades like those during the Day of German Art, the Nazis were able to use a carnival atmosphere to transmit the myth of the Germanic *Volk* worshipping itself and its historical grandeur. This was the kind of nationalist demonstration that served to transcend class divisions and to further strengthen the bonds between rulers and ruled. Art and culture played a crucial role in fostering this mirage and in preserving a harmonious façade of gaiety, rejoicing and spontaneity. By such means the regime could reinforce its claim (which was partly true before 1939) that it relied on consensus and mass support as much as on State repression or terror.

The Nazis could demonstrate to the world and to their own people that the Third Reich leadership was at one with its citizens and that they were heirs to a great 'Aryan' culture, itself the source and the guardian of European civilization. An important part of this strategy had been the restoration to Munich of the cultural pre-eminence it had once enjoyed under the Bavarian kings in the nineteenth century. Another aspect was the ambitious building programme which would demonstrate Hitler's claim that he was constructing the framework for a millennial Reich that stood for 'eternal values'. Equally important, though, was the popular dimension which illustrated the Nazi intention to make art truly accessible to the masses for the first time in German history. What had been achieved politically in welding together a nation through the great Nuremberg Party rallies, was duplicated artistically through spectacular pageants in Munich.

This was the hidden ideological and political agenda which lay behind Nazi Germany's cultural politics.

WEEKEND IN MUNICH

'This film is a rarity - it is unique. My father made it and always kept it in the house. We would see it as children or with friends, but we never released it publicly…This film is a very important historical document and I'm glad that it will be shown to people.'

BERNDT FEIERABEND

'Oddly enough, there was always a clear beautiful day on these festive days and people would always call it "Hitler Wetter" [Hitler weather] - except for that one parade, when there was rain.'

JOSEFA HAMMANN

Munich's House of German Art, one of the Nazis' first official buildings, erected in 1933.

*'That's the main railway station.
Ha! That's the main station. Oh my God, that was
destroyed in the war, very badly. Oh, many things
were destroyed very badly during the war.'*

INGE UNGEWITTER

*'That is the Angel of Freedom. Really,
when I see these pictures, I just can't imagine that
so much time has passed, because this Angel of
Freedom with the fountain looked exactly like it
does today and I find this difficult to accept.'*

CHARLOTTE KNOBLOCH

Munich's principal streets and buildings were richly decorated for the weekend festival of Official German Art.

'It was all ready weeks before that, all this fuss, because everything was being decorated. There were all the preparations to do. Just imagine, so many thousand metres of flags and materials and commemorations, all these things that they put up. I mean it was a great fuss - unbelievable.'

JOSEFA HAMMANN

'This event was extremely exciting. Like today, when something unusual happens, it's filmed because it was great. That's how it was. It certainly was a great event for Munich. The whole city was decorated. After all, I went through the city in an open-topped car and filmed the whole way, and it was a unique experience.'

MARTIN SUMMER

Adolf Hitler's official residence in Munich's Prinzregentenplatz

The Nymphenburg Palace, Munich, the setting for a lavish reception for the national and international press on Friday 14 July 1939.

'It's completely unbelievable to me that people can be so happy here, when twenty kilometres away there's a concentration camp in Dachau already overflowing with people, who hadn't broken any laws and who, just because of their race or the way they looked, were put behind barbed wire and tortured.

It's unbelievable. I could never believe for a moment that a Jew would have dared to come anywhere near this place, unless he was completely unrecognizable as a Jew - but even then he would have feared all these people. You can see that with this mighty machine, they weren't only scared because of the laws. They also feared this might, that this mighty apparatus could do whatever it wanted. After all, they knew what was coming to them.'

CHARLOTTE KNOBLOCH

*'Theatre and concerts, that was all much
too expensive for us and inaccessible, so
these kinds of festivities were really something great, because you could experience all
this for free. These were real dance troupes,
they weren't just ordinary people.'*

JOSEFA HAMMANN

108

Taking tea on the restaurant terrace of the House of German Art, a popular venue in pre-war Munich. The 'English Garden' is in the background.

'If you went into the city, then of course one had to wear a hat and a coat, and gloves and a scarf, and it really was the way one dressed...You had to have a summer coat and a winter coat and you had to be dressed correctly. I really liked going to the theatre, especially the opera, and you'd see a lot of long dresses. It was always a bit festive. I really enjoyed myself then.'

ELSE PEITZ

'You had to wear the star, and when you wore it on the street, you might just be dragged off somewhere. We were outlaws. Even though it was strictly forbidden, we would try to hide the star in some way: put a jacket over it or hide it behind a bag so that we weren't so obviously identifiable as being Jews and were not so easy to pick out. It was a situation in which one cannot imagine the kind of fear in which people lived. Many of the Jewish people in Munich - friends of our family - committed suicide, because they couldn't cope with it any longer.'

CHARLOTTE KNOBLOCH

*'These brown uniforms with their swastikas. I can remember these...
But, of course, that is something a child would remember, these black
uniforms, these SS uniforms, this salute. At that time this was everywhere. Even the landlord, everybody...everybody in the community
quickly got used to this style of greeting.'*

CHARLOTTE KNOBLOCH

OPPOSITE TOP : *The guard of honour outside the House of German Art.*
OPPOSITE BOTTOM : *Guests arrive for the opening of the annual exhibition, Sunday morning, 16 July 1939.*
BELOW : *Hitler inspects the guard of honour as he arrives at the House of German Art.*

'As far as I know, he [Adolf Wagner] provided Mr Feierabend with a pass so that he could film the Day of German Art very close up…When you have a chance as an amateur to do a film like that, then of course you would take advantage of it.'

MARTIN SUMMER

TOP LEFT : *August von Finck, the Munich banker and curator of the House of German Art.*
TOP RIGHT : *Adolf Wagner, the official host of the Day of German Art.*

ABOVE LEFT : *A military throng on the steps of the House of German Art.*
ABOVE RIGHT : *Hitler and Himmler arrive at Munich's Kongresshalle.*

Dr Robert Ley and companion make their entrance.

'Above all Hitler was really quite insecure and desperate for admiration. He somehow had to get publicity for himself through these massive events. That's how I imagine it. Anyway, as I've said, at the time I didn't really think about it.'

JOSEFA HAMMANN

'We got to know him as a good man, but then what
came out at the end was really quite horrible. Well,
perhaps he was just acting.'

ELSE PEITZ

*Freiherr von Finck greets Hitler while Himmler
and other members of the Nazi élite look on.*

*The 1939 event was the last time that Hitler
would officiate at the opening of the Great German
Art Exhibition.*

*Attendance at the Munich arts festival was
obligatory for the top Nazis – Goering was one of
the few absentees.*

'There's Hitler himself, with his followers, his trusted followers, as they were called…I once got quite close to him when I was in Munich and still a young girl. He got out of his car and greeted us all and shook our hands and stroked our heads. Then he drove off again.'

JOSEFA HAMMANN

'He [Hans Feierabend] seemed different. The other film-makers would have cut out the film that didn't look good for Hitler, while he, the amateur, he just filmed everything. He left all of that. He noticed these things.'

MARTIN SUMMER

Hitler, Wagner and Himmler on the steps of the House of German Art.

Inside the House of German Art. Hitler is flanked, on his left, by Wagner and on his right, by von Finck and Hess.

Hitler applauds the 'cleansing' of German art in his official address,
at the opening of the 1939 exhibition.

'The initial aim of German art has now been achieved. The birth of an architectural recovery began here
in Munich three years ago, as did the cleansing of the even more primitive areas of painting and sculpture.
The entire swindle of decadent, nauseous, deceitful and fashionable art has been swept away. A new, decent
and respectable level has now been achieved.'

ADOLF HITLER

TOP : *Hitler is accompanied on a tour of the 1939 exhibition by Dino Alfieri, Gerdy Troost and (on his left) Himmler.*
ABOVE LEFT : *An Italian guest at the Munich exhibition.*
ABOVE RIGHT : *Hitler and his guests admire* Galatea, *a sculpture by Fritz Klimsch.*

'The Nazi painters arranged for Hitler to come to Munich to visit and judge the exhibition. This was in 1937. And then Hitler had one of his famous fits of anger…"Where are the great German artists?" he said. "Yes, well, they are in the cellar." "And why are they there?" And Frau Troost had courage – well, she said, "Because it's kitsch." That didn't impress Hitler very much and he got up on a little buggy and was driven through the various rooms, shouting in every direction, "Out! Out! Out!" And so the whole jury was dismissed and he employed the photographer Hoffmann as the real curator of the exhibition. And so the first exhibition in the Haus der Deutschen Kunst came about with all these over-the-top propaganda pictures, partly farmworkers, partly heroic art, which set the artistic tone for the entire period that they were in charge.'

GÜNTHER GRASSMANN

'Hitler was a bit power-crazy, you know, and wanted to promote himself with these festivals. I've no idea what he really understood about art. Was it art for him? Apparently he was a painter - although I've never seen anything that he painted.'

JOSEFA HAMMANN

'A naked woman plays a very large role in art. After all, this is a theme that has accompanied art for thousands of years. Only this was perverted by the Nazis and was shown in this one-sided way…if you look at all these things…well, there's a knee and an elbow and that's all quite correct, and all the curves and the bones, you can see them all. But it's so driven to the utmost that it's absolutely repulsive… art had just been sold out to propaganda.'

GÜNTHER GRASSMANN

'In the Haus der Kunst - oh, wonderful, you know. They would always show the pretty things, always the pretty things and the interesting things. Never these modernists. I'm not really into all this modern painting, because you can't see anything in it.'

ELSE PEITZ

'We didn't invite Hitler because he usually had something else to do,
but he knew that I was celebrating my engagement and he called up in the
middle of the evening and asked if he could come along. I said,
"Yes, of course, we would love it if you could come." And so he came with
flowers and congratulated me, and that was when he got
to know my husband…He never came alone. He always had a few friends
with him, above all the photographer Hoffmann, who was always with him…
Later on, when it was summer and we had visitors at my parents' in
Tegernsee, he would come with six or eight other people, like Goebbels and
many others from the Party, and they would drink coffee with us, or watch
while all of us young women were swimming around in the lake and all that.
It was a good laugh. But then, of course, when Hitler came to power, it was a
bit more difficult, because a lot of National Socialists also wanted to come and
see the Führer. "Where is my Führer?" they would say. And of course he
wanted things to be much more private.
So we would never say, "Heil, mein Führer", but always
"Good morning, Mr Hitler!"'

ELSE PEITZ

122

'When you're in the middle of it, in that kind of a time, it's really much less clear than it is afterwards. You mustn't forget how little the ordinary citizen knew about the worst aspects of National Socialism. We had a completely controlled press.'

GÜNTHER GRASSMANN

TOP LEFT : *The Führer's motorized salute.*
TOP RIGHT : *Julius Streicher, the Gauleiter of Nuremberg.*

ABOVE LEFT : *Senior Luftwaffe generals leaving the 1939 exhibition.*
ABOVE RIGHT : *The Nazi élite, military and civilian, outside the House of German Art.*

OPPOSITE : *Women and children among the Munich crowds, waiting for a glimpse of Hitler.*

'You couldn't recognize them all individually, but you know, the Bavarian hoi polloi, from Minister
Wagner to Rudolf Hess, who didn't really belong to Bavaria as such, but was an invited guest.
And then all the different gentlemen who were Hitler's personal friends: Gruppenführer so-and-so
and all these people and their wives.'

JOSEFA HAMMANN

TOP LEFT/RIGHT : *Rudolf Hess and Hitler arrive at the Odeonsplatz in the centre of Munich,*
on the afternoon of Sunday 16 July 1939.

ABOVE LEFT : *Adolf Wagner,* Gauleiter *of Bavaria, and his guest Adolf Hitler, with Alfieri and Goebbels.*
ABOVE RIGHT : *The architect Albert Speer with Gerdy Troost on the Odeonsplatz reviewing stand.*

'You wouldn't believe that fifty-five or sixty years ago people were so excited, were taken in by all this grandeur…One would think it was yesterday when you see these people there. Unbelievable. They did this perfectly; they are really perfectionist people, the Germans. I have to say that: whatever they do, they do it perfectly. They also annihilated the Jews perfectly.'

CHARLOTTE KNOBLOCH

'We just marched through the streets to the House of Art and then further on through the city to the Odeonsplatz, where the top men were sitting, who were all waving at us. There was a rainstorm, but then it stopped and we carried on with our parade to the end. In the evening we could then go to the dance, because in all the open areas there was dancing and merriment.'

JOSEFA HAMMANN

Robert Ley joins Nazi officials and their wives to review the 1939 procession.

128

'2,000 YEARS OF GERMAN CULTURE'
THE 1939 PROCESSION

'It was a wonderful day. It was a lovely experience that I haven't forgotten to this day at the age of seventy. And officially, for us, it didn't have anything to do with politics. For us it was just a lovely day, where you met other people and also where we could show ourselves off with different sorts of clothes and really show something - and then we were really quite happy.'

JOSEFA HAMMANN

'I was a rococo lady and belonged to the float with an organ on it. Hitler was enthusiastic about Bayreuth and the music of Wagner. It was a really beautiful day, a sunny day with a blue Bavarian sky, which later ended with a rainstorm. But that didn't really matter to any of us. As a young person you ignore all this. Anyway, it was very nice. A lot of fun really, one can say.'

JOSEFA HAMMANN

The procession featured a series of lavish pageants and tableaux glorifying military, cultural and mythological episodes in the Germanic past. With over 6,000 costumed participants, it included ox-drawn wagons symbolizing 'Blood and Soil' and a golden bust of Pallas Athena, to celebrate Germany's 'classical heritage'.

'Munich had a good tradition of parades. Every Fasching or Carnival Sunday there was a carnival parade and all of us artists put a lot of humour into it…And this tradition, the Nazis wanted to use it for their propaganda, and so they said, "Yes we're going to do parades too"…
They were seen by incredible numbers of people.'
GÜNTHER GRASSMANN

The procession route linked Munich's architectural history with the new Nazi buildings, including the Führerbau and the Ehrentempel.

133

'I'm a painter, I'm a student of art…I was an experienced rider and also did show riding then, and in 1939, when I was fifteen years old, I was asked if I wanted to go on this procession with a horse. Well, of course I said, "Yes, it's interesting, Ja." And I was a Valkyrie, that was the costume, iron pieces around my breast and an iron hat with wings on it. And in one hand I had, how do you say, a "Speer" and a "Schild". And there was a very interesting thoroughbred mare, a beautiful horse and she was a little nervous…And the most important thing about it was…not to get squeezed by this iron business and not to get disturbed by this jumping horse. Because there were a lot of things around, noise and music and people. But when you're fifteen years old it's an adventure - an adventure.'

INGE UNGEWITTER

The Nazi spin on the Crusades, highlighting the Gothic element of the Munich pageants.

'The procession was paid partly by the city and partly by the Reichskulturkammer.
Every German artist, architect or writer had to be a member of the Reichskulturkammer. It was very
expensive: there were more than 4,000 people working for this procession or connected with it. They worked
for 1,700,000 hours to do all the costumes and all the preparations for this procession.'

PROFESSOR WINFRIED NERDINGER

'It's unbelievable how the city glittered…The whole city was shown off at great expense; really the
"Capital City of the Movement" - they were honouring its name…
Where would the Jews have had a place in all these things?
No one would have dared to go there - at least not officially.'

CHARLOTTE KNOBLOCH

OPPOSITE TOP : *A huge golden eagle, to symbolize the steadfast focus on a 1,000-year Nazi Reich.*
OPPOSITE BOTTOM : *A representation of 'Father Rhine', celebrating Germany's 1936 recovery of the Rhineland.*
BELOW : *Nazi standards paraded past the Ehrentempel.*

'The parade went past us. It was all very
tasteful and very beautiful, but just too pretty
to make it really alive. I said even then that
the only thing that really brought this whole
thing to life were the army detachments
who marched with a measured step right at the
very end of the parade.
That's really what showed the life of that time.
Tragically, this perception of mine turned
out to be true.'

GÜNTHER GRASSMANN

'Of course these huge festivals made an enormous
impression on the rest of the world.'

ELSE PEITZ

*Detachments of the SA (LEFT) and SS (ABOVE) from
throughout Germany took part in the procession.*

OVERLEAF : *Over one million people watched the Munich
procession and joined the July 1939 celebrations of Nazi art
and culture.*

139

The haunting images in Hans Feierabend's film show us the surface gloss and also expose to the alert spectator some of the abysses beneath. Under the blazing Bavarian skies, past the clouds of white-clad girls, the prancing horses, the blood-red banners and the marching Brownshirts, the camera takes us back into the eerie world of the 'Aryan' millennium. A world of brutality and kitsch, of concentration camps and *Kultur*, where the great patron of the arts would shortly turn into the mass executioner.

US reporters following the 'Liberation' of Dachau, May 1945.

CHAPTER SEVEN

NATIONALISM ÜBER ALLES

'Whoever thinks about Germany and looks for answers to the German question must also think about Auschwitz.'

GÜNTER GRASS, 1990

O N 9 NOVEMBER 1989 the dismantling of the Berlin Wall, which had divided East from West in the heart of Europe, paved the way for the reunification of Germany. After forty years of partition, the revival of an eighty-million-strong single German nation was a cataclysmic event. It both accelerated and was itself made possible by the collapse of Communism in Eastern Europe and the Soviet Union. Initially greeted with euphoria as a triumph of Western-style democracy and market capitalism, it has thus far proved to be a mixed blessing. Far from heralding the 'end of history', the sudden demise of the *Pax Sovietica* has brought with it the return of some of the uglier aspects of Europe's pre-war past. Feelings of joy at liberation from the yoke of Soviet oppression have been marred by the spectre of a new and violent xenophobia in Germany and the rest of Central and Eastern Europe.[1]

The resurgence of right-wing extremism has produced a chain reaction of fire-bombings, vandalism and murderous assaults on foreigners in Germany during the past few years which raises some agonizing concerns.[2] They were well summarized by German President Richard von Weiszäcker, at a mass rally in Berlin on 8 November 1992:

> Let us not fool ourselves. The events of this year are unprecedented in our post-war history. Malignancy is rife: there have been violent attacks on homes of foreigners, incitement to xenophobic feelings and assaults on young children. Jewish cemeteries have been desecrated, memorials devastated in the concentration camps at Sachsenhausen, Ravensbrück and Überlingen. We are faced with violent right-wing extremism and an increasing number of attacks on the weak, both on foreigners and on Germans. Arsonists and killers are on the prowl.'[3]

The street violence against foreigners had begun to intensify shortly after unification. In October 1991 neo-Nazis and skinheads in the Saxon town of Hoyerswerda besieged 230 foreigners, whose hostel they had subjected to a six-day barrage of stones and Molotov cocktails. To the cheers of many local residents, the foreigners were forced to leave and little was done to punish the perpetrators of the violence. In August 1992 police stood idly by while neo-Nazis mounted a two-day siege of hostels where asylum-seekers lived in the Baltic city of Rostock.[4] This sparked a further wave of savage violence by juveniles.

Altogether, during 1992 more than 2,500 attacks were carried out by neo-Nazis and radical rightists, causing seventeen deaths, injuring 600 and severely damaging many refugee shelters. The assaults were primarily directed against Third World asylum-seekers (Africans, Asians, Arabs), gypsies, Turkish *Gastarbeiter* (guest-workers) and refugees fleeing from the economic and social chaos caused by the collapse of Communism. Though few Jews were direct victims of physical violence, there were many attacks against Jewish synagogues, cemeteries and Holocaust sites. Between October 1990 and the summer of 1992, for example, no less that 367 Jewish cemeteries were vandalized. In Erfurt, the capital of Thuringia, a young neo-Nazi scattered severed pigs' heads in the local synagogue.[5]

At the end of August 1992, a bomb was thrown at a Holocaust memorial site in Berlin, the place from which fifty years earlier thousands of Jewish Berliners had been deported to death camps in the East. Not long afterwards, the Jewish cemetery in Berlin-Weissensee was desecrated. Such incidents sent a chilling message to the small German Jewish community of around 60,000 (about one-tenth of its size when the Nazis came to power in 1933) that its security could no longer be taken for granted. They also suggested a close connection between the dramatic rise in xenophobia and the revival of anti-Semitism in the new Germany.

By the end of 1992 the attacks against foreigners, minority groups and even the physically disabled, had reached a scale not seen since the Nazi era. The most murderous incidents took place against Turkish *Gastarbeiter*, so-called 'foreigners' who had lived in Germany for a generation and had contributed much to the post-war German 'economic miracle'. In the West German town of Mölln a fire-bombing on 22 November 1992 caused the deaths of a 51-year-old Turkish woman, her granddaughter and niece.[6]

The fire this time. Solingen, June 1993.
Aftermath of an arson attack on a Turkish household in northern Germany, in which five people died. The protest banner reads, 'This arson attack in Solingen has taken place because of the German Government's immigration policies. As a result I will not be sending my children to school tomorrow.'

Five more people died following an arson attack on a Turkish household at Solingen in May 1993. According to the *Verfassungsschutz*, (Office for the Protection of the Constitution), in 1993 there were altogether 2,232 incidents of neo-Nazi and skinhead violence, a slight decrease over the previous year.[7] But the overall number of general offences by the extreme Right increased and anti-Semitic incidents rose, including seventy-two violent acts against Jews.[8] Taken in the perspective of the last decade, the figures still tell a shocking story of escalation, especially since unification. In 1983, only seventy-three acts of racist violence were recorded, in 1989 (the last year of German partition) the number was 264, and by 1992 it had climbed steeply to 2,584.[9] There were also more desecrations of Jewish cemeteries than on the eve of the Nazi seizure of power in 1933.

Initially the Kohl government failed to take the neo-Nazi threat seriously and only in 1993 did a stricter police and legal crackdown on far-right extremists become evident.[10] Some government officials had, at first, appeared to blame the victims of the racist attacks more than the perpetrators. They focused mainly on the numbers of foreigners and stressed their wish to change the ultra-liberal asylum laws, rather than the need to curb the extreme Right. The Ministry of the Interior finally banned two neo-Nazi parties (the National Front and German Alternative) and five neo-Nazi rock groups, but only after mass protests. The Mölln tragedy had belatedly jolted many Germans to take to the streets in protest against neo-Nazi violence. Hundreds of thousands of marchers, bearing candles or lanterns, walked silently through the centre of Berlin, Munich, Frankfurt and other German cities. These demonstrations did much to improve the atmosphere and restore post-war Germany's somewhat scarred image for tolerance and democracy.[11]

The German government, chastised by this public reaction, toughened its measures against the neo-Nazis but it also severely restricted the flow of non-residents into the country. Like neighbouring governments in France, Great Britain and Holland, its answer to popular xenophobia was to echo far-right themes and promptly implement them through legislation. The assumption was that the presence of large numbers of foreigners *explained* the increase in support for neo-Nazi groups and populist or neo-fascist movements. By limiting immigration and reducing the number of asylum seekers the impact of the extreme Right could be neutralized.[12] In fact, restrictive asylum laws have failed to stop the attacks on Turkish *Gastarbeiter*, foreigners or Jews. The reason is not difficult to grasp. The real problem is race, not immigration – the inclination across Europe to treat people of different colour, religion and ethnic background as 'foreign bodies'.[13] Without this deep-rooted xenophobia, the toleration of neo-Nazi violence and the tacit willingness of different governments in Europe to let the radical Right set the immigration agenda would be difficult to fathom.

It is, of course, true that Germany, with six million foreign residents (one-third of them Muslim Turks) and two million asylum seekers since 1989, has had a special problem.[14] Most of those asking for asylum are in fact economic refugees, wanting entry into Europe's richest welfare state. In 1992, the peak year of neo-Nazi violence, there were 438,000 asylum seekers in Germany (60 per cent of the total within the European Community), knocking on the door of an already overstrained economy.[15] The costs of unification, involving huge transfers of capital to salvage the bankrupt East German economy, rising unemployment and indebtedness, created a growing backlash against foreigners in general. The collapse of the entire East German infrastructure after the rapid unification produced not only high unemployment, insecurity and fear of change, but deep demoralization.[16] Disoriented by the aggressive new capitalist ethos, despised by their richer West German cousins, feeling cheated by promises of an economic miracle and suffering from a poor self-image, East Germans had real grounds for resentment.[17] Sympathy for right-wing extremism naturally grew on this fertile soil, despite the anti-fascist tradition of the German Democratic Republic. Although there are today very few foreign workers and even fewer Jews in the ex-GDR, both xenophobia without foreigners and anti-Semitism without Jews proved to be easily transplanted in conditions of crisis.[18]

Neo-Nazism based on young street gangs and soccer-fan groups had in fact existed in the GDR since the early 1980s as an expression of profoundly negative feelings towards the Communist authorities. There was also a more widespread, latent pan-German sentiment and an everyday racism directed at imported foreign workers, Third World students and blacks in particular. East German sports prowess was often seen by the working population, for example, as a mark of white world supremacy.[19] Labels like 'Negermusik' (a pejorative term for Anglo-Saxon rock, jazz and blues, which were officially banned in East Germany) were taken from the vocabulary of the Third Reich and even used by the Communist regime in its fight against American 'imperialist' culture.[20]

Although the East German Stalinists initially carried out a more far-reaching de-Nazification programme than had occurred in post-war West Germany, their anti-fascism ended up as more of a ritualized ceremony than an effective pedagogy. A totalitarian regime which relied on police state methods and whose indoctrination and propaganda produced nothing but double-think was unlikely to inspire genuine anti-fascism. Its army had adopted a goose-step reminiscent of the Wehrmacht and its

youth parades bore more than a passing resemblance to those of the Third Reich.[21] The blue-shirted Communist youth might claim to stand for proletarian 'internationalism' but their stress on group conformity and paramilitary training echoed the Nazi past as much as the promise of a new socialist dawn. Both systems, with their regimented good order, their guarantee of permanent employment and their endemic hostility to pluralistic Western liberalism, offered similar attractions. At the same time, the sheer mendacity of East German propaganda encouraged a part of rebellious youth to turn, after the Communist collapse, to neo-Nazism – as the polar opposite and 'brother-enemy' of the old regime. A similar dynamic can be found in the aggressive nationalism, anti-Semitism and neo-fascist trends that have swept across Russia and eastern Europe since 1989.

Youth disaffection and alienation in the ex-GDR were more rapidly channelled into a neo-Nazi direction by the active post-unification recruitment drives of West German extreme Right groups. By mid-1991 it was estimated that the level of general support for the extreme Right among young people in the East had reached around 50,000.[22] Saxony, Saxony-Anhalt and parts of Brandenburg were already considered neo-Nazi strongholds, with the city of Dresden vying for the title of 'Capital of the Movement'. According to youth surveys in Saxony at the end of 1990, about 15 to 20 per cent of young people had a 'closed authoritarian attitude' and half of the total sample approved of the ultra-nationalist war cry, 'Germany for the Germans!'[23] Forty-six per cent of apprentices and 23 per cent of those still in school also agreed with the more radical neo-Nazi slogan 'Ausländer raus!' ('Foreigners Out'). Such data revealed a deep confusion, disorientation and frustration among the youth – a severe state of economic, moral and psychological deprivation following the collapse of the old regime.

Violent rejectionism, alienation and bitterness at disappointed expectations, as well as fear of the future, produced the desperate need for scapegoats and the growing attraction to the extreme Right. This has particularly been the case among young, white working-class males in the bleak concrete wastelands of Dresden, Leipzig and other East German cities. The predisposition towards neo-Nazism also exists in areas bordering Poland, both because of traditional anti-Polish sentiments and fear of an influx of asylum seekers from the East.[24] Much of the inflammatory neo-Nazi propaganda comes, it is worth noting, from Gary Rex Lauck's NSDAP–AO in the United States and from Ernst Zundel, a German exile in Toronto, Canada, through his Munich 'agent' Bela Ewald Althans.[25]

The neo-Nazi movement, whether based in the East or the West, has become increasingly entrenched in the skinhead subculture. The skinhead gangs, especially brutal and thuggish in the East, often assume local policing activities, taking over whole neighbourhoods and terrorizing opposition into silence. Youth centres and bars are their battlefields and also serve as recruiting centres. Many skinheads are unemployed or work at marginal jobs, are poorly educated, come from broken homes and have juvenile criminal records.[26] The primitive slogans of German nationalism based on blood, race and the folk community provide them both with a crude ideology and with a new sense of belonging.

Music is a key element in this subculture, serving as a celebration of the gang ethic, a tool for recruitment, a propaganda weapon and an incitement to violence and racism.[27] Even though German law officially forbids the dissemination of neo-Nazi propaganda, the songs recorded on tape cassettes, compact discs or record albums are available through mail-order houses, the most successful having been Rock-O-Rama records. Through this rock music, skinheads are initiated into a world of neo-Nazi bigotry, into an ideology of 'white power' and the 'heroic' struggle for race and nation. The nihilist message of these bands is already in their names like Störkraft (Disturbing Force), Volkszorn (People's Wrath), Endsieg (Final Victory), Reich 'n' Roll, Bomber, Stuka or Werwolf. The lyrics deliberately arouse hatred of Turks, Jews, homosexuals and other 'un-German' elements. They speak of sending Turks to concentration camps, plunging the knife into Jewish stomachs, defending the white race. The rock group Volkszorn sings: 'Muslim, oh Muslim, you are only a swine that stinks of garlic. On how many Germans have you already played a dirty trick?' Endsieg's notorious Kanakan song (Kanakan is slang for Turks) is openly genocidal: 'Kill your children, abuse your women, annihilate your race.' The Frankfurt band Böhse Onkelz (some of whose albums have been bestsellers in Germany) tells its listeners that 'we are writing history with our blood'.[28]

These and other lyrics glorify violence, street warfare, racism and anti-Semitism. Some songs lament Germany's defeat in the Second World War, or pay tribute to Hitler's former deputy and a renowned Nazi 'martyr', Rudolf Hess. This skinhead music, whether in Germany, Italy, France, Britain or the USA, has an unmistakably neo-Nazi message and the power to arouse raw emotions. Swastika-emblazoned banners decorate the bandstands, skinheads, arms outstretched, shout 'Sieg Heil!', the beer flows and so, too, does the blood of

Mob rules Britannia. *The skinhead hardcore of the British National Party (BNP) celebrates the September 1993, Millwall election victory of BNP Councillor Derek Beacon.*

the victims. Here is an extract from an ADL investigative report on the open-air concert in Massen on 3 October 1992, sponsored by the neo-Nazi group, German Alternative:

> It attracted more than 1,500 Skinheads, many armed with knives, axes, baseball bats and material for manufacturing fire-bombs. After several hours of listening to the thumping beat of the self-proclaimed 'Fascho bands' and augmented by a flood of alcohol, intoxicated teenagers attacked a busload of Polish tourists, smashing windows and beating anyone in the vicinity.[29]

Similar scenes of violence (in Britain as in Germany) are common at sporting events. Skinheads display Nazi flags, shout racist slogans and launch brutal assaults, resulting in the maiming or crippling of dozens of victims. During the wave of attacks on asylum seekers, foreign workers and Jewish targets in Germany, the skinheads naturally joined the mob action. In 1993, the number of far-right skinhead youths engaged in such violence, who were known to the police, was estimated at approximately 5,600. But the total number is certainly very much higher, and still growing.[30]

After the Rostock attack in August 1992, destructive street riots and fire-bombings by neo-Nazi groups spread rapidly – encouraged by police laxity and some open sympathy from the populace, especially in former East Germany. These were not spontaneous attacks by small groups of drunken youths happening to fall on chance victims, contrary to the claims at the time by the authorities. They were organized and prepared acts of violence by well-armed gangs motivated by extreme nationalist rhetoric against foreigners and Jews.[31] Indeed, the neo-Nazi groups in the East, with their sophisticated cellular phones and fax hook-ups, often seemed better equipped and certainly far more motivated than the poorly trained, understaffed East German police. Since the demise of the hated Stasi (secret police) after the collapse of the GDR, their democratic successors have been manifestly unable to cope. Nor have they been immune to the rising tide of German nationalism. In both East and West Germany, a section of the police sympathizes with the radical-right Republikaner Party, which may help to explain their low-profile response to mob violence against foreigners.

According to the Office for the Protection of the Constitution, in 1993 there were no fewer than seventy-seven different far-right extremist groups in Germany with 42,400 members (multiple memberships are disregarded) – of which about one-third were militant neo-Nazis. In December 1992 two of these organizations, the National Offensive and the German Alternative, were banned for possession of weapons and explosives. They had openly campaigned against liberal democratic institutions and in favour of a *völkisch* state, while training for violent action against foreigners, Jews and asylum seekers.[32] The German National Democratic Party (NPD) with 5,000 members, the German Workers' Freedom Party (FAP) and the small German League for Volk and Heimat still continue, however, to hold the neo-Nazi banner aloft. One of their more successful actions was the

planning and execution of the Rudolf Hess Memorial March on 14 August 1993. They managed to outwit the police and to hold their banned rally in the city centre of Fulda in Hesse, to the great embarrassment of the authorities.

The German neo-Nazis have also succeeded in consolidating some of their international contacts with various extreme right-wing organizations in Russia and Eastern Europe. The internationalization of contacts, exchanges and racist propaganda has in general been a growing feature of the neo-Nazi scene, favoured by the use of electronic media, difficult to monitor and even harder to stop. Racist and anti-Semitic material are now often distributed through computer networks and bulletin board systems; through various public-access TV channels and radio programmes; or by the production and distribution of video cassettes. There are neo-Nazi telephone networks and hot-lines, as well as computer games that spread the new gospel of Holocaust denial.[33] Thus 'electronic' fascism helps keep the Nazi poison alive, to circumvent public bans and censorship by the authorities, as well as providing mutual aid between members of the Neo-Nazi International.

Nevertheless, a sense of proportion needs to be maintained about the current scale of the neo-Nazi threat. Television cameras may be attracted like magnets to the sight of neo-Nazis rampaging on the streets of Germany and other European countries. The insignia, the marching, the uniforms, the salutes and the slogans are instantly recognizable. Chillingly they remind us of Brownshirts and Blackshirts, of Nazis and fascists, something we think that we know about and can deal with. The violence is real enough and shocking, as we have seen; so, too, is the blind, primitive racism behind it.[34] But in itself, it cannot bring down a stable democratic system like that of contemporary Germany. The threat from contemporary neo-Nazis certainly cannot be compared with the massed army of Brownshirts who controlled the streets in the last years of the Weimar Republic.

The neo-Nazis are still isolated and totally outside the political mainstream, confronted by a German government committed to liberal democracy and the rule of law. Neither in official government circles, nor among the mainstream political parties, the established press, the business community, the bulk of intellectuals or respectable public opinion, is there any hint of genuine nostalgia for the Third Reich. The kind of limitless national ambition and rampant militarism that provoked two world wars seems well and truly dead. The newly unified Germany is, perhaps for the first time in its history, something like a 'normal' nation-state – if anything, almost too placid, passive and pacific for its own good.[35]

But if militarism is scarcely visible and the Federal Republic has, until very recently, been a remarkably peaceful, consumerist society, there is still room for concern about the present and the future.[36] For forty years, after 1949, the West Germans zealously applied themselves to building a stable, prosperous democracy. They voluntarily muted their national consciousness in the framework of NATO and the Common Market, becoming model Europeans. Gradually they emerged as the economic dynamo of the European Community. Today, Berlin looks set once more to become the continent's economic and political centre of gravity, as it was in 1900 and again under vastly different circumstances in 1940. Will new burdens of power and responsibility change the German orientation to the West and bring a new self-assertive nationalism in its wake which could

unhinge Europe? Are the fears of a Fourth Reich, heard at times in neighbouring European capitals, entirely misplaced? Will the frantic German desire for 'normalization' and calls for a robust, healthy national identity, increasingly heard on the conservative Right, lead to a flight from responsibility?[37] Will they not erase the memory of the Holocaust in favour of a more comfortable, comforting and misleading sense of the German past? Günter Grass's warning to his compatriots that 'whoever thinks about Germany and looks for answers to the German question must also think about Auschwitz' is surely pertinent.[38] But in the euphoria over unification it went largely unheeded.

The new Germany has proved to be no more immune to the nationalist virus than its neighbours in western, central or eastern Europe. Moreover, the effects of unemployment, recession and large-scale immigration have once more created a space in Germany for a more potentially viable national-populist movement of the radical Right, whose main slogan is 'Germany for the Germans'. Since 1989, this political vacuum has been filled by the Republikaner Party, led until recently by the portly ex-Waffen SS officer, Franz Schönhuber.[39] His movement, like Jean-Marie Le Pen's Front National in France, Jörg Haider's growing Freedom Party in Austria and the Vlaams Blok in Belgium, is fundamentally xenophobic and opposed to the very existence of a multi-cultural, multi-ethnic society.[40] At the same time, Schönhuber had publicly opposed anti-Semitism in order to dissociate himself from other extreme Right parties, especially the neo-Nazis. This more respectable façade has paid some electoral dividends. Thus at the local elections in Hesse in March 1993 the Republikaners gained 8.6 per cent of the vote. Their appeals for law and order, and for the immediate expulsion of 'foreign criminals', even won them 9.8 per cent of the vote in Frankfurt am Main.[41] This corresponded to similar performances in state elections over the past few years in Baden-Württemberg, Berlin and their Bavarian stronghold.

Their membership has remained solid at around 23,000, but internal factionalism has undermined their cohesion and prospects, as it has that of other far-right parties. Their predictably poor performance in the 1994 German national elections does not, however, signify that the problem of racism and neo-Nazism has been resolved. The Republikaner Party often competes for votes with its bitter rivals, the Deutsche Volksunion (DVU, German People's Union) – an extreme right-wing party led by the millionaire Munich publisher Gerhard Frey. The DVU membership has risen slightly to 26,000 and its chairman maintains close links with the Russian fascist Vladimir Zhirinovsky and with the British Holocaust denier, David Irving. The *Deutsche National Zeitung*, the weekly publication of the DVU, with a self-declared circulation of 130,000, remains the most widely read newspaper of the German far Right.

Populist ultra-nationalists like Frey and Schönhuber in Germany or Haider in Austria, are not openly fascist and seek to maintain some tactical distance from neo-Nazism. They play by the rules of the democratic game, claim to express the *vox populi* on immigration and to represent a healthy nativist resistance to the 'evils' of a multicultural society. They are also preoccupied with banishing once and for all the burden of German guilt and demonstrating (in Schönhuber's words) that 'Germans have given the world far more than Auschwitz can ever wreck.'[42] In the case of the *Deutsche National Zeitung*, the rejection of what is

branded as continuous Allied 'war propaganda' against Germany slides over into outright denial of the Holocaust.

The implicit belief in an international Jewish conspiracy is what lies behind the accusation on the far Right that the 'Zionists' deliberately fostered the 'Auschwitz lie' to squeeze money from Germany.[43] Once this monstrous 'Holocaust myth' has been nailed, not only Germany but the entire far-right ideology can be rehabilitated. World Jewry will become once again the aggressors and persecutors, Germans (and Nazis) the innocent victims. If there were no gas chambers, the greatest stumbling block in the German past to the coming national rebirth has gone. No more *angst*, no more guilt, the Truth makes you free![44] With German innocence re-established, the road is open to ultra-nationalism, fascism and neo-Nazism. Racism can acquire a shiny new gloss without the accompanying stench of mass murder. Hence the great and insidious importance that Holocaust denial has assumed on the far Right in the post-war period.[45]

The conservative Right, for its part, has never tried to deny German responsibility for the Holocaust, but has sought to relativize and normalize the Nazi past. One of Chancellor Helmut Kohl's priorities during the past decade has been to end Germany's negative self-image. The Bitburg affair of 1985 grew directly out of his overly impatient desire to emerge from the dismal shadow of the Third Reich as the standard-bearer of a robust, healthy German patriotism. The emphasis on the *uniqueness* of the Holocaust was perceived by Kohl and some of his advisers as an obstacle to this goal. After all, it was argued, the crimes of Nazism were not fundamentally different from those of other totalitarian terror regimes. Kohl's former ally, the late Franz Josef Strauss (leader of the Bavarian

Christian Social Union), even declared that to leave out the 'barbarism' of others was a 'historical forgery' that would destroy German national identity!

During the so-called 'Battle of the Historians' in the summer of 1986, the connection between history and this kind of political agenda became clearer. A leading conservative historian, Ernst Nolte, in an article of June 1986 entitled 'The Past that Will Not Pass Away', maintained that the Nazi mass murder of Jews was merely a 'copy' of the crimes of the Gulag Archipelago.[46] Moreover, he argued, Hitler's Holocaust was essentially a preventative action, taken out of fear that the Germans would otherwise suffer a similar fate at the hands of 'Jewish' Bolsheviks! Worse still, Nolte even claimed that the Zionist leader Chaim Weizmann had officially declared war on Nazi Germany by supporting Britain in September 1939, thereby justifying Hitler's treatment of the Jews.

Such puerile 'revisionist' arguments by a leading German historian were grist to the mill of the neo-Nazis and the beer-hall crowd. So too, in a different way, were the efforts of another distinguished German historian, Andreas Hillgrüber. He portrayed the battle of the Wehrmacht on the Eastern Front in 1944–5 as a *Nibelungen*-like saga of loyalty to protect the Germans against the 'mass rape' and 'orgy of revenge' of the Red Army.[47] The German Army was fighting for a noble goal, to preserve the Third Reich's Great Power status, which Roosevelt, Stalin and Churchill were malevolently seeking to smash. In this revisionist version of history all of the European Centre was needlessly lost in 1945 because it had been liberated from Nazi imperialism![48] At the same time, while the German Reich was being militarily destroyed, European Jewry was coming to 'the end', as if by some natur-

al process. The innocent reader would barely be aware that it was Hitler's Third Reich which had virtually destroyed European Jewry and that the Wehrmacht's 'heroic' resistance permitted the extermination of Jews to continue to the bitter end.[49]

Nolte and Hillgrüber were not without their academic defenders. Some suggested that Stalin's liquidation of the 'Kulaks' provided a model for Hitler or at least a backdrop for his 'extirpation fantasies'. Others agreed with Nolte that until 1939 the Nazi State was 'a constitutional and liberal idyll' compared to Soviet totalitarianism. Yet others stressed that apart from the gas chambers there was no essential difference between Nazi and Soviet annihilation practices. Such efforts to normalize and relativize the Nazi past have thus far failed, only because a substantial body of German historians strongly opposed them.[50] They sharply rejected the attempt to exonerate the Germans by comparisons with the ex-USSR, Cambodia, Algeria, Vietnam or other post-war tragedies; they were openly sceptical about conservative nostalgia for the German national past and the desire to forge from it a healthy national identity; and they staunchly defended Germany's post-war integration into the West. But the polemics and subsequent analyses of German opinion showed that the desire for normalization of the past is becoming ever stronger in Germany.

On the eve of unification, a detailed survey of public opinion indicated that 69 per cent of West Germans definitely wanted a line drawn under the Nazi past.[51] A clear majority also felt that harping on German guilt abroad was an expression of resentment at German prosperity and success. With regard to the Third Reich, 43 per cent felt it had both good and bad sides, 38 per cent saw more bad sides than good, 16 per cent saw only the bad sides and 3 per cent saw only positive aspects. On Hitler, opinions were generally more negative, although 26 per cent of West Germans still had a positive opinion of him.[52] This percentage rose when the question was rephrased to exclude the Second World War and the Holocaust. West Germans were asked, if Hitler had died or if he had been assassinated at the end of 1938, would he today be considered one of the greatest statesmen in German history? A majority (60 per cent) rejected this proposition but 38 per cent agreed that he *would* have been rated a great statesman. Two-thirds of the respondents did, however, consider National Socialism to have been harmful from the very beginning.[53]

Other results of the survey were more evenly balanced and some were clearly troubling in their implications. Thus, only 34 per cent thought that six million Jews had died in the Nazi Holocaust; 42 per cent could not say exactly; 13 per cent thought the figure was much too high and 10 per cent believed it was too low.[54] Forty-eight per cent of West Germans felt that there was already enough education about the Third Reich, but 45 per cent disagreed; 47 per cent of the population did not object to the reparations paid to Jews, but 46 per cent did think they were too high. Eighty-three per cent of West Germans discounted the chances of a new Hitler (37 per cent were categorical), but half of the population was against race-mixing and in favour of preserving the purely German character of the country. Among supporters of the Republikaner Party, of course, the desire for the complete exclusion of foreigners was far higher.[55] A clear correlation between a positive attitude to Hitler and hostility towards foreigners (*Fremdenhass*) emerged from the survey.

In a government-sponsored survey conducted in September 1993, it is undoubtedly significant that far more Germans than four years earlier agreed there was a danger of a return to National Socialism. Thirty-four per cent of West Germans and 49 per cent of East Germans, as against 54 per cent of Americans (polled at the same time) thought the threat was real.[56]

But do the revival of xenophobia and anti-Semitism, the neo-Nazi outrages or the desire to forget the Holocaust, indicate the possibility of a second coming for Nazism? Does the new national consciousness and signs of German assertiveness, the existence of well-established right-wing extremist structures and the erosion of many taboos about the Nazi past, represent a serious danger to German democracy?[57] These are important questions, but the data that might be helpful in answering them are necessarily incomplete. The historian finds himself here in the position of an interpreter trying to make sense of a long sentence in German. Only at the end does he know what the verb is going to be. In the meantime he is like a prophet in reverse – confident about predicting the past and reasonably sure that history never exactly repeats itself the second time around.

Nevertheless a number of historical observations may be useful in understanding the present. The new united Germany with its solid democracy, its stable two-party system, respect for civil liberties and still powerful economy, is very different from Hitler's Reich, which expired in the rubble of Berlin fifty years ago. Nationalism, although it has revived in Germany and even more in other parts of Europe, is not yet the integrative, mobilizing force which it was after the Treaty of Versailles in the 1920s. Potentially, it could easily have had this strength, given the Allied occupation after 1945, the division of Germany and the expulsion of millions of Germans from east of the 'Reich', but its immediate effects were successfully contained. Unlike Weimar, the Federal Republic was rapidly integrated into the victorious Western alliance and East Germany coerced into the Soviet bloc. The decisive nature of the military defeat put paid to any 'stab in the back' legends, such as had developed after 1918. The German civilian suffering during the Second World War was also a sobering experience which largely discredited National Socialism. The break in continuity in both East and West was substantially greater after 1945 than it had been in 1918, though it was by no means complete.

The catastrophic aspects of National Socialism – the total ruin of the cities, the exile of so many Germans from their homelands after 1945 – had exposed many German nationalist illusions.[58] The material success of the Federal Republic, on the other hand, showed the benefits of integration into the European Common Market and the Western system and of a pacific foreign policy. Increasingly, patriotism was based on economic and sporting success (the strength of the deutschmark, of German athletes and football teams, and so on) and respect for the universalist values of liberal democracy.

Nevertheless, the historic events of 1989 did constitute a major watershed and they quickly led to the revival of some previously dormant national slogans. The costs of unification resulted, for the first time in decades, in a diminution in living standards. The proliferation of neo-Nazi and radical Right militancy in Germany and across Europe, however fissiparous and fragmented, was also a symptom of serious malaise. It pointed, moreover, to the existence of a dormant but tenacious

'Neo-fascist' chic. Alessandra Mussolini, granddaughter of Italian dictator Benito Mussolini, takes her seat in the Italian Parliament, following her April 1992 election victory as a member of the far-right Italian Socialist Movement (MSI).

subculture of fascism and Nazism that had survived the débâcle of 1945.[59] True, the recession of the 1990s is not comparable in severity with the Great Depression (1929–1933), which transformed Hitler's Nazis into a mass movement. There are no more powerful Communist parties to provide, as in the 1930s, the sense of acute political polarization; there are no Russian Revolutions to panic the middle classes; no great inflations to wipe out their savings. Unlike under Weimar, German liberal democracy is still strong and the parliamentary system (in contrast to Italy's) capable of surviving periodic crises in confidence.[60]

Above all, there are no charismatic fascist leaders in Europe today like Mussolini or Hitler, able to mobilize the irrational cravings of the masses, to translate the diffuse sense of cultural malaise into an all-out assault on liberal values and modern civilization. The cosmetic trappings, the nihilistic violence and 'street theatre' of fascism are still there in a minor key, but not its visionary ideal and the propagandist flair able to turn it into political reality.

The beery Bavarian joviality of Schönhuber, the 'yuppie' populism of Jörg Haider, the rousing rhetoric of Le Pen and the clean-cut Italian 'neo-fascists' in Berlusconi's government, need careful watching. But they ultimately seem like a pale echo of the demagogic talents of the inter-war fascist leaders in Italy and Germany. Of the current crop of xenophobic nationalists, the photogenic 43-year-old Jörg Haider, who won more than 22 per cent of the national vote in the 1994 Austrian elections, is clearly the most dangerous. He is well positioned to enter a coalition government and even to win the Chancellorship in 1998 by exploiting vehement anti-immigrant feelings in Austria.

Heil Haider! *The glamorous face of Austria's far right. Jörg Haider, leader of the Freedom Party, launches the controversial anti-foreigner petition at his party's January 1993 conference.*

One has, however, to go to the Third World dictators in the post-war era to find more authentic echoes of the fascist and Nazi experience. The style, the rhetoric, the public behaviour and the official ideologies may be different, but the techniques, the 'totalitarian' nationalism and the underlying phenomenon are not so dissimilar. There is the same worship of the nation as *ersatz* god, the same blind faith in the Leader and the single Party as the embodiment of exact scientific wisdom, and the same tendency to persecute alien minorities or else to invent fictive enemies that are threatening the regime.[61] Third World dictators in the post-war era like Peron, Castro, Nkrumah, Idi Amin, Mao Tse-tung, Kim Il Sung, Pol Pot, Nasser, Qaddafi and Saddam Hussein learnt much from the fascist, Nazi and Stalinist examples. In backward societies they mobilized the masses in developmental dictatorships that have combined ideology and organization, ancient national tradition and modern technology. As in the case of pre-war European fascisms, the combination of a hybrid form of bastardized nationalism and socialism, combined with the repressive machinery of the authoritarian State and a ruthless use of violence, have produced some very nasty outcomes.[62]

Perhaps the best example today of a potential dictator on the model of Mussolini or Hitler, combining European and Third World attributes, is Vladimir Zhirinovsky. The leader of the Liberal Democratic Party (it is obviously neither) in Russia, he is operating in an environment that has some real analogies with the last years of Weimar. The disintegration of a great empire, a devastating economic crisis, political instability and a strong sense of national humiliation in Russia are ideal preconditions for a local version of Nazism. The cultural climate, too, with its mystical irrationalism, its return to Russia's religious and national past, the rabid anti-Westernism of the reactionary intelligentsia and the backlash against rootless modernity, has obvious echoes of pre-Hitler Germany.[63] Already by June 1991 Zhirinovsky had come from nowhere to win six million votes by appealing to an ultra-nationalism which could attract both skinheads and intellectuals, the underclass in the cities and the impoverished in the countryside.[64] In December 1993 he garnered nearly 25 per cent of the popular vote in parliamentary elections thanks to a skilful populist television campaign, which proved his mastery of the medium. Cultivating the clown image to attract media attention, he manipulated it cleverly to his own ends, while conveying a simple, forceful message.

Zhirinovsky's constituency includes many disgruntled members of the humiliated Red Army, neglected rural residents, poorly educated workers from smaller towns and well-educated young males from the larger cities. His programme calls for

Führer of the Russian Right. *Vladimir Zhirinovsky campaigning for the Russian Presidency in Gorky Park, Moscow, in June 1991. By December 1993 his improbably named Liberal Democratic Party had attracted nearly 25 per cent of the popular vote.*

a crack-down on Mafia crime, for law and order, a strong Russian State, and he fiercely condemns free-market liberal democracy. Zhirinovsky is an open expansionist, in favour of restoring Russia's imperial frontiers of 1900, annexing territories to the west and south, and ruthlessly 'Russifying' the ethnic minorities. He advocates a form of State capitalism to counter Russia's economic chaos, poverty, disorder and hyperinflation, which he blames on decadent Western-style liberalism.

Zhirinovsky and his followers are undoubtedly impressed by Hitler's National Socialism. Like Hitler, Zhirinovsky sees himself as called to be the sole Führer of the Russian Right.[65] Abroad, he seeks to build an anti-Semitic and anti-American alliance. The American cosmopolitan world order must be undermined and the 'Jewish-Zionist consipiracy' in Russia and abroad decisively checked. The future order he envisages will be dominated by an ethnically purified and restored Russian Empire in alliance with *Grossdeutschland* and the Japanese. Only such a revolutionary transformation can supposedly save the civilization of the white race.[66]

As such examples reveal, the contemporary world is indeed full of would-be heirs to the age of fascism, who take up in different ways and in many different combinations the legacy of the past. They remind us that Nazism and fascism were no traffic accidents of history, no freak aberrations which were safely and permanently interred in 1945. Not only is fascism a distinctive child of the twentieth century, it is an integral part of Western intellectual, cultural and political history.[67] Most of its ingredients are still present today, whether it be the call for strong leaders, militarism, racism, populist nationalism or the fear that civilization itself is threatened by irrevocable decadence and decline. In the last resort, the *national* myth is probably the most potent of all these elements and it shows no signs of fading.[68] All fascisms are obsessed by national symbols and the belief that the nation can be born anew through the destruction of the old order.[69] Nazism also built on this core myth of national rebirth, which was the positive side of its broad crusade against cultural degeneration. The swastika was the symbol of this national awakening, containing the promise to draw on mythic energies and to inaugurate a new 'Aryan' millennium. Hermann Rauschning recalls that Hitler told him in 1934: 'Those who see in National Socialism nothing more than a political movement know scarcely anything of it. It is even more than a religion: it is the will to create mankind anew.'[70]

Fascism and Nazism were cultural rebellions before they became political revolutions. Fifty years after their military defeat they remain a more or less permanent feature of modern political culture. The power and success of Hitler's Reich until 1942 gave Nazism a particular strength, just as its biological racism made it a distinct branch grafted onto the fascist tree. In addition to its ideology, what made it attractive to so many young people between the wars was its special political style, its rhetoric, symbolism, chants, ceremonies and paramilitary ethos.[71] Something of that appeal to emotion, myth and action for its own sake still subsists for those least integrated into contemporary Western society. Moreover, as a movement which was and still is anti-liberal, anti-bourgeois, anti-conservative, anti-Marxist, anti-Semitic and anti-democratic, it had the attraction to youth of *total* opposition to the system. At the same time, the nationalist core sentiment (fortified by racism) provided it with a broader, supra-class, positive appeal that is still very much alive today, though other movements and parties are no less capable of exploiting it.

Nazism (like other forms of fascism) has relied greatly in the past on romantic components such as the love of heroism and adventure, the exaltation of violence and even death.[72] It was closely linked with the military experience of the First World War, the love of uniforms and the search for a new kind of community that could maintain the camaraderie of the trenches. This 'heroic' style has gone out of fashion in post-1945 Germany, though it has continued elsewhere in different modes and under different labels. But the accent on a confused sense of virility, the male chauvinism, militarism and homosexual undertones are still present in many contemporary neo-Nazi movements.[73] So, too, is the need for loyalty, obedience and submission to the leader.

In this book we have focused on art, myth and the role of images in the Nazi appeal. The emphasis on rhetoric, style, romanticism and seductive cultural forms drew many academics, literary intellectuals and artists to fascism and Nazism in an earlier period. This aspect has diminished, though it has by no means disappeared, in today's neo-fascist and neo-Nazi movement. The scale of Nazi crimes and the sheer destruction they wreaked have fortunately dampened some of the amoral aestheticization of violence, war and mass mobilization so common in the past. The youthful enthusiasm, the nihilistic activism and the utopian dreams which intoxicated so many pre-war intellectuals have been irrevocably tainted by the evils which Nazism wrought.[74]

Hitler, of course, personified in many ways the specific political style of National Socialism. His talents as an orator, a propagandist and publicist, his political fanaticism and the gigantic energies he unleashed, continue to exercise an undeniable fascination. The disaster into which he plunged Germany and Europe, the systematic mass murder of the Jews and the ghastly inhumanity of his rule, have none the less done much to discredit fascism. Hitler and his movement were fatally underestimated for most of his career, with catastrophic results. Relatively few observers realized at the time with what sinister skill he took respectable middle-class virtues and reversed them in revolutionary fashion to serve his system of terror.

Hitler and the other Nazi leaders were the product not only of German (and Austrian) culture, but of a European Christian-bourgeois system of values. Their core beliefs, ideology, tastes and sentiments were formed in the European *fin de siècle* as a radical alternative to the prevailing liberal status quo. They espoused ideas which were eminently respectable before 1914 and became even more current in Central Europe after the First World War. Admittedly, both Nazism and fascism were bound up with the post-1918 crisis of liberal democracy and built their mass support on the politics of fear. But their respective movements also drew great strength from the feeling that they had a coherent world-view and that they represented a 'total revolution' that would renew a decadent civilization.[75] Many of the ills of modern industrial mass society against which they revolted are still with us, as are the conditions which originally produced the Nazi and fascist backlash.

The aesthetic politics of the Nazis were part of an overarching vision of man and the community. Their social utopia climaxed in exterminatory acts of 'ethnic cleansing' on a hitherto unprecedented scale. The singularity of those crimes can never be erased and they are a warning as to where the cult of instinct, irrational feelings and brutal violence can lead. The revival of fascism, racism, nationalism and anti-Semitism in contemporary Europe is a timely reminder to those who would forget that the Nazi legacy is still with us. But without a deeper understanding of its cultural roots, the seeds of a resurgent fascism will be difficult to eradicate. In particular, a failure to appreciate the sources of

its aesthetic appeal and its connection with nationalism may prove costly. The *völkisch* mutation of the German nationalist ideal turned out to be a crucial element in the descent towards Nazism; so, too, did the deification of the artist, the rapturous pursuit of the Absolute and the irrationalist metaphysic of destruction in so much romantic art. Nowhere was the cult of frenzied feeling, the delirium of the senses and the dream of a 'total work of art' more evident than in the music of Richard Wagner, Hitler's cultural hero. Nazi propaganda techniques drew heavily on the intoxicating effects of the Wagnerian theatrics and on his racially exclusivist ideal of the *Volk* community. Hitler, as a political 'artist' in the neo-romantic mould, translated this Wagnerian vision with terrifying literalness into the realm of the mass spectacle. In a simular manner, the Nazis hijacked the traditions of classical antiquity, yoking Hellenic aesthetic ideals of pure form and bodily perfection to the 'Aryan' myth of a Nordic Superman.

At first sight, our post-modern electronic age of media networks and instant communications seems far removed from these racist phantasmagorias, romantic excesses and dreams of aesthetic purity harboured by the Nazis. The very concept of 'culture', and even more of 'eternal values' or permanent ideals of beauty, has come to seem more than questionable. We live in a society where the fragmentary is an integral part of our social, cultural and even psychic condition. In the contemporary society of the spectacle, the boundaries between the real and the imaginary have begun to dissolve and crumble. Image has become destiny, style replaces substance and the culture of the word is increasingly threatened with demise.

In this image-centred world of the post-modern lies danger as well as liberating potential. The

Nazis may indeed serve as salutary warning for the uses and abuses of image-making, for in certain respects they were the unacknowledged pioneers and masters of modern media philosophy – itself a symptom of the value–vacuum in contemporary society. In their manipulation of modern technologies and media, their mastery of crowd psychology, of aesthetic illusion and the visual orchestration of the masses, they were ahead of their time. Contemporary post-modernism, with its assault on objectivity, abstraction, rational thought and systematic analysis, has some disturbing, if non-ideological, echoes of these fascist premises. The Nazis, with their predilection for the mythical and the irrational, for exploiting unconscious sexual drives and demonstrating the supremacy of the visual image, did at certain points inadvertently anticipate our own post-modernist predicament. If this condition is 'inescapably superficial' and all media philosophy is ultimately 'kitsch', then they are our contemporaries more than we might like to think. If 'posing-for', as one contemporary media philosophy puts it, lies at the heart of post-modern modernity, then the Nazis were extremely modern.[76] They posed for the cameras, they posed for posterity, they endlessly posed before the masses, and for a time they stole the show.

Nazism was perhaps the first mass movement to exploit fully the power of the media, which it did with all the finesse and vulgarity of Hollywood. Not for nothing were Hitler and Goebbels film addicts, who instantly recognized the importance of the new media of their time in amplifying their ideology. Their racist message proved perfectly compatible with sophisticated media techniques, just as their romantic ideas about the profundity of the 'German soul' fused readily with the most advanced military technology. Most disturbing of all, torturers and sadists in the death camps were able to perform mass killings in the daytime, yet listened to Mozart and Schubert by night. The much-vaunted humanizing effects of culture proved to be a weak reed incapable of immunizing mass murderers and collaborators against implementing a monstrous genocide. Indeed, beauty itself became the accomplice of bestiality and a primary desensitizing agent against the tormented cries of oppressed humanity.

The politicized aesthetic of the Nazis provided the fatal attraction that seduced a highly civilized nation and plunged it into the abyss of inhumanity. The Nazi myth of the reborn nation, which calls for eradicating the 'impurities' in its midst, contains a powerful warning for the present. We would therefore do well to hearken to the lesson in the Book of Exodus: 'And a stranger shalt thou not wrong, neither shalt thou oppress him.'[77] In the Hebrew Bible the commandment to love the stranger is repeated no less than thirty-six times. Commenting on this remarkable fact, the German Jewish philosopher Hermann Cohen aptly observed that it is in the alien that man first discovers the idea of humanity.

HITLER'S CIRCLE

JOSEPH GOEBBELS (1897–1945)

The master propagandist and cultural czar of the Third Reich for twelve years, Goebbels came from a strict Catholic, working-class family in the Rhineland. Rejected for military service in the First World War because of a crippled foot, he was tormented by an acute sense of physical inadequacy, which he overcompensated for with his political radicalism and exceedingly venomous rhetoric. The most educated and intelligent of the leading Nazis (he had studied history and literature at the University of Heidelberg), his oratorical gifts and flair for theatrical effects blossomed in the late 1920s in  the street battles with Communists in Berlin. Goebbels was the creator of the Führer myth - the public image of Hitler as the political Messiah and Redeemer of the German people. His stage management and manipulative talents were indispensable to the Nazis' rise to power and their subsequent ability to retain the enthusiasm and support of the masses. As Reich Minister for Public Enlightenment and Propaganda after 1933, he had broad control of the radio, press, publishing, literature, cinema and the other visual arts.

A consummate organizer, a master of the techniques of mass persuasion, a complete cynic and a relentless Jew-baiter, Goebbels remained close to Hitler – despite a brief falling out in 1938 over his adulterous love affairs with beautiful actresses. During the war years he never lost his nerve or fighting spirit, remaining with Hitler until the bitter end in the Berlin bunker in 1945. After Hitler's suicide, he decided to follow suit, having his six children poisoned by an SS doctor and then himself and his wife shot by an SS orderly. Shortly before his death he declared, 'We shall go down in history as the greatest statesmen of all time, or as the greatest criminals.'

RUDOLF HESS (1894–1987)

The Deputy Leader of the Nazi Party, which he had joined in 1920, Hess had studied at the University of Munich, where he was strongly influenced by the geopolitical theories of Professor Karl Haushofer. He was one of the first advocates in the Nazi movement of the need for German *Lebensraum* (living space). Imprisoned with Hitler following the abortive beer-hall *putsch* in Munich in 1923, he took down most of the dictation for *Mein Kampf* and helped with some of the writing of the book. As Hitler's private secretary between 1925 and 1932,  Hess showed a naïve, sincere and dogged devotion to his Führer.

In 1933 he was rewarded with the post of Reich Deputy Leader. He would usually introduce Hitler from the tribunal at mass meetings, with the wide-eyed, ecstatic enthusiasm of the true believer. National Socialism, for Hess, meant above all uncritical loyalty and complete surrender to the orders of the Leader. By the summer of 1939, Hess had reached the apex of his career, being made successor designate to Hitler and Goering. His bizarre solo flight to Scotland on 10 May 1941 to convince the British to allow Hitler a free hand in the East put an end to his career. He was imprisoned and held as a prisoner of war. Hitler repudiated him as insane and the Nazi press ridiculed him as a deluded idealist. At Nuremberg Hess was sentenced to life imprisonment and kept at the insistence of the Russians in the Allied military prison in Berlin, Spandau, until his death at the age of ninety-two. Rudolf Hess became a martyr for neo-Nazis all over the world and his burial place in northern Bavaria is a shrine for extremist movements of the radical Right.

HEINRICH HIMMLER (1900–1945)

The head of the Gestapo and *Reichsführer* of the SS, Heinrich Himmler became the second most powerful man in the Nazi empire during the Second World War. A Bavarian Catholic, who had at one time been a chicken farmer (he studied agriculture at Munich Technical High School between 1918 and 1922), Himmler participated in the beer-hall *putsch* of November 1923. In 1929 he became head of Hitler's personal bodyguard, the black-shirted *Schutzstaffel* (SS), which later rose under his leadership to become a veritable state within the State. In 1933 Himmler was appointed Munich Police President and shortly afterwards Commander of the political police throughout Bavaria. He masterminded the purge of June 1934, which

smashed the rival SA. A very able organizer, meticulous, calculating and efficient, Himmler perfected the techniques of State terrorism against political and other opponents of the regime. He set up the concentration camp at Dachau in 1933, and constantly extended the camp network and the number of prisoners. During the Second World War he was the supreme overlord of the death-camp system and the organizational architect of the 'Final Solution', responsible to Hitler alone.

A small, diffident man of pedantic demeanour and quiet, unemotional gestures, Himmler looked more like a humble bank clerk than the police dictator of Germany. Even in 1939 he was relatively unknown in Germany and still more in the outside world, though this changed with the outbreak of war. A fanatical racist who regarded the Greater Germanic Reich as the guardian of 'Nordic' supremacy and the custodian of a higher human culture, Himmler organized the systematic extermination of Jews and Slavs in Poland, Russia and other parts of Eastern Europe.

After having been captured by British troops, he committed suicide on 23 May 1945 by swallowing a poison vial which he had concealed in his mouth, before he could be brought to trial.

ROBERT LEY (1890–1945)

The Leader of the German Labour Front (DAF) between 1933 and 1945, Ley had been a chemist by profession and joined the Nazi Party in 1924. A personal friend of Hitler's and a bitter anti-Semite, Ley was notorious for his habitual drunkenness, uncouth behaviour and involvement in both street and public brawls during the early days of the movement. The prototype of the plebeian radical and anti-bourgeois Nazi, he was appointed Reich Organization Leader in November 1932. Less than a year later he was put in charge of what became the Third Reich's largest single mass organization, the *Deutsche Arbeitsfront*. This monolithic labour organization eventually had twenty-five million German workers under its aegis. Its aim was to abolish the class struggle, restore 'social peace' and win over the workers to Nazi ideals by looking after their social welfare and creating the 'right' cultural atmosphere. Through organizations like *Kraft durch Freude* (Strength through Joy), also headed by Ley, the DAF opened up new cultural vistas to the masses. The German Labour Front offered subsidized visits to the theatre and opera, free lectures, travel to foreign lands at minimal prices, sport and recreational activities as part of its drive towards a 'classless' utopia. Employers and employees wore the same, simple blue uniform,

though the State froze wages and salaries and obliged workers to pay increasingly large gifts to a variety of Nazi 'charities'.

Workers also paid on the instalment plan before delivery for the People's Car (Volkswagen) project, which was taken in hand by the DAF in 1938. Not one single car was produced for a civilian customer in the Third Reich, but Ley and his organization pocketed the profits. This was a good example of the fraudulent façade of Nazi socialism. Ultimately the militant phraseology of the DAF was part of a huge propaganda exercise to maximize productivity and erase the political consciousness of German workers.

Ley committed suicide on 24 October 1945 in his prison cell while he was awaiting trial at Nuremberg.

ALBERT SPEER (1905–1981)

The Reich Minister of Armaments and War Production from 1942 to 1945, Speer was the prototype of the intelligent technocrat who loyally and efficiently serves a totalitarian regime.

Born into a prosperous, upper-middle-class family of master-builders, Speer studied at the Institute of Technology in Karlsruhe and completed his architectural studies in Munich and Berlin. He became a member of the Nazi Party in 1931 after coming under the hypnotic spell of Hitler's oratory. After 1933 Speer was responsible for the designs and decorations used in the large Party rallies, beginning with the May Day celebration of the Tempelhofer field. He perfected the Nazi style of public parade, the monumental liturgy of the movement, using inventive lighting effects and rapidly erected flagpoles with great skill at the Nuremberg Reich Party rallies. His organizing ability, technological expertise and artistic imagination greatly impressed Hitler, who came to regard

him as an 'architect of genius'. He saw in Speer a youthful disciple who would transform his own artistic dreams and visions of a grandiose German Reich into an imposing architectural reality. Speer was soon given a stream of projects to design, including the impressive new Reich Chancellery in Berlin, completed in January 1939. He was also commissioned to oversee the rebuilding of Berlin and other German cities in the neo-classical, monumental style which both he and Hitler had always favoured. In 1942 he succeeded Fritz Todt as Minister of Armaments and War Production, achieving miracles in rapidly expanding the war production of the Reich despite massive Allied bombing attacks. Speer was sentenced to twenty years' imprisonment at Nuremberg. His best-selling memoirs (published in 1970) provided one of the most impressive descriptions of the inner workings of the Third Reich.

JULIUS STREICHER (1885–1946)

The founder and editor of the Third Reich's most notorious anti-Semitic newspaper, *Der Stürmer*, Julius Streicher was born in Upper Bavaria. An elementary school teacher by profession, he joined the Nazi Party in 1921. Four years later, he was appointed *Gauleiter* for Franconia, and transformed Nuremberg into his personal fiefdom and one of the centres of violent anti-Semitism in Germany. A tireless speaker and plebeian rabble-rouser, Streicher was highly regarded by Hitler, who declared that *Der Stürmer* was the only paper he read avidly from first to last page. Though more educated Germans were often repelled by the coarse prose style, the pornography, the crude cartoons and

the rabid anti-Semitism of the paper, Hitler found Streicher's material amusing and very clever. The impact of the paper was increased by a nationwide system of display cases in public squares, at bus stops and street corners, in factory canteens and parks. The racist slogans and scandal-mongering drew substantial crowds.

The Nuremberg anti-Semitic laws of 1935 were influenced by Streicher's vehement campaign to remove the Jews from all spheres of German public life. In 1937 the circulation of his paper had reached half a million copies and he made a personal fortune by enlarging his newspaper business and expropriating Jewish property. By 1939, however, Party officials were constantly complaining about his psychopathic behaviour and sexual peccadilloes. His aspersions on the virility of other Nazi potentates finally brought about his dismissal from all Party posts in 1940. But he continued his anti-Semitic incitement until the end of the war. He was eventually indicted and hanged at Nuremberg on 16 October 1946. As he went to the scaffold he proclaimed his eternal loyalty to Hitler and his undying hatred of the Jews.

FRAU PROFESSOR GERDY TROOST

Frau Troost was the widow of Paul Ludwig Troost (1878–1934), who had been Hitler's favourite architect and the man whom he had personally commissioned to build the House of German Art in Munich. Hitler's relationship to Troost was that of a pupil to an admired teacher and he would frequently visit the architect's studio in a battered backyard of the Theresienstrasse in Munich. Troost's death on 21 March 1934, after a severe illness, was a painful blow, but the Führer remained close to his widow, an

interior decorator and fierce defender of her husband's work. Together with the architect Professor Leonhard Gall, Frau Troost took over her husband's *atélier* and completed his plans for the House of German Art and various other commissions. On Hitler's forty-eighth birthday (20 April 1937) she was rewarded with the title of Professor. Her taste in architecture was very close to Hitler's and was expressed in two handsome volumes entitled *Das Bauen im neuen Reich* (1938), printed by the Party publisher in Bayreuth. This amalgam of *völkisch* ideas and Nazi political jargon is one of the definitive statements on what was considered acceptable architecture in the Third Reich. Frau Troost was one of the arbiters of artistic taste in Munich and always highly visible at the Great German Art Exhibitions in the city. In 1937 she protested vigorously at

Hitler's one-sided selection of works for the first exhibition held at the House of German Art, but to no avail. Albert Speer described her as a woman of refinement and character, fearless in standing up for her opinions in artistic matters. But although Hitler frequently listened to her, she was unable to influence his abominable taste in painting.

ADOLF WAGNER (1890–1944)

Gauleiter of Munich and Bavarian State Minister, Adolf Wagner was one of Hitler's *Alte Kämpfer* (Old Guard fighters) from the early days of the Nazi movement. A coarse, despotic and unattractive Bavarian with a duelling scar from his student days and a wooden leg, Wagner was notorious for his drunkenness and womanizing. This did not prevent him from rising steadily in the Nazi hierarchy in Bavaria. In November 1929 he was appointed *Gauleiter* of the NSDAP for Munich–Upper Bavaria. In March 1933 he was made *Staatskommissar* (State Commissioner) and then, in April, Minister of the Interior and Deputy Prime Minister of Bavaria. He was a member of the clique who helped to massacre the SA leaders during the Night of the Long Knives in June 1934. In November 1936 he was made Bavarian Minister of Education and Culture. Adolf Wagner was deeply involved in the administrative and organizational arrangements for the establishment of the House of German Art. He helped to secure financial pledges

from wealthy industrialists and bankers, which made its implementation possible. Determined to revive Munich's nineteenth-century role as a new 'Athens on the Isar', Wagner was highly visible as a speaker and host of the Day of German Art. At the opening of the Great German Art Exhibition in 1937 he declared pompously that only the most perfect works by German artists could henceforth be shown at the House of German Art. It was Wagner who commissioned Hans Feierabend to make the colour film in 1939 of the Day of German Art from which the images in this book are taken.

For years Wagner had been the real strongman of Bavaria, highly valued by Hitler, to whom he had constant access and who often placed a special plane at his disposal for trips to Berlin. In June 1942, however, the despotic *Gauleiter* had a stroke from which he would never recover. He died on 12 April 1944 and Adolf Hitler personally attended his state funeral at the Feldernhalle.

SELECT BIBLIOGRAPHY

Adam, Peter, *Art of the Third Reich* (New York, 1992).

Alff, Wilhelm, *Der Begriff Faschismus und andere Aufsätze zur Zeitgeschichte* (Frankfurt/M, 1973).

Arendt, Hannah, *The Origins of Totalitarianism* (New York, 1951).

Backes, Klaus, *Hitler und die bildenden Künste: Kulturverständnis und Kunstpolitik im Dritten Reich* (Cologne, 1988).

Baldwin, Peter (ed.), *Reworking the Past: Hitler, the Holocaust and the Historians' Debate* (Boston, 1990).

Balfour, Michael, *Propaganda in War 1939–45. Organizations, Policies and Publics in Britain and Germany* (London, 1979).

Bankier, David, *The Germans and the Final Solution. Public Opinion under Nazism* (Cambridge, 1992).

Barron, Stephanie, *et al.*, *'Degenerate Art': The Fate of the Avant-Garde in Nazi Germany* (Los Angeles/New York, 1991).

Baynes, Norman (ed.) *The Speeches of Adolf Hitler, April 1922 to August 1939*, 2 vols (London/Oxford, 1942).

Behne, Adolf, *Entartete Kunst* (Berlin, 1947).

Benjamin, Walter, *Gesammelte Schriften* vol.3 (Frankfurt/M, 1977).

Benn, Gottfried, *Kunst und Macht* (Stuttgart/Berlin, 1934).

Berger, John, *The Success and Failure of Picasso* (London, 1965).

Bessel, Richard, *Political Violence and the Rise of Nazism* (NewHaven/London, 1984).

Bleuel, Hans Peter, *Sex and Society in Nazi Germany* (Philadelphia, 1973).

Bracher, Karl Dietrich, *The German Dictatorship: The Origins, Structure and Consequences of National Socialism* (London, 1991).

Brady, Robert, *The Spirit and Structure of German Fascism* (London, 1937).

Bramsted, Ernest K., *Goebbels and National Socialist Propaganda 1925–45* (London, 1965).

Breker, Arno, *Paris, Hitler et Moi* (Paris, 1970).

—— *Im Strahlungsfeld der Ereignisse* (Preussisch-Oldendorf, 1972).

Brenner, Hildegard, *Die Kunstpolitik des Nationalsozialismus* (Hamburg, 1963).

Broszat, Martin, *German National Socialism 1919–45* (Santa Barbara, 1966).

Bullock, Alan, *Hitler: A Study in Tyranny* (London, 1962).

Burden, Hamilton T., *The Nuremberg Party Rallies: 1923–39* (London, 1967).

Busch, Günter, *Entartete Kunst – Geschichte und Moral* (Frankfurt/M, 1969).

Canetti, Elias, *Crowds and Power* (London, 1981).

—— *The Conscience of Words and Earwitness* (London, 1987).

Castriota, David (ed.), *Artistic Strategy and the Rhetoric of Power* (Southern Illinois University, 1986).

Cecil, Robert, *The Myth of the Master Race: Alfred Rosenberg and*

Nazi Ideology (New York, 1972).

Cheles, Luciano, *et al.* (ed.), *Neo-Fascism in Europe* (London, 1992).

Claus, Jürgen (ed.), *Entartete Kunst: Bildersturm vor 25 Jahren* (Munich, 1962).

Courtade, Francis, and Cadars, Pierre, *Le Cinéma Nazi* (Paris, 1972).

Crew, David (ed.), *Nazism and German Society 1933–1945* (London, 1994).

Darré, Richard Walther, *Neuadel aus Blut und Boden* (Munich, 1930).

—— *Das Bauerntum als Lebensquell der Nordischen Rasse*, 7th edn (Munich, 1929).

Dawidowicz, Lucy, *The War Against the Jews* (New York, 1975).

—— *The Holocaust and the Historians* (Harvard, 1981).

Domarus, Max (ed.), *Hitler: Reden und Proklamationen 1932–45* (Wiesbaden, 1973).

Doucet, Friedrich, *Im Banne des Mythos – Die Psychologie des Dritten Reiches* (Esslingen, 1979).

Dresler, Adolf (ed.), *Deutsche Kunst und entartete 'Kunst': Kunstwerk und Zerrbild der Weltanschauung* (Munich, 1938).

—— *Das Braune Haus und das Verwaltungsgebäude der Reichsleitung der NSDAP*, 3rd edn (Munich, 1939).

Dreyer, E.A., *Deutsche Kultur im Neuen Reich – Wesen, Aufgaben und Ziele der Reichskulturkammer* (Potsdam, 1934).

Eberlin, K., *Was ist Deutsch in der Deutschen Kunst?* (Leipzig, 1934).

Elgar, Dietmar, *Expressionism: A Revolution in German Art* (Cologne, 1989).

Evans, Richard J., *In Hitler's Shadow: West German Historians and the Attempt to Escape from the Nazi Past* (New York, 1989).

Farias, Victor, *Heidegger and Nazism* (Philadelphia, 1989).

Feder, G., *Die neue Stadt* (Berlin, 1939).

Feistel-Rohmeder, Bettina, *Im Terror des Kunstbolschewismus* (Karlsruhe, 1938).

Fest, Joachim, *The Face of the Third Reich* (London, 1972).

—— *Hitler* (New York, 1974).

Frazer, Graham and Lancelle, George, *Zhirinovsky: The Little Black Book* (London, 1994)

Friedländer, Saul, *L'Antisémitisme Nazi* (Paris, 1971).

—— *Reflections of Nazism: An Essay on Kitsch and Death* (New York, 1984).

Gamm, Hans-Jochen, *Der braune Kult* (Hamburg, 1962).

Giesler, Hermann, *Ein anderer Hitler – Bericht eines Architekten* (Leoni, 1978).

Gilman, Sander, *The Jew's Body* (London/New York, 1991).

Glaser, H., *Spiesserideologie: Von der Zerstörung des deutschen Geistes im 19. und 20. Jahrhundert* (Freiburg, 1964).

Goebbels, Joseph, *Goebbels spricht: Reden aus Kampf und Sieg* (Odenburg, 1933).

—— *Signale der neuen Zeit: 25 ausgewählte von Dr Joseph Goebbels* (Munich, 1938)

—— *Vom Kaiserhof zur Reichskanzlei* (Munich, 1934).

—— *The Goebbels Diaries* (London, 1948).

Gombrich, E.H., *Ideals and Idols: Essays on Values in History and in Art* (Oxford, 1979).

Gottschewsky, L., *Männerbund und Frauenfrage: Die Frau im Neuen Staat* (Munich, 1978).

Graml, Hermann, *Anti-Semitism in the Third Reich* (Oxford, 1992).

Gregor-Dellin, Martin (ed.), *Richard Wagner: Mein Denken* (Munich/Zurich, 1982).

Griffin, Roger, *The Nature of Fascism* (London, 1993).

Grosse Deutsche Kunstausstellung, 1937 (Munich, 1937), catalogue; 1938 (Munich, 1938), catalogue; 1939 (Munich, 1939), catalogue.

Grosshans, Henry, *Hitler and the Artists* (New York, 1983).

Grunberger, Richard, *A Social History of the Third Reich* (London, 1974).

Guyot, Adelin, and Restellini, Patrick, *L'Art Nazi* (Paris, 1987).

Haffner, Sebastian, *The Meaning of Hitler* (New York, 1979).

Hale, Oran J., *The Captive Press in the Third Reich* (Princeton, 1964).

Hart-Davis, Duff, *Hitler's Olympics: The 1936 Games* (London, 1988).

Hartmann, Wolfgang, *Der historische Festzug* (Munich, 1976).

Heartfield, John, *Krieg im Frieden: Fotomontagen zur Zeit 1930–38* (Frankfurt/M, 1982).

Heer, Friedrich, *Der politische Glaube des Adolf Hitler: Anatomie einer politischen Religiosität* (Munich, 1968).

Heiber, Helmut, *Joseph Goebbels* (Berlin, 1962).

Heidegger, Martin, *Nietzsche: The Will to Power as Art* (New York, 1979).

Herf, Jeffrey, *Reactionary Modernism: Technology, Culture and Politics in Weimar and the Third Reich* (Cambridge, 1987).

Hillgrüber, Andreas, *Zweierlei Untergang: Die Zerschlagung des Deutschen Reiches und das Ende des europäischen Judentums* (Berlin, 1986).

Hinkel, Hans (ed.), *Handbuch der Reichskulturkammer* (Berlin, 1937).

Hinz, Berthold, *et al.* (ed.), *Die Dekoration der Gewalt: Kunst und Medien im Faschismus* (Giessen, 1979).

—— *Art in the Third Reich* (New York, 1979).

Hitler, Adolf, *Die Rede unseres Führers Adolf Hitlers bei der Grundsteinlegung des Hauses der deutschen Kunst in München am 15. Oktober 1933* (Munich, 1937).

—— *Die Reden Hitlers am Parteitag der Freiheit 1935* (Munich, 1935).

—— *Reden des Führers am Parteitag der Ehre 1936* (Munich, 1936).

—— *Reden des Führers am Parteitag der Arbeit 1937* (Munich, 1938).

—— *Reden des Führers am Parteitag Grossdeutschland* (Munich,

1939).

—— *Mein Kampf* (New York/London, 1939).

—— *Hitler's Table Talk 1941–4* (Oxford, 1988).

Hochman, Elaine S., *Mies van der Rohe and the Third Reich* (New York, 1989).

Hofer, Walther (ed.), *Der Nationalsozialismus: Dokumente 1933–45* (Frankfurt/M, 1957).

Huber, Engelbert, *Das ist Nationalsozialismus* (Stuttgart, 1933).

Hull, David S., *Film in the Third Reich* (Berkeley, 1969).

Jäckel, E., and Kuhn, A. (ed.), *Hitler, Sämtliche Aufzeichnungen 1905–24* (Stuttgart, 1980).

Jäckel, Eberhard, *Hitlers Weltanschauung* (Stuttgart, 1981).

Joachimedes, C. M., *et al.* (ed.), *German Art in the Twentieth Century: Painting and Sculpture 1905–85* (London, 1985).

Joachimsthaler, Anton, *Hitler in München 1908–20* (Munich, 1992).

Jones, J. Sydney, *Hitler in Vienna 1907–13* (New York, 1983).

Kaes, Anton, *From Hitler to Heimat: The Return of History as Film* (Cambridge, Mass., 1989).

Kershaw, Ian, *Popular Opinion and Political Dissent in the Third Reich: Bavaria 1933–45* (New York, 1983).

—— *The Hitler Myth: Image and Reality in the Third Reich* (Oxford, 1989).

Klaus, M., *Mädchen im Dritten Reich: Der Bund Deutscher Mädel* (Cologne, 1983).

Kochan, Lionel, *Pogrom: 10 November 1938* (London, 1957).

Kokoschka, Oskar, *Mein Leben* (Munich, 1971).

Koonz, Claudia, *Mothers in the Fatherland: Women, the Family and Nazi Politics* (London, 1987).

Kracauer, Siegfried, *From Caligari to Hitler: A Psychological History of the German Film* (Princeton, 1947).

—— *Das Ornament der Masse* (Frankfurt/M, 1963).

Krier, L. (ed.), *Albert Speer: Architektur 1933–42* (Brussels, 1985).

Lacone-Labarthe, Philippe, *Heidegger, Art and Politics* (Oxford, 1990).

Laqueur, Walter, *Weimar: A Cultural History* (London, 1974).

—— (ed.), *Fascism: A Reader's Guide* (London, 1976).

Lehmann-Haupt, Helmut, *Art under a Dictatorship* (Oxford, 1954).

Leiser, Erwin, *Nazi Cinema* (London, 1974).

Lepper, Barbara, *Verboten, verfolgt: Kunstdiktatur im Dritten Reich* (Duisberg, 1983).

Ley, Michael, *Genozid und Heilserwartung: Zum Nationalsozialistischen Mord am Europäischen Judentum* (Vienna, 1993).

Lotz, Wilhelm, *Schönheit der Arbeit im Deutschland* (Berlin, 1940).

Lyotard, Jean-François, *Heidegger et 'les juifs'* (Paris, 1988).

Maccoby, Hyam, *The Sacred Executioner* (New York, 1982).

McLuhan, Marshall, *Understanding Media: The Extensions of Man* (New York, 1964).

Mann, Thomas, *Gesammelte Werke*, 13 vols (Frankfurt/M, 1974).

Maser, Werner, *Adolf Hitler, Legende – Mythos – Wirklichkeit* (Munich, 1974).

Merker, Reinhard, *Die bildende Künste im Nationalsozialismus: Kulturideologie, Kulturpolitik, Kulturproduktion* (Cologne, 1983).

Miller Lane, Barbara, *Architecture and Politics in Germany 1918–45* (Cambridge, Mass., 1968).

Milza, Pierre, and Roche-Pézard, Fanette (ed.), *Art et Fascisme* (Paris, 1989).

Möller van den Bruck, A., *Der preussische Stil* (Breslau, 1931).

Mosse, George L. (ed.), *Nazi Culture* (London, 1966).

—— *The Crisis of German Ideology* (New York, 1966).

—— *The Nationalization of the Masses* (New York, 1975).

—— *Nationalism and Sexuality* (New York, 1985).

—— (ed.), *International Fascism: New Thoughts and New Approaches* (London, 1979).

Nipperdey, Thomas, *et al.* (ed.), *Weltbürgerkrieg der Ideologien* (Frankfurt/Berlin, 1984).

Noakes, Jeremy, and Pridham, Geoffrey (ed.), *Nazism 1919–45: A Documentary Reader*, 2 vols (Exeter, 1984).

Nolte, Ernst, *The Three Faces of Fascism* (London, 1965).

Nordau, Max, *Entartung* (Berlin, 1892).

Nye, Robert A., *The Origins of Crowd Psychology: Gustave Le Bon and the Crisis of Mass Democracy in the Third Republic* (London/Beverly Hills, 1975).

Ohana, David, *Misdar Ha-Nihilistim* (The Order of the Nihilists, Jerusalem, 1993).

Orwell, George, *The Collected Essays, Journalism and Letters of George Orwell: My Country Right or Left*, vol.2, 1940–43 (London, 1971).

Padfield, Peter, *Hess. Flight for the Führer* (London, 1991).

Petsch, Joachim, *Kunst im Dritten Reich: Architektur, Plastik, Malerei* (Cologne, 1983).

Peukert, Detlev, *Inside Nazi Germany: Conformity, Opposition and Racism in Everyday Life* (New Haven/London, 1987).

Poliakov, Léon, *Le Mythe Aryen* (Paris, 1971).

Probst, V.G., *Arno Breker: 60 ans de sculpture* (Paris, 1981).

Proctor, Robert N., *Racial Hygiene: Medicine under the Nazis* (Cambridge, Mass., 1988).

Rauschning, Hermann, *The Revolution of Nihilism* (New York, 1939).

—— *Gespräche mit Hitler* (Zurich, 1940).

Rave, Paul Ortwin, *Kunstdiktatur im Dritten Reich* (Hamburg, 1947).

Reich, Wilhelm, *Massenpsychologie des Faschismus* (Copenhagen, 1933; reprinted Frankfurt/M, 1972).

Reichel, Peter, *La Fascination du fascisme* (Paris, 1993).

Riefenstahl, Leni, *Hinter den Kulissen des Reichsparteitagfilms* (Munich, 1935).

Rittich, Werner, *Architektur und Bauplastik der Gegenwart* (Berlin, 1936).

Roh, Franz, '*Entartete' Kunst: Kunstbarberei im Dritten Reich* (Hanover, 1962).

Rose, Paul, *Wagner: Race and Revolution* (London, 1992).

Rosenberg, Alfred, *Revolution in der bildenden Kunst* (Munich, 1934).

—— *Der Mythos des XX. Jahrhunderts* (Munich, 1938).

Rosenfeld, Alvin, *Imagining Hitler* (Bloomington, Indiana, 1985).

Schirach, Baldur von, *Zwei Reden zur Deutschen Kunst* (Munich, 1941).

Schmeer, K., *Regie des öffentlichen Lebens im Dritten Reich* (Munich, 1956).

Schmidt, Matthias, *Albert Speer. The End of a Myth* (London, 1985).

—— *The New Reich* (London, 1993).

Schoenbaum, David, *Hitler's Social Revolution: Class and Status in Nazi Germany 1933–39* (NewYork/London, 1980).

Scholz, Robert, *Architektur und bildende Kunst 1933–45* (Preussisch Oldendorf, 1977).

Schönleben, Eduard, *Fritz Todt: der Mensch, der Ingenieur, der Nationalsozialist* (Oldenbourg, Stalling, 1943).

Schrade, H., *Bauten des Dritten Reiches* (Leipzig, 1937).

Schroeder, Rudolf, *Modern Art in the Third Reich* (Offenburg, 1952).

Schultze-Naumburg, Paul, *Kunst und Rasse* (Munich, 1928).

—— *Kampf um die Kunst* (Munich, 1932).

—— *Die Kunst der Deutschen* (Stuttgart, 1934).

Schuster, Peter-Klaus (ed.), *Die 'Kunststadt' München 1937: Nationalsozialismus und 'Entartete Kunst'* (Munich, 1988).

Seidel, Gil, *The Holocaust Denial* (Leeds, 1986).

Silva, Umberto, *Ideologia e arte del fascismo* (Milan, 1973).

Sontag, Susan, *Under the Sign of Saturn* (New York, 1980).

Speer, Albert (ed.), *Die neue Reichskanzlei* (Munich, 1940).

—— *Inside the Third Reich* (London, 1971).

Spengler, Oswald, *Der Untergang des Abendlandes*, 2 vols (Munich, 1922).

Staudinger, Hans, *The Inner Nazi: A Critical Analysis of Mein Kampf* (Baton Rouge, 1981).

Stephenson, Jill, *Women in Nazi Society* (London, 1975).

Stern, Fritz, *The Politics of Cultural Despair* (Berkeley, 1961).

Stern, J.P., *Hitler: The Führer and the People* (London, 1975).

Sternhell, Zeev (ed.), *L'Éternel Retour* (Paris, 1994).

—— with Mario Snajder and Maia Asheri, *The Birth of Fascist Ideology* (Princeton, 1994).

Syberberg, Hans-Jürgen, *Hitler: A Film from Germany* (New York, 1982).

Tabor, Jan (ed.), *Kunst und Diktatur: Architektur, Bildhauerei, und Malerei in Österreich, Deutschland, Italien und der Sowjet-union 1922–56*, 2 vols (Baden, 1994).

Taylor, Brandon, and van der Will, Wilfried (ed.), *The Nazification of Art: Art, Design, Music, Architecture and Film in the Third Reich* (Winchester, 1990).

Taylor, Fred (ed.), *The Goebbels Diaries 1939–41* (London, 1982).

Taylor, Mark C. and Saarinen, Esa, *Imagologies. Media Philosophies* (London, 1994).

Taylor, Robert R., *The Word in Stone: The Role of Architecture in National Socialist Ideology* (Berkeley/Los Angeles, 1974).

Teut, Anna, *Architektur im Dritten Reich 1933–45* (Berlin, 1967).

Theweleit, Klaus, *Male Fantasies*, 2 vols (Minneapolis, 1989).

Thies, Jochen, *Architekt der Weltherrschaft: Die 'Endziele' Hitlers* (Düsseldorf, 1980).

Troost, Gerdy (ed.), *Das Bauen im Neuen Reich*, 2 vols (Bayreuth, 1938).

Tyrell, Albrecht, *Vom Trommler zum Führer* (Munich, 1975).

Vidal-Naquet, Pierre, *Les Assassins de la mémoire* (Paris, 1987).

Vondung, Klaus, *Magie und Manipulation: Ideologischer Kult und Politische Religion des Nationalsozialismus* (Göttingen, 1971).

Waite, Robert G., *The Psychopathic God: Adolf Hitler* (New York, 1977).

Watson, Alan, *The Germans. Who Are They Now?* (London, 1992).

Welch, David, *Nazi Propaganda* (London/Canberra, 1983).

—— *Propaganda and the German Cinema 1933–45* (Oxford, 1983).

—— *The Third Reich: Politics and Propaganda* (London/New York, 1993).

Wernert, E., *L'Art dans le IIIe Reich* (Paris, 1936).

Willrich, W., *Säuberung des Kunsttempels: eine Kunstpolitische Kampfschrift zur Gesundung deutscher Kunst im Geist nordischer Art* (Munich/Berlin, 1937).

Wistrich, Robert (ed.), 'Theories of Fascism', *Journal of Contemporary History* (October 1976, special issue).

Who's Who in Nazi Germany (New York/London, 1982).

—— *Hitler's Apocalypse: Jews and the Nazi Legacy* (London, 1985).

—— *Between Redemption and Perdition* (London, 1990).

—— *Anti-Semitism: The Longest Hatred* (London/New York, 1991).

Wolbert, Klaus, *Die Nackten und die Toten des 'Dritten Reiches'. Folgen einer politischen Geschichte des Körpers in der Plastik des deutschen Faschismus* (Giessen, 1982).

Wolin, Richard (ed.), *The Heidegger Controversy: A Critical Reader* (Cambridge, Mass./London, 1993).

Wolters, Rudolf, *Albert Speer* (Oldenburg, 1943).

Wülf, Josef (ed.), *Musik im Dritten Reich* (Guterslöh, 1963).

—— (ed.), *Die Bildenden Künste im Dritten Reich: Eine Dokumentation* (Guterslöh, 1963).

—— (ed.), *Theater und Film im Dritten Reich* (Guterslöh, 1964).

—— (ed.), *Presse und Funk im Dritten Reich* (Guterslöh, 1964).

Zbryek, Z., *Selling the War: Art and Propaganda in World War II* (London, 1982).

Zelinsky, Hartmut, *Richard Wagner – ein deutsches Thema: Eine Dokumentation zur Wirkungsgeschichte Richard Wagners 1876–1976* (Frankfurt/M, 1976).

—— *Sieg oder Untergang: Sieg und Untergang* (Munich, 1990).

Zeman, Zbynek, *Nazi Propaganda*, 2nd edn (London/New York, 1964).

—— *Heckling Hitler: Caricatures of the Third Reich* (London, 1984).

Zimmerman, Michael, *Heidegger's Confrontation with Modernity* (Bloomington, Indiana, 1990).

NOTES ON THE TEXT

Chapter One: Nazism: Image, Icon and Myth

1 Detlev Peukert, *Inside Nazi Germany: Conformity, Opposition and Racism in Everyday Life* (New Haven/London, 1987), pp.208–35

2 See Richard J. Evans, *In Hitler's Shadow: West German Historians and the Attempt to Escape from the Nazi Past* (New York, 1989), pp.65–91. Also the exchange between Martin Broszat and Saul Friedländer, in Peter Baldwin (ed.), *Reworking the Past: Hitler, the Holocaust and the Historians' Debate* (Boston, 1990), pp.102–34 and in the same volume the articles by Dan Diner, 'Between Aporia and Apology: On the Limits of Historicizing National Socialism', pp.135–45 and Mary Nolan, 'The *Historikerstreit* and Social History', pp.224–48. Nolan emphasizes the need for social history to explore more closely the links between everyday life and terror, and the ways in which memory is structured and legitimated by the culture and the political system. While defending the overall record of *Alltagsgeschichte*, she admits that it has problems, especially in relation to the Holocaust. They are most evident in 'its narrow focus on subjective experience, its lack of context, its overemphasis on normality and *Resistenz*, its failure to link victims and non-victims, and its inattention to racism . . . ', p.242.

3 See Alvin Rosenfeld, *Imagining Hitler* (Bloomington, Indiana, 1985), pp.103–12 for a suggestive analysis of pop culture, politics and the 'iniquity of images'. Rosenfeld shows that the ghost of Hitler is very much alive in popular fiction but in a morally debilitating way. Fantasies about Nazism have become mixed with exaggerated dreams of power and submission, erotic conquest and the pornography of violence.

4 Ibid., p.104. 'In sum, Hitler has become a gag, an adornment, a piece of the fun.'

5 Quoted in ibid., p.105.

6 Saul Friedländer, *Reflections of Nazism: An Essay on Kitsch and Death* (New York, 1984), pp.18–19.

7 See 'The Game and the Show', *Guardian Weekend* (20 November 1993), pp.6–14 for an enlightening investigation of image makers in contemporary American politics.

8 Zbyněk Zeman, *Nazi Propaganda* (London, 1964), p.5.

9 Ibid., p.28ff.

10 Marshall McLuhan, *Understanding Media: The Extensions of Man* (New York, 1964), p.261.

11 Ibid., pp.262–3.

12 See the discussion in Robert R. Taylor, *The Word in Stone: The Role of Architecture in National Socialist Ideology* (Berkeley/Los Angeles, 1974), p.199.

13 Werner Rittich, *Architektur and Bauplastik der Gegenwart* (Berlin, 1936), p.21ff.

14 Eduard Schönleben, *Fritz Todt: der Mensch, der Ingenieur, der Nationalsozialist* (Oldenbourg, Stalling, 1943), p.56.

15 Ibid. As a reward for building the *Autobahnen* and the Western Wall, Todt was decorated by Hitler with the 'German Order' for special

services to the German people. He was the first German to be so honoured. During the Second World War he was, until his death in 1942, Reich Minister of Armaments and Munitions, responsible for all the major technical tasks concerning the German war effort. See Robert Wistrich, *Who's Who in Nazi Germany* (New York/London, 1982), pp.318–19. For Todt's views on the relation between aesthetics, engineering and technology in general, see Jeffrey Herf, *Reactionary Modernism: Technology, Culture and Politics in Weimar and the Third Reich* (Cambridge, 1987), pp.199–204.

16 Herf, *Reactionary Modernism*, pp.204–7.

17 Speech by Joseph Goebbels, 17 February 1939, at the opening of the Berlin Auto Show, quoted in ibid., p.196.

18 Orwell's essay, 'The Frontiers of Art and Propaganda', was originally a radio talk, reprinted in the *Listener* (29 May 1941). See *The Collected Essays, Journalism and Letters of George Orwell: My Country Right or Left*, vol.II 1940–43 (London, 1971), pp.149–53.

19 Ibid., p.152.

20 George Orwell, 'Literature and Totalitarianism', a broadcast talk in the BBC Overseas Service, printed in the *Listener* (19 June 1941); *Collected Essays*, pp.161–64.

21 See George L. Mosse, *The Crisis of German Ideology* (New York, 1964) for the development of the Volkish myth in German culture at the end of the nineteenth century.

22 Walter Benjamin 'Theorien des deutschen Faschismus' in Walter Benjamin, *Gesammelte Schriften*, Vol.3 (Frankfurt/M, 1977), pp.238–50.

23 Quoted in Herf, *Reactionary Modernism*, p.36.

24 See Robert S. Wistrich, *Anti-Semitism: The Longest Hatred* (London/New York, 1991), for the historic background to these archetypes.

25 Adolf Hitler, *Mein Kampf* (New York/London, 1939), p.221.

26 John Berger, *The Success and Failure of Picasso* (London, 1965), p.70.

27 This has changed in the last five to ten years, as can be seen from the bibliography at the back of this book. See also the remarks in Brandon Taylor and Wilfried van der Will (ed.) *The Nazification of Art* (Winchester, 1990), pp.4–5.

28 There is much controversy and a growing literature on this topic. See for example Jean-François Lyotard, *Heidegger et 'les juifs'* (Paris, 1988); Victor Farias, *Heidegger and Nazism* (Philadelphia, 1989); Michael Zimmerman, *Heidegger's Confrontation with Modernity* (Bloomington, Indiana, 1990); and Philippe Lacone-Labarthe, *Heidegger, Art and Politics* (Oxford, 1990). For an overall survey, see Richard Wolin (ed.), *The Heidegger Controversy: A Critical Reader* (Cambridge, Mass./London, 1993).

29 Wistrich, *Who's Who in Nazi Germany*, pp.88,143,304–5.

30 Richard Grunberger, *A Social History of the Third Reich* (London, 1974), p.523.

31 Ibid., p.517.

32 Michael Meyer, 'The Nazi

Musicologist as Myth-Maker in the Third Reich', *Journal of Contemporary History*, vol.10, no.4 (October 1975), pp.649–65.

33 Martin Heidegger, *Nietzsche: The Will to Power as Art* (New York, 1979), pp.85–6. These Nietzsche lectures were given at the end of the 1930s when Heidegger had distanced himself somewhat from Nazism. He had initially believed that the National Socialists would bring about a cultural revolution, returning a decadent German and Western civilization to the sources of being. The German Volk, by going back to the great beginning made by the ancient Greeks, would reverse the false path taken by soulless Western rationalism. He saw Nazism as a possible road to salvation between the 'bankrupt' solutions of American technocracy and Russian Bolshevik materialism. By the late 1930s he was convinced that the cultural 'essence' of National Socialism had in fact been betrayed, but he was still in sympathy with its ideal.

34 Meyer, 'Nazi Musicologist as Myth-Maker', p.664.

35 Friedländer, *Refelections*, pp.42–3.

36 Ibid., pp.41-2; Joachim Fest, *Hitler* (New York, 1974), pp.699–700.

37 Peter Reichel, *La Fascination du fascisme* (Paris, 1993), p.23.

38 Peukert, *Inside Nazi Germany*, pp.42–57.

39 Anton Kaes, *From Hitler to Heimat: The Return of History as Film* (Cambridge, Mass., 1989).

40 See Lacone-Labarthe, *Heidegger: Art and Politics*, for an evaluation of National Socialism as a form of 'national aestheticism' referring back to Greek ideals. There are some interesting parallels between Hitler and Heidegger in this and other respects.

41 David Low, *Low's Autobiography* (London, 1956), p.250. For information about Low, the caricaturist of the London *Evening Standard* and examples of his brilliant cartoons of Hitler and the Third Reich, see Zbyněk Zeman, *Heckling Hitler: Caricatures of the Third Reich* (London, 1984). Low firmly rejected the common underestimations of Hitler as an inconsequential clown, a windbag or a certifiable lunatic. Nor did he regard the German leader as an inexplicable enigma.

Chapter Two: Adolf Hitler: Art and Megalomania

1 See Anton Joachimsthaler, *Hitler in München 1908–20* (Munich, 1992), for an account of his early years in Munich.

2 Joachim C. Fest, *The Face of the Third Reich* (London, 1972), p.35ff.

3 See Albrecht Tyrell, *Vom Trommler zum Führer* (Munich, 1975).

4 E. Jäckel and A. Kuhn (ed.), *Hitler, Sämtliche Aufzeichnungen 1905–24* (Stuttgart, 1980), p.939.

5 Ian Kershaw, *The Hitler Myth: Image and Reality in the Third Reich* (Oxford, 1989), p.39.

6 *Völkischer Beobachter* (27 February 1933).

7 Kershaw, *The Hitler Myth*, pp.80–82.

8 *Reden des Führers am Parteitag der Ehre vom 8 bis 14 September 1936* (Munich, 1936), pp.246–7. See also J.P. Stern, *Hitler: The Führer and the People* (London, 1975), for an analysis of this kind of rhetorical flourish in Hitler's speeches.

9 Alan Bullock, *Hitler: A Study in Tyranny* (London, 1962), pp.312–71; Kershaw, *The Hitler Myth*, pp.121–47.

10 *Völkischer Beobachter* (8 November 1938), p.2. For a useful general account, see Hermann Graml, *Anti-Semitism in the Third Reich* (Oxford, 1992), pp.5–29.

11 Peter Loewenberg, 'The Kristallnacht as a Public Degradation Ritual', Leo Baeck Yearbook, XXXII (1987), pp.309–23.

12 Lionel Kochan, *Pogrom: 10 November 1938* (London, 1957), p.15.

13 Loewenberg, 'Kristallnacht', p.313.

14 Graml, *Anti-Semitism*, pp.142–4.

15 Robert Wistrich, *Hitler's Apocalypse: Jews and the Nazi Legacy* (London, 1985).

16 Ian Kershaw, *Popular Opinion and Political Dissent in the Third Reich: Bavaria 1933–45* (New York, 1983), p.275.

17 Graml, *Anti-Semitism*, p.141.

18 Kershaw, *The Hitler Myth*, p.142.

19 Ibid.

20 Max Domarus (ed.), *Hitler: Reden und Proklamationen 1932–45* (Wiesbaden, 1973), p.1178.

21 Albert Speer, *Inside the Third Reich* (London, 1971), p.235.

22 On the subject of propaganda, see Zbyněk Zeman, *Nazi Propaganda*, 2nd edn (London/New York, 1964), and David Welch, *Nazi Propaganda* (London/Canberra, 1983).

23 George L. Mosse (ed.), *Nazi Culture* (London, 1966), pp.xxii–xxvi.

24 Ibid., p.xxix.

25 Adolf Hitler, *Mein Kampf* (New York/London, 1939), p.398.

26 Ibid., p.392.

27 Ibid., p.406.

28 Ibid., p.418.

29 See Wistrich, *Hitler's Apocalypse*; pp.34–6.

30 Hans Staudinger, *The Inner Nazi: A Critical Analysis of Mein Kampf* (Baton Rouge, 1981), pp.72–7.

31 Ibid. See also Lucy Dawidowicz, *The War Against the Jews* (New York, 1975); Sebastian Haffner, *The Meaning of Hitler* (New York, 1979); Wistrich, *Hitler's Apocalypse*.

32 Wistrich, *Hitler's Apocalypse*, p.40ff. See also Michael Ley, *Genozid und Heilserwartung: Zum Nationalsozialistischen Mord am Europäischen Judentum* (Vienna, 1993).

33 Mosse (ed.), *Nazi Culture*, p.7.

34 'Hitlers Rede' (2 September 1933), quoted in Josef Wülf (ed.), *Die Bildenden Künste im Dritten Reich: Eine Dokumentation* (Gütersloh, 1963), pp.64–7.

35 *New York Times* (3 September 1933).

36 For the best general account, see Stephanie Barron *et al.*, *Degenerate Art: The Fate of the Avant-Garde in Nazi Germany* (Los Angeles/New York, 1991).

37 Richard Grunberger, *A Social*

History of the Third Reich (London, 1974), pp.535–6.

38 For a complete list of the artists, see Peter-Klaus Schuster (ed.), *Die 'Kunststadt' München 1937: Nationalsozialismus und 'Entartete Kunst'* (Munich, 1988), pp.122–216.

39 'Entartete Kunst am Pranger', *Völkischer Beobachter* (20 July 1937), p.1.

40 *Die Reden Hitlers am Parteitag der Freiheit 1935* (Munich, 1935), p.29. On the broader theme, see Rudolf Schroeder, *Modern Art in the Third Reich* (Offenburg, 1952), and Reinhard Merker, *Die bildende Künste im Nationalsozialismus: Kulturideologie, Kulturpolitik, Kulturproduktion* (Cologne, 1983).

41 See John Heartfield, *Krieg im Frieden: Fotomontagen zur Zeit 1930–38* (Frankfurt/M, 1982), and Peter Halko, 'Zurück zur Ordnung: Der revolutionäre Shock der Moderne und die reaktionäre Antwort' in Jan Tabor (ed.), *Kunst und Diktatur*, vol. I (Baden, 1994), pp.24–9.

42 Peter-Klaus Schuster, 'München – das Verhängnis einer Kunststadt', in Schuster (ed.), *Die 'Kunststadt' München*, p.22ff.

43 See Walter Laqueur, *Weimar: A Cultural History* (New York, 1974), pp.162–82.

44 Paul Schultze-Naumburg, *Kunst und Rasse* (Munich, 1928), and *Kampf um die Kunst* (Munich, 1932).

45 Barbara Miller Lane, *Architecture and Politics in Germany 1918–45* (Cambridge, Mass., 1968), pp.133–40, 156–9.

46 Ibid., p.157.

47 See Hildegard Brenner, *Die Kunstpolitik des Nationalsozialismus* (Hamburg, 1963), pp.78–86.

48 For the evolution of Hitler's views on art and architecture, see Franz Roh, 'Entartete Kunst': *Kunstbarbarei im Dritten Reich* (Hanover, 1962), pp.41–8. See also Klaus Backes, *Hitler und die bildenden Künste: Kulturverständnis und Kunstpolitik im Dritten Reich* (Cologne, 1988), and Henry Grosshans, *Hitler and the Artists* (New York, 1983).

49 See August Kubizek, *The Young Hitler I Knew* (Boston, 1955), and J. Sydney Jones, *Hitler in Vienna 1907–13* (New York, 1983), pp.46–7.

50 Speer, *Inside the Third Reich*, p.123.

51 Adelin Guyot and Patrick Restellini, *L'Art Nazi* (Paris, 1987), p.56.

52 Robert Wistrich, *Between Redemption and Perdition* (London, 1990), pp.56–67.

53 For a sharply drawn contrast between the atmosphere of Berlin and Munich, see Thomas Mann, 'Betrachtungen eines Unpolitischen', in his *Gesammelte Werke*, vol. XII (Frankfurt/M, 1974), p.140ff.

54 Eva von Seckendorff, 'Erster Baumeister des Führers: Die NS-Karriere des Innenarchitekten Paul Ludwig Troost', in Tabor (ed.), *Kunst und Diktatur*, vol. II, pp.580–85.

55 Adolf Dresler, *Das Braune Haus und das Verwaltungsgebäude der Reichsleitung der NSDAP* (Munich, 1939).

56 Peter Adam, *Art of the Third Reich* (New York, 1992), pp.228–38.

57 *Die Rede unseres Führers Adolf Hitler bei der Grundsteinlegung des Hauses der deutschen Kunst in München am 15 Oktober 1933* (Munich, 1937). For its significance, see *Das Bauen im Dritten Reich* (Bayreuth, 1938; 3rd edn, 1941) pp. 10–20. This book was edited by Frau Professor Gerdy Troost.

58 Domarus, *Hitler: Reden*, p.707 (speech of 19 July 1937 at the opening of the House of German Art). Also, speech of 22 January 1938, ibid., p.779.

59 Robert R. Taylor, *The Word in Stone: The Role of Architecture in National Socialist Ideology* (Berkeley/Los Angeles, 1974), p.67.

60 Speer, *Inside the Third Reich*, p.79.

61 Jones, *Hitler in Vienna*, p.52, notes that the Makart style had a real attraction for Hitler. So steeped was he in nineteenth-century classicism and historicism that the artistic revolt in *fin-de-siècle* Vienna completely passed him by.

62 Elaine S. Hochman, *Mies van der Rohe and the Third Reich* (New York, 1989), describes in detail the complexity and ambiguities in the relations between the Nazi regime and modernist architects like Mies van der Rohe.

63 Speer, *Inside the Third Reich*, p.80.

64 Taylor, *The Word in Stone*, p.69ff.

65 Anson Rabinbach, 'The Aesthetics of Production in the Third Reich', in Robert Wistrich *et al*. (ed.), *Theories of Fascism, Journal of Contemporary History* (October 1976, special issue), pp.43–74.

66 Ibid. p.50.

67 Ibid. p.66.

68 Adam, *Art of the Third Reich*, p.239.

69 Taylor, *The Word in Stone*, p.129.

70 Speer, *Inside the Third Reich*, pp.96–7.

71 Taylor, *The Word in Stone*, pp.138–9.

72 Ibid., p.140.

73 See Norman Baynes (ed.), *The Speeches of Adolf Hitler, April 1922 to August 1939* (London/Oxford, 1942), p.601. Speech of 9 January 1939 at the opening of the Chancellery.

74 Hermann Giesler, 'Bauen im Dritten Reich', *Kunst im Dritten Reich* (September 1939). Quoted in Adam, *Art of the Third Reich*, p.256.

75 Werner Rittich, *Architektur und Bauplastik der Gegenwart* (Berlin, 1936) p.32.

76 Troost, *Das Bauen im Dritten Reich*, vol. I, p.20.

77 Rittich, *Architektur*, p.36.

78 Domarus, *Hitler: Reden*, p.707 (19 July 1937).

79 Troost, *Das Bauen im Dritten Reich*, vol. I, p.24.

80 Franz Hofmann, quoted in Taylor, *The Word in Stone*, p.266.

81 See Miller Lane, *Architecture and Politics in Germany*, p.147. See also Joachim Petsch, *Kunst im Dritten Reich: Architektur, Plastik, Malerei* (Cologne, 1983).

82 Miller Lane, *Architecture and Politics in Germany*, p.147.

83 Otto Dietrich, 'Adolf Hitler als Künstlerischer Mensch', *Nationalsozialistische Monatshefte*, III (1933), p.473. Joseph Goebbels, 'Die grosse Kundgebung der deutscher

Künstler am Samstag', *Völkischer Beobachter* (19 July 1937). In a speech in 1938 Thomas Mann acknowledged that Hitler, with all his recalcitrance, bohemianism, rage at the world, revolutionary instinct and 'subconscious storing up of explosive cravings for compensation', had the temperament of an artist. Mann, a firm opponent of Nazism, admitted that this artistic bent was 'a thoroughly embarrassing kinship', but one that should not be ignored. See Thomas Mann, *Gesammelte Werke*, vol. XII (Munich, 1953), p.775ff.

84 Quoted in Miller Lane, *Architecture and Politics in Germany*, p.159.

85 *Reden des Führers am Parteitag der Arbeit 1937* (Munich, 1937). In 1942 Hitler was still expounding in his table talk on the importance of art and architecture. He told his entourage that he had become a politician against his will. 'To my mind politics is just a means to an end. Wars come and go. The only lasting things are cultural values. Are not music and architecture the forces that will guide the footsteps of future generations?' Quoted in Henry Picker, *Hitler's Tischgespräche im Führerhauptquartier* (Stuttgart, 1976), p.167.

86 Miller Lane, *Architecture and Politics in Germany*, p.189.

87 Ibid., p.215.

88 See Jeffrey Herf, *Reactionary Modernism: Technology, Culture and Politics in Weimar and the Third Reich* (Cambridge, 1987), pp.189–216. Also Andrew Graham-Dixon, 'As if Hitler never existed', *The Independent*, 24 September 1994, p.29. In this provocative review of the *Deutsche Romantik* festival on London's South Bank, Graham-Dixon describes the 'Final Solution' as 'the appalling translation into genetics, of that idealizing strain within German Romantic aesthetics that dreamed of total purity. Where almost all the German Romantics dreamed of changing the world, Hitler went about the job of doing so... in the radical Romantic artist's spirit of nutty but single-minded fanaticism.'

89 Jochen Thies, *Architekt der Weltherrschaft: Die 'Endziele' Hitlers* (Düsseldorf, 1980), pp.76–9.

90 Ibid., p.79.

91 Jochen Thies, 'Hitler's European Building Programme', *Journal of Contemporary History*, vol. XIII (1978), pp.413–31.

92 Speer, *Inside the Third Reich*, p.121.

93 Elias Canetti, 'Hitler, According to Speer', *The Conscience of Words and Earwitness* (London, 1987), pp.66–91.

Chapter Three: The Mass Seduction

1 David Schoenbaum, *Hitler's Social Revolution: Class and Status in Nazi Germany 1933–39* (New York/London, 1980), pp.56–9.

2 See Martin Broszat, *German National Socialism 1919–45* (Santa Barbara, 1966), and the classic work by Karl Dietrich Bracher, *The German Dictatorship: The Origins, Structure and Consequences of National Socialism* (London, 1991), pp.108–42.

3 For a portrait of Röhm and the SA mentality, see Joachim C. Fest, *The Face of the Third Reich* (London, 1972), p.207ff. On the broader question of violence, see Richard Bessel, *Political Violence and the Rise of Nazism* (New Haven/London, 1984).

4 Gabriele Petricek, 'Auf die Uniform ist Verlass: Die NS-Disziplinierung durch die Kleidung', in Jan Tabor (ed.), *Kunst und Diktatur*, vol. I, (Baden, 1994), pp.56–64.

5 Ibid. For the socio-psychological implications, it is still worth consulting the pioneering study of Wilhelm Reich, *Massenpsychologie des Faschismus* (Copenhagen, 1933; reprinted Frankfurt/M, 1972).

6 Joseph Goebbels, *Vom Kaiserhof zur Reichskanzlei* (Munich, 1934), p.174.

7 T. Aich, *Massenmensch und Massenwahn* (Munich, 1947), p.83.

8 Petricek, 'Auf die Uniform ist Verlass', p.63.

9 Hans-Jochen Gamm, *Der braune Kult* (Hamburg, 1962), pp.43–56.

10 George L. Mosse, *Confronting the Nation* (Hanover/London, 1993), pp.52–3.

11 Klaus Theweleit, *Male Fantasies*, vol. II, *Male Bodies: Psychoanalyzing the White Terror* (Minneapolis, 1989), p.189.

12 Adolf Hitler, *Mein Kampf* (New York/London, 1939), p.47.

13 Ibid., pp.48–50.

14 Ibid., p.283.

15 Ibid., p.317.

16 See Robert A. Nye, *The Origins of Crowd Psychology: Gustave Le Bon and the Crisis of Mass Democracy in the Third Republic* (London/Beverly Hills, 1975), pp.71ff.

17 Ibid., p.178. For these and other French influences on Mussolini, see Zeev Sternhell *et al*., *The Birth of Fascist Ideology* (Princeton, 1994), and the review by Robert S. Wistrich, 'How Fascism Began', *The Times Literary Supplement* (3 June 1994), pp.27–8.

18 Nye, *Origins of Crowd Psychology*, p.179.

19 Alan Bullock, *Hitler: A Study in Tyranny* (London, 1962), p.68.

20 Ibid., p.71.

21 Quoted in Fest, *The Face of the Third Reich*, p.39.

22 Gamm, *Der braune Kult*, p.24ff.

23 Klaus Vondung, *Magie und Manipulation: Ideologischer Kult und Politische Religion des Nationalsozialismus* (Göttingen, 1971), p.34ff.

24 Robert S. Wistrich, *Hitler's Apocalypse: Jews and the Nazi Legacy* (London, 1985), pp.136–53.

25 See Friedrich Heer, *Der politische Glaube des Adolf Hitler: Anatomie einer politischen Religiosität* (Munich, 1968).

26 Vondung, *Magie und Manipulation*, pp.42–3.

27 Gamm, *Der braune Kult*, p.141; Vondung, *Magie und Manipulation*, pp.61–3. The quote is from Richard Grunberger, *A Social History of the Third Reich* (London, 1974), p.105.

28 Gamm, *Der braune Kult*, p.142.

29 Michael Ley, *Genozid und Heilserwartung: Zum Nationalsozialistischen Mord am Europäischen Judentum* (Vienna, 1993), pp.185–212, and Hyam

Maccoby, *The Sacred Executioner* (New York, 1982), p.174.

30 George L. Mosse, *The Nationalization of the Masses* (New York, 1975), pp.100–14.

31 Paul Lawrence Rose, *Wagner: Race and Revolution* (London, 1992), p.182.

32 Ibid.

33 Albert Speer, *Inside the Third Reich* (London, 1971), p.219.

34 Thomas Mann's extraordinary remarks are quoted in Rose, *Wagner*, p.184.

35 Mosse, *The Nationalization of the Masses*, p.193. See also Michael Meyer, 'The Nazi Musicologist as Myth Maker in the Third Reich', *Journal of Contemporary History*, vol. X, no. 4 (October 1975), pp.649–66. Meyer points out that Wagner's 'political conception of a genuine *Volksgemeinschaft*, which was to be held together by the spell of his ritualistic music drama, was appropriated by the Nazis in 1933 to demonstrate their affinity to it and – due to their proclaimed intention of realizing it by revolutionary means – in justification of their power' (p.650). Wagner was not only the centre of the most popular music cult during the Third Reich, celebrated at popular events and reinforced by official representatives of the State, he was also highly regarded as a spiritual leader and political visionary.

36 Mosse, *The Nationalization of the Masses*, pp.194–5.

37 Stuart Woolf, 'Les cérémonies du fascisme', in Pierre Milza and Fanette Roche-Pézard (ed.), *Art et Fascisme* (Paris, 1989), pp. 245–6.

38 Brandon Taylor and Wilfried van der Will, 'Aesthetics and National Socialism', in their volume entitled *The Nazification of Art: Art, Design, Music, Architecture and Film in the Third Reich* (Winchester, 1990), pp.1–13.

39 For questions of comparability, see Umberto Silva, *Ideologia e arte del fascismo* (Milan, 1973), Milza and Roche-Pézard, *Art et Fascisme*, and especially the two volumes of Tabor (ed.), *Kunst und Diktatur*, which examine art in Nazi Germany, Austria and Fascist Italy during the 1930s, and also in the Soviet Union. One important difference between the Nazi and Soviet aesthetic was the deliberately archaic utopia which the National Socialists espoused as part of their revolt against industrialism. Nazi art purged the cities, the factories, the combines, the large dams and the theme of 'electrification' from its field of vision. As Saul Friedländer in his *Reflections of Nazism: An Essay on Kitsch and Death* (New York, 1984), p.29, neatly puts it: 'This is far from the Soviet ideal, where the iconography of singing tomorrows avoids themes of death and destruction.' The romantic kitsch of death and even of the apocalypse, one of the bedrocks of Nazi aesthetics, had no real parallel in Stalinist Russia.

40 Andreas Fleischer and Frank Kämpfer, 'The Political Poster in the Third Reich', in Taylor and van der Will (ed.), *The Nazification of Art*, p.183ff.

41 Quoted in Jeremy Noakes and Geoffrey Pridham (ed.), *Nazism 1919–45: A Documentary Reader*, vol. II (Exeter, 1984), p.408.

42 Robert Wistrich, *Who's Who in Nazi Germany* (London, 1985), p.98.
43 Ibid., p.96ff.
44 Fest, *The Face of the Third Reich*, pp.130–51.
45 Ernest K. Bramstead, *Goebbels and National Socialist Propaganda 1925–45* (London, 1965). See also Joseph Goebbels, *Signale der neuen Zeit: 25 ausgewählte Reden von Dr Joseph Goebbels* (Munich, 1938).
46 Speech on 'The Tasks of German Theatre', Berlin, 8 May 1933, in Joseph Goebbels, *Goebbels spricht: Reden aus Kampf und Sieg* (Oldenburg, 1933).
47 See Žbyněk Zeman, *Nazi Propaganda*, 2nd edn (London/New York, 1964).
48 David Welch, *The Third Reich: Politics and Propaganda* (London/New York, 1993).
49 Kristian Sotriffer, 'Deutsche Gottsucher: Die Gründe für die Verfolgung der Moderne in der NS-Zeit', in Tabor (ed.), *Kunst und Diktatur*, vol. II, pp.534–45.
50 Catherine Milian, 'Deutsche Kunstbetrachtung: Das Verbot der Kunstkritik im Nationalsozialismus', in ibid., pp.546–9.
51 See Welch, *The Third Reich*, pp.168–9, for the text of the ban on art criticism.
52 See ibid., p.136ff. for the relevant documents.
53 Ibid. p.139.
54 Ibid., pp.154–5.
55 Ibid., p.146.
56 Quoted in Grunberger, *A Social History*, p.510.
57 E. H. Gombrich, 'Myth and Reality in German Wartime Broadcasts', in his *Ideals and Idols: Essays on Values in History and in Art* (Oxford, 1979), pp.92–111.
58 Siegfried Kracauer, *From Caligari to Hitler: A Psychological History of the German Film* (Princeton, 1947), p.272.
59 Francis Courtade and Pierre Cadars, *Le Cinéma Nazi* (Paris, 1972), pp. 193–202.
60 David Welch, '"Jews Out!" Anti-Semitic Film Propaganda in Nazi Germany and the "Jewish Question"', in *The British Journal of Holocaust Education*, vol. I, no. 1 (Summer 1992), pp.55–73.
61 Speech of 28 March 1933, reprinted in Welch, *The Third Reich*, pp.149–54.
62 Ibid., p.150. Though Goebbels obviously did not sympathize in 1933 with the Bolshevik message in Eisenstein's film epic, it is worth remembering that in the mid-1920s he had himself been a very left-wing Nazi.
63 Bernd Sösemann, 'Ein tiefer geschichtlicher Sinn aus dem Wahnsinn' in Thomas Nipperdey et al. (ed.), *Weltbürgerkrieg der Ideologien* (Frankfurt/Berlin, 1993), pp.136–74.
64 Leni Riefenstahl, *Hinter den Kulissen des Reichsparteitagfilms* (Munich, 1935), p.84.
65 Kracauer, *From Caligari to Hitler*, p.301.
66 Ibid. See also Peter Reichel, *La Fascination du fascisme* (Paris, 1993), pp.125–8.
67 Kracauer, *From Caligari to Hitler*, pp.302–3.
68 Theweleit, *Male Fantasies*, vol. II, pp.412–13.
69 Jacqueline Austin, 'A Battle of Wills: How Leni Riefenstahl and Frank Capra Fought a War with Film and Remade History', in David Castriota (ed.), *Artistic Strategy and the Rhetoric of Power* (Southern Illinois University, 1986), pp.157–61.
70 Kracauer, *From Caligari to Hitler*, p.300.
71 Susan Sontag, 'Fascinating Fascism', *New York Review of Books* (6 February 1975).

Chapter Four: The Culture of Barbarism

1 Wilhelm Alff, 'Die Angst vor der Dekadenz', in his *Der Begriff Faschismus und andere Aufsätze zur Zeitgeschichte* (Frankfurt/M, 1973), pp.124–41. On the wider role which the ideology of 'decadence' played in the assault on liberal democracy and in the incubation of fascism, see Zeev Sternhell (ed.), *L'Eternel Retour* (Paris, 1994).
2 Max Nordau, *Entartung* (Berlin, 1892). See the essay by Jan Tabor, 'Der Irrweg eines wahnsinnigen Wortes: Entwicklung und Anwendung des Begriffes Entartung', in Jan Tabor (ed.), *Kunst und Diktatur*, vol. I, (Baden, 1994), pp.90–97, for the use and abuse of Nordau's concepts by the Nazis.
3 Ibid., p.90.
4 Franz Roh, *'Entartete' Kunst: Kunstbarbarei im Dritten Reich* (Hanover, 1962), p.5.
5 Hildegard Brenner, *Die Kunstpolitik des Nationalsozialismus* (Hamburg, 1963), p.12.
6 Walter Laqueur, *Weimar: A Cultural History* (London, 1974), p.80.
7 Paul Ortwin Rave, *Kunstdiktatur im Dritten Reich* (Hamburg, 1947), p.13.
8 Adolf Hitler, *Mein Kampf* (New York/London, 1939), p.354.
9 *New York Times* (6 September 1934).
10 Ibid. (13 September 1935).
11 Wolf Willrich, *Säuberung des Kunsttempels: Eine Kunstpolitische Kampfschrift zur Gesundung deutscher Kunst im Geist nordischer Art* (Munich/Berlin, 1937).
12 Richard Grunberger, *A Social History of the Third Reich* (London, 1974), p.534.
13 Ibid., p.535. See also Rave, *Kunstdiktatur*, p.50.
14 Mario-Andreas von Lüttichau, 'Deutsche Kunst und "Entartete Kunst": Die Münchner Ausstellungen 1937', in Peter-Klaus Schuster (ed.), *Die 'Kunststadt' München 1937: Nationalsozialismus und 'Entartete Kunst'* (Munich, 1988), pp.83–118.
15 See the speech by Adolf Ziegler, opening the 1937 exhibition of 'degenerate art', ibid., pp.217–18.
16 Ibid.
17 From the guide to the exhibition, reproduced in J. Wülf (ed.), *Die Bildenden Künste im Dritten Reich: Eine Dokumentation* (Gütersloh, 1964), pp.320–21.
18 Bruno E. Werner, 'Die Ausstellung Entartete Kunst', *Deutsche Allgemeine Zeitung* (20 July 1937).
19 *Hamburger Tageblatt* (20 July 1937), quoted in Wülf, *Die Bildenden Künste*, p.330.
20 Dr Wilhelm Spael, 'Das Haus der deutschen Kunst', *Kölnische Volkszeitung* (22 July 1937).
21 'Wiedergeburt der deutschen Kunst', *Kieler Neueste Nachrichten* (20 July 1937), quoted in Wülf, *Die Bildenden Künste*, p.330.
22 George L. Mosse (ed.), *Nazi Culture* (London, 1966), pp.151–9.
23 Ibid., p.157.
24 Ibid., p.152.
25 Ibid., p.159.
26 Norman Baynes (ed.), *The Speeches of Adolf Hitler, April 1922 to August 1939*, vol. II(London/Oxford, 1942), pp.584–93. Full text in *Völkischer Beobachter* (19 July 1937 and in Schuster (ed.), *Die 'Kunststadt' München*, pp.242–52.
27 Baynes, *Speeches of Adolf Hitler*, p.585.
28 Ibid., p.588.
29 Ibid., p.590.
30 Ibid.
31 Ibid., p.591.
32 Ibid., p.592.
33 Barbara Lepper, *Verboten, verfolgt: Kunstdiktatur im Dritten Reich* (Duisberg, 1983). See also Ulrike Aubertin and Annick Lantenois, 'La Grande Exposition de "L'Art Allemand" et "L'Art dégénéré": Fondement et symbolique d'une confrontation', in Pierre Milza and Fanette Roche Pézard (ed.), *Art et Fascisme* (Paris, 1989), p.139ff.
34 Aubertin and Lantenois, 'La Grande Exposition', pp.145–6.
35 Mosse (ed.), *Nazi Culture*, p.133ff.
36 Karl Arndt, 'Das "Haus der Deutschen Kunst" – ein Symbol der neuen Machtverhältnisse', in Schuster (ed.), *Die 'Kunststadt' München*, pp.61–82.
37 Rave, *Kunstdiktatur*, p.56.
38 Berthold Hinz, *Art in the Third Reich* (New York, 1979), pp.40–41.
39 Ibid., p.58.
40 Rave, *Kunstdiktatur*, p.57.
41 Peter Adam, *Art of the Third Reich* (New York, 1992), p.114.
42 Hinz, *Art in the Third Reich*, p.10.
43 Ibid., p.44.
44 Bruno E. Werner, 'Erster Gang durch die Kunstausstellung', *Deutsche Allgemeine Zeitung* (20 July 1937), in Wülf (ed.), *Die Bildenden Künste*, pp.190–91.
45 Quoted in Hinz, *Art in the Third Reich*, p.79.
46 For the position of women in the Third Reich, see Jill Stephenson, *Women in Nazi Society* (London, 1975), and Claudia Koonz, *Mothers in the Fatherland: Women, the Family and Nazi Politics* (London, 1987). For the iconography of women, see Annie Richardson, 'The Nazification of Women in Art', in Brandon Taylor and Wilfried van der Will (ed.), *The Nazification of Art: Art, Design, Music, Architecture and Film in the Third Reich* (Winchester, 1990), pp.53–79, and Andrea Theresia Schwaiger, 'Weibliche Bestformen: Das Bild der Frau in der NS-Malerei', in Tabor (ed.), *Kunst und Diktatur*, vol. II, pp.550–53.
47 Richardson, 'Nazification of Women in Art', pp.67–70.
48 Mosse (ed.), *Nazi Culture*, pp.39–56.
49 Alfred Rosenberg, *Der Mythos des XX Jahrhunderts* (Munich, 1938), p.512.
50 Engelbert Huber, *Das ist Nationalsozialismus* (Stuttgart, 1933), pp.121–2.
51 See Koonz, *Mothers in the Fatherland*. She points out that Nazi electoral propaganda systematically sought to refute charges of misogyny, and largely succeeded, despite the exaggerated masculine ethos of the movement. Hitler's appeal to women is well documented. He skilfully played on their emotions and exploited the fact that he was a non-smoking, anti-alcoholic bachelor, who had gone to prison for his convictions and for the defence of German honour. The pseudo-religious aura and mood of mass hysteria created around Hitler appeared to intensify his charisma for women. Unlike other Nazi leaders such as Streicher or Rosenberg, he carefully avoided insulting them in public and always praised their patriotism. The collaboration of women was essential to his goal of nurturing an 'Aryan' master-race!
52 Ibid.
53 *Völkischer Beobachter* (25 December 1938).
54 Ibid. (15 September 1935).
55 *Der SA-Mann* (18 September 1937), quoted in Mosse (ed.), *Nazi Culture*, p.47ff.
56 Mosse (ed.), *Nazi Culture*, p.52. For the impact of 'swing' jazz and other forms of unorganized resistance or 'deviancy' in the Third Reich, see Detlev Peukert, *Inside Nazi Germany: Conformity, Opposition and Racism in Everyday Life* (New Haven/London, 1987), pp.154–74. Peukert points out that 'swing' was a middle-class form of youth protest in Nazi Germany. Members listened to jazz, jitterbugged, used English phrases, let their hair grow a little and carried umbrellas, whatever the weather. The girls painted their nails. There were also more aggressive marks of 'deviancy' or opting out of the thought-control and conformist pressures of public life in the Third Reich. The Edelweiss Pirates or youth gangs in Leipzig would indulge in sex or having a good time, hitch-hiking around the country or even beating up members of the Hitler Youth where they could find them. Though these were marginal phenomena, the existence of such 'sub-cultures' showed that the Nazis, even after several years in power, did not have a complete grip on German society.
57 Henri Nannen, *Die Kunst im Dritten Reich* (1937), p.62.
58 Brenner, *Die Kunstpolitik*, p.67.
59 Georg Bussmann, '"Degenerate Art" – A Look at a Useful Myth', in C. M. Joachimides et al. (ed.), *German Art in the Twentieth Century: Painting and Sculpture 1905–85* (London, 1985), pp.113–24.
60 The resemblance to the book burnings is even stronger when one takes into account that in 1939 about 4,000 of the 'degenerate' canvases were reputedly burned in the courtyard of the Berlin fire brigade's headquarters. See Grunberger, *A Social History of the Third Reich*, p.535.
61 *Völkischer Beobachter* (17 July 1937).
62 Mario-Andreas von Lüttichau, in Schuster (ed.), *Die 'Kunststadt'*

München, pp.88–9. See also W. Hartmann, *Der historische Festzug* (Munich, 1976), and the comments in Hinz, *Art in the Third Reich*, pp.2–4.
63 *Völkischer Beobachter* (17 July 1937). Translation in Hinz, *Art in the Third Reich*.
64 Ibid.
65 Ibid.

Chapter Five: A Glittering Façade

1 *Manchester Guardian* (15 July 1939).
2 *Völkischer Beobachter* (17 July 1939), p.2.
3 Ibid.
4 *Münchner Neuesten Nachrichten* (17 July 1939). See also 'Grossdeutschlands stolze Geschichte im festlichen Zug', in *Münchner Stadtanzeiger* (17 July 1939).
5 'Hitler on Aim of Nazi Art', *Daily Telegraph and Morning Post* (17 July 1939).
6 Ibid.
7 *Manchester Guardian* (15 July 1939).
8 'Our One Desire Peace: Daladier's Speech', in ibid.
9 *Daily Telegraph* (17 July 1939).
10 'Tag der Deutschen Kunst: Schwert schützt Kunst', *Münchner Zeitung* (15/16 July 1939).
11 Ibid.
12 Ibid.
13 'Der Gauleiter spricht', ibid.
14 *New York Times* (17 July 1939).
15 *Münchner Zeitung* (15/16 July 1939).
16 Ibid. See also 'Nazi "True Liberty" is Art Show Theme', *New York Times* (15 July 1939).
17 *Münchner Zeitung* (15/16 July 1939), p.2.
18 'Reichspressechef Dr. Dietrich empfängt', ibid.
19 Ibid.
20 'Goebbels sees Art restored to Folk', *New York Times* (16 July 1939).
21 Ibid.
22 Ibid.
23 Ibid.
24 'Art Limps in Nazi Germany', *New York Times* (23 July 1939).
25 Klaus Backes, *Hitler und die bildenden Künste: Kulturverständnis und Kunstpolitik im Dritten Reich* (Cologne, 1988).
26 *New York Times* (23 July 1939).
27 Ibid. For examples, see the official German catalogue of the exhibition in the House of German Art, *Grosse Deutsche Kunstausstellung, 1939* (Munich, 1939).
28 Peter Adam, *Art of the Third Reich* (New York, 1992), p.97.
29 *Die Kunst im Dritten Reich* (April 1939), p.122. Translation in Adam, *Art of the Third Reich*, p.133.
30 *Völkischer Beobachter* (15 September 1935).
31 Adam, *Art of the Third Reich*, p.150.
32 For Ziegler, see Robert Wistrich, *Who's Who in Nazi Germany* (London, 1982), p.347.
33 Adam, *Art of the Third Reich*, p.153.
34 *Time* (24 July 1939), p.20. *Time* called Padua's painting 'the Munich show's sensation'. It also sardonically recalled Hitler's purchase of a Ziegler painting two years earlier at the Munich art exhibition, to show its readers what was currently con-

sidered high art in the Third Reich: 'Reportedly to decorate his bedroom, he paid 15,000 marks for Professor Adolph Ziegler's (President of the Reich Chamber of Graphic & Plastic Arts) full-length, photographic female nude *Terpsichore*. Prior to its purchase, its voluptuous model had accompanied the Reich Leader through the exhibition. Almost anywhere else in the world *Terpsichore* would be considered the kind of thing to put on a beer ad calendar.'
35 *New York Times* (16 July 1939).
36 Walter Horn, 'Vorbild und Verpflichtung: Die grosse deutsche Kunstausstellung 1939 in München', *Nationalsozialistische Monatshefte* (September 1939), pp.830–33, also quoted in J. Wülf (ed.), *Die Bildenden Künste im Dritten Reich: Eine Dokumentation* (Gutersloh, 1963), pp.192–3.
37 Ibid.
38 Willibald Sauerländer, 'The Nazis' Theater of Seduction', *New York Review of Books* (21 April 1994).
39 Klaus Wolbert, *Die Nackten und die Toten des 'Dritten Reiches': Folgen einer politischen Geschichte des Körpers in der Plastik des deutschen Faschismus* (Giessen, 1982), p.131. See also Peter Reichel, *La Fascination du Nazisme* (Paris, 1993), pp.341–7. The sculptors adopted an excessively formal language and monumentalism in order to represent the Nazi body ideal of beauty, strength, youth and will-to-power. The result often resembled body-building athletes more than the dignity of classical sculpture. The Nazi obsession with 'eternal', absolute values reduced all relative and conditional forms to the realm of the vulgar and worthless. Klaus Wolbert observed that the more the exclusive ideal of 'perfect beauty' became dominant in the Third Reich, the less the 'real man' and the individual human being was protected in practice. It is tempting to see a connection between the 'heroic' Nazi mysticism of the superhuman, the monumental and idealized bodily forms and their readiness to destroy everything deemed to be weak, blemished, inferior or less than physically perfect.
40 *Völkischer Beobachter* (24 November 1938).
41 Oliver Rathkolb, 'Ganz gross und monumental: Die Bildhauer des Führers: Arno Breker und Josef Thorak' in Jan Tabor (ed.), *Kunst und Diktatur: Architektur, Bildhauerei, und Malerei in Österreich, Deutschland, Italien und der Sowjetunion 1922–56*, vol. II (Baden, 1994), p.586ff. See also Adelin Guyot and Patrick Restellini, *L'Art Nazi* (Paris, 1987), p.137ff., and Adam, *Art of the Third Reich*, p.176ff.
42 See Werner Rittich, 'Zum 40. Geburtstag Arno Brekers', *Völkischer Beobachter* (18 August 1940) and 'Der Lyriker Arno Breker', *Völkischer Beobachter* (15 June 1944). Also Breker's memoir, *Im Strahlungsfeld der Ereignisse* (Preussisch Oldendorf, 1972).
43 *Völkischer Beobachter* (19 July 1937). Translation in Norman Baynes (ed.), *The Speeches of Adolf Hitler, April 1922 to August 1939*, vol. II (London/Oxford, 1942), pp.584–92.
44 Baynes, *Speeches of Adolf Hitler*,

p.591.
45 Ibid., pp.591–2.
46 Goebbels at the Day of German Art, 9 July 1938, quoted in Adam, *Art of the Third Reich*, p.114.
47 Peter Reichel, *La Fascination du Fascisme* (Paris, 1993), p.340.
48 Adam, *Art of the Third Reich*, p.114.
49 Wolfgang Hartmann, 'Der historische Festzug zum "Tag der deutschen Kunst"', in Berthold Hinz et al. (ed.), *Die Dekoration der Gewalt: Kunst und Medien im Faschismus* (Giessen, 1979), pp.87–100.
50 Ibid.
51 Robert R. Taylor, *The Word in Stone: The Role of Architecture in the National Socialist Philosophy* (Berkeley/Los Angeles, 1974), pp.58, 92–3, 95.
52 Paul Schultze-Naumburg, *Die Kunst der Deutschen* (Stuttgart, 1934), p.44.
53 Taylor, *The Word in Stone*, p.98.
54 Hartmann, 'Der historische Festzug'.
55 On the influence of Friedrich Gilly and Karl Friedrich Schinkel, see Taylor, *The Word in Stone*, pp.99–100. Their Prussian neo-classical style had been much praised by the conservative theorist, Möller van den Bruck, in his influential book *Der preussische Stil*, 3rd edn (Breslau, 1931). Van den Bruck, who popularized the term 'The Third Reich' in the early 1920s, was much admired by Hitler and the Nazis. See Fritz Stern, *The Politics of Cultural Despair* (Berkeley, 1961), pp.263–6.
56 Gerdy Troost (ed.), *Das Bauen im neuen Reich*, vol. I (Bayreuth, 1938), p.9.
57 Hartmann, 'Der historische Festzug', p.99.
58 Adam, *Art of the Third Reich*, p.115.
59 Ibid., p.114.
60 Hartmann, 'Der historische Festzug', p.95.
61 'Schmuck für grosse Tage', *Völkischer Beobachter* (3 June 1939).
62 *Tag der Deutschen Kunst* (Munich, 1938), pp.18–19, official programme.

Chapter Six: Brown Shirts, Blue Skies

1 The Nazis were very interested in developing colour film and photography, though it was only during the Second World War that they first produced feature films in colour like *Baron von Münchhausen* (1943) and Veit Harlan's *Kolberg* (1945). The first documentary newsreels in colour also appeared at the end of the war, but dealt with relatively anodyne themes from everyday life such as folk dancing, the Berlin zoo or relaxing on the beaches. Colour at that time had a sort of 'magical' effect of unreality, in comparison with black and white – rather different from our contemporary experience. It was still rarely used, its cost was prohibitive and it was beyond the access of most amateurs. See the interesting remarks of André Gunthert, 'La Couleur de l'utopie: La peinture officielle du IIIe Reich', in Pierre Milza et Fanette Roche-Pézard (ed.), *Art et Fascisme* (Paris, 1989), pp.193–207.
2 Craig Brown, 'The Evil that

Men Do', *Sunday Times* (23 May 1993). Review of *Good Morning, Mr Hitler*.
3 Isabel Hilton, 'Filming Hitler: July 1939', *Independent on Sunday* (16 May 1993).
4 Transcript of interview with Charlotte Knobloch, Munich. *Good Morning, Mr Hitler*, Channel Four.
5 Transcript of interview with Berndt Feierabend, Munich, ibid.
6 For details about Dachau in this period, see Paul Berben, *Dachau: The Official History 1933–45* (London, 1975).
7 Transcript of interview with Martin Summer, Munich. *Good Morning, Mr Hitler*, Channel Four.
8 Ibid.
9 Transcript of interview with Peter Feierabend, Munich, ibid.
10 Ibid.
11 Ibid.
12 Telephone conversation with Dr Ernst Eisenmann, Ramat Gan, Israel, September 1993.
13 Transcript of interview with Berndt Feierabend, Munich. *Good Morning, Mr Hitler*, Channel Four.
14 Transcript of interview with Peter Feierabend, ibid.
15 Ibid.
16 Ibid.
17 Transcript of interview with Professor Nerdinger, Munich.
18 Transcript of interview with Charlotte Knobloch, Munich. *Good Morning, Mr Hitler*, Channel Four. On the self-image and alienation of those Jews who stayed on in Germany after 1945 and whose image of the Germans can never be the same again, see Frank Stern, 'Antagonistic Memories: The Post-War Survival and Alienation of Jews and Germans', in Luisa Passerini (ed.), *Memory and Totalitarianism*, vol.1, *International Yearbook of Oral History and Life Stories* (Oxford, 1992), pp.22–43.
19 Knobloch, ibid. For information about current German attitudes to Jews, see David A. Jodice, *United Germany and Jewish Concerns: Attitudes Towards Jews, Israel, and the Holocaust* (American Jewish Committee Working Papers on Contemporary Anti-Semitism, New York, 1991). The data, taken as a whole, are disturbing. They show that attitudes among West Germans are surprisingly negative, given the Federal Government's efforts to come to terms with the Holocaust, and its 'special relations' with Israel. For example, 65 per cent of West Germans wished to put the memory of the Holocaust behind them, 44 per cent agreed that 'Jews exert too much influence on world events', 39 per cent thought that Jews exploit the Holocaust (including 29 per cent of the younger respondents) and 46 per cent rejected the idea of a special relationship with Israel. East Germans were more open on these issues, contrary to what is generally believed.
20 Knobloch, ibid. For a grim overview of the 'Jewish Question' within the 'German Question' since 1945 and the persistence of anti-Semitism in Germany, see Henryk M. Broder, *Der Ewige Antisemit: Über Sinn und Funktion eines beständigen Gefühls* (Frankfurt/M, 1987). Broder coined the bitter but striking phrase that 'the Germans will never

forgive the Jews for Auschwitz', ibid., p.164.

21 Ibid.

22 See Hilton, 'Filming Hitler'.

23 Transcript of interview with Inge Ungewitter, Munich. *Good Morning, Mr Hitler*, Channel Four. It is remarkable how frequently in personal conversation, memories and in oral testimonies, Germans deny any knowledge of the fate of the Jews. Their language becomes vague and abstract, giving the impression that the Jews simply vanished from pre-war Germany or were invisible to begin with. On the other hand, they do have sharp memories of wartime destruction caused by bombing raids and of German collective suffering. The Allied bombing was for them *the* great disaster, whereas for Jews in occupied Europe the raids were a ray of hope. This point is well made by Stern, 'Antagonistic Memories' pp.28–9.

24 Transcript of interview with Josefa Hammann, Munich. *Good Morning, Mr Hitler*, Channel Four.

25 Ibid.

26 Ibid.

27 Ibid.

28 Ibid. It is interesting that the violence of the *Kristallnacht* made some impression and did arouse a general, if vague sense of sympathy with the harassed Jews in some Germans. But this feeling appears to have faded very quickly and one rarely, if ever, gets any note of German solidarity with Jews in the interviews. For a historical analysis of this syndrome, see David Bankier, *The Germans and the Final Solution. Public Opinion under Nazism* (Cambridge, 1992).

29 Ibid.

30 Ibid.

31 Transcript of interview with Else Peitz, Munich. *Good Morning, Mr Hitler*, Channel Four.

32 Ibid.

33 Ibid.

34 Ibid. It is uncanny how Frau Peitz's memories reflect the image of a petty bourgeois Mr Everyman that Hitler himself often liked to radiate. In the eyes of the masses, he was the projection of their own desires and tastes – whether for operettas, adventure stories, sentimental films or chocolate and cream cakes. As Saul Friedländer shrewdly observes, the photo albums assembled by his personal photographer, Heinrich Hoffman, 'are full of images of bourgeois serenity'. See Saul Friedländer, *Reflections of Nazism: An Essay on Kitsch and Death* (New York, 1984), pp.66–7. What are completely missing in this imagery are Hitler's sadism, his revolutionary nihilism and will to destruction.

35 Transcript of interview with Else Peitz, Munich. *Good Morning, Mr Hitler*, Channel Four.

36 Ibid.

37 Ibid. Here we are confronted with a whole array of stereotypical perceptions which appear impervious to the impact of the Holocaust and the passage of time. The Jews are recalled as wealthy and clannish, as owning the big stores and running hospitals even in the Nazi period. The ignorance is simply mind-boggling. Already by 1935 German Jews had been stripped of their rights; they were second-class citizens living

under a system of racial apartheid, humiliated and harassed. By the summer of 1939, which the German interviewees recall with euphoric nostalgia, Jews were in a state of hopeless despair, the last shreds of their economic existence and human dignity torn up by the roots.

38 Ibid. There is no perception in this or other memories of the daily terror perpetrated against the Jews since the Nazis came to power. The chillingly evasive talk about Nazi 'discretion' gives no hint of the obsessive racist propaganda, the violence of the SA, the draconian anti-Jewish laws or the brutally effective 'Aryanization' programme. Nevertheless, a glimpse of the total Jewish social isolation does come through without, however, any honest recognition of German guilt or responsibility.

39 Ibid. In many German oral accounts, as Stern points out ('Antagonistic Memories', p.39), knowledge of concentration camps is admitted, but *awareness* is postponed until after 1945. Thus the Nazi crimes are pushed aside, along with any personal responsibility. In this context it is worth quoting President Richard von Weiszäcker's speech in the Bundestag on 8 May 1985, as a corrective. The German President noted that at the root of the Nazi tyranny was 'Hitler's immeasurable hatred' against our Jewish compatriots', which he had 'never concealed from the public'. Von Weiszäcker asked pointedly: 'Who could remain unsuspecting after the burning of the synagogues, the plundering, the stigmatization with the Star of David, the deprivation of rights, the ceaseless violation of human dignity? ... When the unspeakable truth of the Holocaust then became known at the end of the war, all too many of us claimed that they had not known anything about it or even suspected anything.'

40 Transcript of interview with Else Peitz, Munich. *Good Morning, Mr Hitler*, Channel Four.

41 Transcript of interview with Günter Grassmann, Munich.

42 Ibid.

43 Willibald Sauerländer, 'The Nazis' Theater of Seduction', *New York Review of Books* (21 April 1994).

Chapter Seven: Nationalism Über Alles

1 See Human Rights Watch, 'Foreigners Out': Xenophobia and Right-Wing Violence in Germany (New York, 1992), and Robert S. Wistrich, 'Nationalism and Anti-Semitism in Central and Eastern Europe Today', in *Anti-Semitism in Post-Totalitarian Europe* (Prague, 1993), pp.35–49.

2 See, for example, *Sunday Times* (29 November 1992), p.16, *Daily Telegraph* (26 November 1992), *The Times* (28 November 1992), p.10, and (14 December 1992), pp.6–7. Also *Newsweek* (21 September 1992), p.26, and *Der Spiegel*, 2 (1993), pp.36–48.

3 Quoted in *The German Neo-Nazis: An ADL Investigative Report* (New York 1993), p.1.

4 Tom Reiss, 'Strange World of Germany's Neo-Nazi Youth', *Wall Street Journal* (17 December 1992).

See also Murray Gordon, 'Racism and Anti-Semitism in Germany: Old Problem, New Threat', *Congress Monthly*, vol. 60, no. 3 (March/April 1993), pp.3–7.

5 Gordon, 'Racism and Anti-Semitism in Germany'.

6 *The Times* (24 November 1992), p.15. See also 'Fanatics of Fire', *Newsweek* (4 January 1993), p.30.

7 Figures quoted in *Anti-Semitism: World Report 1994* (Institute of Jewish Affairs, London, 1994), p.38.

8 Ibid.

9 These are official figures from the Office for the Protection of the Constitution. See *Response* (The Wiesenthal Centre World Report), vol. 14, no. 2 (Summer 1993), p. 2, for a more detailed breakdown.

10 See Peter Schneider, 'Neo-Nazi Violence: Stop It Now, Explain it Later', *Harper's* (June 1993).

11 Gordon, 'Racism and Anti-Semitism in Germany', p.6. The Solingen fire-bombing aroused fierce protests by Turkish immigrants as well. They were furious at government denials of an organized Nazi campaign.

12 *Anti-Semitism: World Report 1994*, p.x.

13 Scott Sullivan, 'Time to Tell the Truth', *Newsweek* (27 April 1992), p.12.

14 'Germany: Including the Ausländers', *Newsweek* (28 June 1993).

15 See Steve Vogel, 'The Politics of Hate', *American Legion Magazine* (April 1993).

16 Cornelia Dieckmann and Mario Kessler, 'Right-Wing Extremism and Anti-Semitism after the Transformation: The Case of the New German States', in *Anti-Semitism in Post-Totalitarian Europe*, pp.259–71.

17 For West German arrogance to their Eastern cousins, see *Der Spiegel* (11 February 1991), p.81.

18 Dieckmann and Kessler, 'Right-Wing Extremism', p.262. They note that less than 1 per cent of all the GDR's residents were foreigners and that they had virtually no contact with East Germans outside the work place. The Jewish community of East Germany has been estimated at between 2,500 to 3,000. The Communist regime claimed to have uprooted anti-Semitism, but pursued an aggressively hostile policy to Israel and Zionism. Until shortly before its demise, it refused to accept any responsibility for the Holocaust or to pay any reparations to Jews outside the country. This contrasted sharply with the West German policy of material restitution since the early 1950s.

19 Ibid., p.263.

20 Ibid.

21 Peter Millar, 'Still Proud to Be German', *The Times* (24 November 1992), p.15.

22 *Süddeutsche Zeitung* (6/7 July 1991).

23 Christoper T. Husbands, 'Neo-Nazis in East Germany: The New Danger?', *Patterns of Prejudice*, vol. 25, no. 1 (1991), pp.3–17.

24 Ibid., p.14.

25 For the Zundel–Althans connection, see the controversial documentary film *Beruf neo-Nazi* by

Winfried Bonengel. Zundel, a German who emigrated to Canada to escape military service, made a living as a commercial artist and expert in retouching photos. An open admirer of Hitler and a Holocaust denier, he sells tapes of speeches by Nazi 'greats' and video cassettes abroad to a neo-Nazi constituency. Very media-conscious, he shows off his 'concentration camp' pyjamas in the film. On Zundel's Holocaust denial, see *Hitler's Apologists: The Anti-Semitic Propaganda of Holocaust 'Revisionism'* (ADL, New York, 1993), pp.37–40. Althans, a tall, blond, much younger neo-Nazi, runs a sales and publicity company in Munich, offering among other things, 'action shots' of paramilitary neo-Nazis to the media for a price. He also operates the German Youth Education Project with a following of nearly 40,000 and acts as a German booking agent for British Holocaust denier, David Irving. For some of these connections and a good general picture of the neo-Nazi subculture in Germany, see Michael Schmidt, *The New Reich* (London, 1993).

26 German Neo-Nazis, p.4.

27 Sounds of Hate: *Neo-Nazi Rock Music from Germany* (New York, 1992). One skinhead band leader is quoted as saying: 'Music is the number one. It's just the best way to reach people. Through music people can start educating them [the skinheads]. Politics through music.' The hard-driving rock sound is known sometimes as 'Oi music', or in the USA as 'White Power'. (The politics is that of the extreme Right.)

28 *German Neo-Nazis*, p.4.

29 Ibid.

30 *Anti-Semitism: World Report 1994*, p.37.

31 Husbands, 'Neo-Nazis in East Germany', p.6.

32 *Anti-Semitism: World Report 1994*, pp.36–79.

33 Ibid., p.xiv.

34 Commentators have frequently noted the parallels with the 1930s, suggesting that foreigners are targeted today, just as the Jews were at that time by the Nazis. The old slogan *'Juden Raus!'* (Jews out!) has simply been replaced by the skinhead chant *'Ausländer Raus!'* (Foreigners Out!). See Charles P. Cozic (ed.), *Nationalism and Ethnic Conflict* (San Diego, 1994), p.151.

35 See Peter Pulzer, 'Unified Germany: A Normal State?' *German Politics*, vol. 3, no. 1 (April 1994), pp.1–17, and the remarks by Norman Stone, 'Use and Abuse of the Memory of War', *The Times* (18 July 1994) in response to Ian Buruma's book, *Wages of Guilt* (London, 1994), comparing German and Japanese attitudes to war crimes.

36 See the interview with Elie Wiesel, expressing doubts about German moral and political maturity. 'Deutschland ist nicht bereit', *Der Spiegel*, 1 (1990), pp.105–10.

37 For the importance of history as the anchor of a healthy German national identity, see Michael Stürmer's article, 'Geschichte in geschichtslosen Land', *Frankfurter Allgemeine Zeitung* (25 April 1986). For the link between the *Historikerstreit* and German nationalism, see Anson Rabinbach, 'German

38 Günter Grass, 'Kurze Rede eines vaterlandslosen Gesellen', *Die Zeit* (9 February 1990).

39 Uwe Backes, 'The West German Republikaner: Profile of a Nationalist, Populist Party of Protest', *Patterns of Prejudice*, 24/1 (1990), pp.3–16, and the interview with Schönhuber by Anatol Lieven, 'Rabble-Rouser in a Suit', *The Times* (24 November 1992).

40 Robert S. Wistrich, 'The Shadow of Schindler's List', *European Brief* (March/April 1994), pp.14–15, and also my Frank Green Lecture, published by the Oxford Centre for Hebrew and Jewish Studies, *Anti-Semitism in the New Europe* (Oxford, 1994).

41 *Anti-Semitism: World Report 1994*, p.36.

42 Quoted in Dieckmann and Kessler, 'Right-Wing Extremism', p.268.

43 For Holocaust negation, see Gil Seidel, *The Holocaust Denial* (Leeds, 1986), and Pierre Vidal-Naquet, *Les Assassins de la mémoire* (Paris, 1987). This is, of course, an *international* phenomenon, with particularly active branches in Britain, France and the United States.

44 Schmidt, *The New Reich*, p.197. The great popularity of David Irving on the German far Right derives from this need for psychological liberation. He gives them a clean conscience about their past. As a relentless British defamer of Churchill's reputation and now as a Holocaust denier, his 'truth' is grist to the neo-Nazi and far-right mill in Germany.

45 For a valuable analysis, see Roger Eatwell, 'The Holocaust Denial: A Study in Propaganda Technique' in Luciano Cheles *et al.* (ed.), *Neo-Fascism in Europe* (London, 1992), pp.120–46.

46 Ernst Nolte, 'Vergangenheit, die nicht vergehen will', *Frankfurter Allgemeine Zeitung* (6 June 1986). For a good discussion of Nolte, see Evans, *In Hitler's Shadow*, pp.24–46.

47 Andreas Hillgrüber, *Zweierlei Untergang: Die Zerschlagung des deutschen Reiches und das Ende des europäischen Judentums* (Berlin, 1986). On Hillgrüber, see Evans, *In Hitler's Shadow*, pp.47–65; Rabinbach, 'German Historians Debate the German Past', p.192ff; Saul Friedländer, 'West Germany and the Burden of the Past: The Ongoing Debate', *Jerusalem Quarterly*, no. 42 (Spring 1987), pp.4–18.

48 Josef Joffe, 'The Battle of the Historians', *Encounter* (June 1987), pp.72–7.

49 The point is well made by Friedländer, 'West Germany and the Burden of the Past', p.8ff.

50 The best answer to those historians who denied the singularity of the Holocaust was given by the Stuttgart historian, Eberhard Jäckel, 'Die elende Praxis der Untersteller', *Die Zeit*, no. 38 (12 September 1986). Jäckel wrote *inter alia*: 'The Nazi extermination of the Jews was unique, because never before did a state under the responsible authority of its leader, decide and announce that a specific human group, including the old, the women, the children, the newborn, would be killed in its totality and implement this decision with all the means a state has at its disposal. . .'

51 'Mit Gestrigen in die Zukunft?' (Spiegel-Umfrage über Hitler, die NS-Zeit und die Folgen), *Der Spiegel*, no. 15 (1989), pp.150–60. This finding has been confirmed in all polls since unification. The data show that West Germans are keener than their compatriots in the East to forget the Nazi past and more resentful of Jews for what they consider an 'exploitative' attitude to the Holocaust. See Jennifer L. Golub, *German Attitudes Towards Jews: What Recent Survey Data Reveal* (New York, 1991), and David A. Jodice, *United Germany and Jewish Concerns: Attitudes Towards Jews, Israel and the Holocaust* (American Jewish Committee Working Papers on Contemporary Anti-Semitism, New York, 1991) pp.5–6, 15–16, 23–5.

52 *Der Spiegel*, no. 15 (1989), p.150. 6.4 million West Germans had a good opinion of Hitler and another 5.5 million were neutral.

53 Ibid. The levels of ignorance about Hitler and National Socialism are disturbing, however. 25 per cent admitted that they knew little or nothing about Hitler; 22 per cent claimed to know a lot and 53 per cent to know something. The most exaggerated finding was the claim by one-third of all West Germans that their families had been against Hitler!

54 Ibid.

55 The Republikaner showed consistently higher anti-foreigner and anti-Semitic attitudes than most West Germans. 52 per cent had a negative opinion of Jews (in 1993 this had risen to over 60 per cent) as against 18 per cent of the West German population; 72 per cent thought that the German race must be kept pure against foreigners; 67 per cent considered Hitler a great man without the war and the Holocaust; and 51 per cent had a good general opinion of Hitler.

56 *See Anti-Semitism: World Report 1994*, pp.41–2. Questioned in the same survey about Jews, 20 per cent of *all* Germans thought that their compatriots were anti-Semitic. 52 per cent of all Americans in a poll carried out simultaneously believed Germans to be anti-Semitic.

57 For an interesting controversy on this question, see the remarks by Frank Stern, in *German Unification and the Question of Anti-Semitism* (American Jewish Committee, New York, 1993) and the replies by his critics. See also the essays in Hajo Funke (ed.), *Von der Gnade der Geschenkten Nation* (Berlin, 1988), which provide a useful background for the issues as they appeared on the eve of unification.

58 Heinrich August Winkler, 'Nationalism and the Nation-State in Germany', in Mikuláš Teich and Ray Porter (ed.), *The National Question in Europe in Historical Context* (Cambridge, 1993), pp.181–95.

59 For an illuminating attempt to examine post-war fascisms and their subculture in a broader historical and theoretical context, see Roger Griffin, *The Nature of Fascism* (London, 1993), pp.161–79. See also David Childs, 'The Far Right in Germany since 1945', in Cheles *et al.* (ed.), *Neo-fascism in Europe*, pp.66–85.

60 The corruption in Italian politics has produced a backlash which has opened the door to a new right-wing alliance. For the first time since 1945 there are neo-fascists (calling themselves the National Alliance) in the government coalition. At the end of 1993 their leader Gianfranco Fini gained 47 per cent of the votes in Rome, and Alessandra Mussolini (granddaughter of the dictator) received 44 per cent in Naples. Fini's supporters gave up their blackshirts some time ago and condemn Mussolini's race laws of 1938 as an aberration. But their anti-immigrant platform panders to Italian xenophobia, and after the 1994 general elections right-wingers in Rome chanted 'Duce! Duce!' and gave the Nazi salute at victory celebrations. It remains to be seen whether the National Alliance can truly emancipate itself from the fascist legacy and become a respectable right-wing conservative party. See *Anti-Semitism: World Report 1994*, pp.48–58 on Italy.

61 See Hugh Seton-Watson, 'The Age of Fascism and Its Legacy', in George L. Mosse (ed.), *International Fascism: New Thoughts and New Approaches* (London, 1979), p.369.

62 Walter Laqueur, 'Fascism – the Second Coming', *Commentary* (February 1976), pp.57–62.

63 Walter Laqueur, 'From Russia With Hate', *New Republic*, 5 (February 1990), pp.21–5. See also his recent *Black Hundred: The Rise of the Extreme Right in Russia* (New York, 1993), pp.204–71, and Robert S. Wistrich, *Anti-Semitism: The Longest Hatred* (London/New York, 1992), pp.171–91.

64 Roger Boyes, 'Russia Invaded by a New Army of Fascist Rabble-Rousers', *The Times* (13 February 1992), p.10.

65 Jacob W. Kipp, 'The Zhirinovsky Threat', *Foreign Affairs* (May/June 1994), pp.72–86.

66 Ibid., p.84.

67 See Zeev Sternhell *et al.*, *The Birth of Fascist Ideology* (Princeton, 1994), and Robert S. Wistrich, 'How Fascism Began', *Times Literary Supplement* (3 June 1994).

68 Mosse, introduction to *International Fascism*, p. 31. See also Griffin, *The Nature of Fascism*, pp.32–6, 38–40, 98–106 for an analysis of the 'palingenetic myth' (of national rebirth) and its relevance for understanding fascism and Nazism.

69 Ibid.

70 Hermann Rauschning, *The Revolution of Nihilism* (New York, 1939), pp.240–42. On the subject of nihilism and its importance for twentieth-century totalitarian theories, movements and regimes, see also David Ohana, *Misdar Ha-Nihilistim* (The Order of the Nihilists, Jerusalem, 1993) in Hebrew.

71 Martin Broszat, *German National Socialism 1919–45* (Santa Barbara, 1966), p.62, recognized this when he wrote: 'It was the dynamics of the Party, its parades, the ceremonial blessing of banners, the marching columns of the SA, the uniforms, the bands, etc., which captured the imagination of the masses.'

72 See Saul Friedländer, *Reflections of Nazism: An Essay on Kitsch and Death* (New York, 1984), p.20ff., for the ways in which these romantic and kitsch elements still fascinate artists seeking to capture the Nazi experience from within. Hans-Jürgen Syberberg's *Hitler, A Film from Germany* (New York, 1982), an eight-hour epic film on the subject, is a case in point. Susan Sontag already noted Syberberg's intoxication with ravishing images and 'voluptuous anguish'; Friedländer also observes some disquieting aspects in his aesthetic approach and that of Rainer Werner Fassbinder in *Lili Marleen*. Both artists sought in their respective ways a synthesis of kitsch and death, both saw the necessary relationship, in the Nazi era and now, between myth and kitsch. Both also managed to blur any moral distinction between the Jews and the Nazis. The controversy in 1985 over Fassbinder's banned play, *Garbage, the City and Death*, with its stereotypical image of the 'rich Jew', was a good example of his ambiguity. See Heiner Lichtenstein (ed.), *Die Fassbinder-Kontroverse* (Frankfurt/M, 1986) for all the relevant materials. See also Robert S. Wistrich, *Between Redemption and Perdition* (London, 1990), pp.121–9.

73 Schmidt, *The New Reich*, p.64.

74 Syberberg is again an exception to this rule. See, for example, his call for a new, unifying aesthetic in *Von Unglück und Glück der Kunst in Deutschland nach dem letzten Kriege* (Munich, 1990), which contains some very strange, not to say anti-Semitically tinged assertions. Although he does not invite sympathy for the Nazi past, Syberberg calls for an authentically *German* art, one which takes its cue from 'the people' and is not imposed (like the prevailing culture that, in his view, typified post-war Germany) from outside. The assumption is that since 1945, as a result of Allied and also 'Jewish' domination, the German soul has been unable to express itself. It was strangled by an 'ill-fated alliance of a Jewish-left aesthetics' and a 'Jewish interpretation of the world'. Since 1990, a whole 'Jewish epoch of European cultural history' has come to an end, according to Syberberg. The Germans can finally be rid of 'the Auschwitz of the merchants' and 'the Sunday speeches of our educators'. One must hope that this kind of metaphysically obscurantist and pseudo-philosophical discourse about aesthetics will remain an isolated phenomenon, though it has a long tradition in Germany.

75 On this topic, see the classic essay by Zeev Sternhell, 'Fascist Ideology', in Walter Laqueur (ed.), *Fascism: A Reader's Guide* (London, 1976), pp.315–76.

76 Mark C. Taylor and Esa Saarinen, *Imagologies. Media Philosophy* (London, 1994).

77 Exodus 22:21.

INDEX

175

PICTURE CREDITS

T = TOP
B = BOTTOM
L = LEFT
R = RIGHT

Bayerische Staatsbibliothek,
Munich: pp 26T, 77T
Bildarchiv Preussischer
Kulturbesitz, Berlin:
12, 13 (both)
Die Kunst im Dritten Reich:
34R, 79
Josefa Hammann: 94
Luke Holland: 84, 89, 90, 91,
92, 93, 95, 98

Hulton Deutsch Collection
Ltd, London: 26B, 28, 47,
143, 161T, 163T, 164T,
165
Hulton/Reuters, London:
155, 156
Imperial War Museum,
London: 17L, 23, 25, 34L,
35, 37, 54, 68, 70, 71, 73,
74, 86, 161B, 162, 163B
Network Photographers:
145 (Frieder Blickle),
149 (Justin Leighton),
157 (Nikolai Ignatiev)
Private collection: 33

Presseillustrationen Heinrich
R. Hoffmann: 77B
Ernst Reinhold/Artothek: 76
Stadtarchiv, Munich: 45, 83
Ullstein, Berlin: 62
Weimar Archive, Telford: 63
(both)
Wiener Library, London:
17R, 52, 58, 59, 164B

All the colour illustrations
are based on the original
colour archive footage that
featured in the Channel Four
documentary *Good Morning,*

Mr Hitler!, as stated on p.4.

Every reasonable effort has
been made to acknowledge
the whereabouts of illustrative material included in this
volume. Any errors that may
have occurred are inadver-
tent, and will be corrected
in subsequent editions
provided notification is sent
to the publisher.